Lighthouse Horrors

Lighthouse Horrors

TALES OF ADVENTURE, SUSPENSE, AND THE SUPERNATURAL

EDITED BY CHARLES G. WAUGH,
MARTIN HARRY GREENBERG,
AND JENNY-LYNN AZARIAN

Down East Books

ISBN 0-89272-340-8
Library of Congress Catalog Card Number 93-73752

Printed and bound at Capital City Press, Montpelier, Vt.
Color separation by Four Colour Imports
Cover illustration by Chris Van Dusen

9   8   7   6   5   4   3

Down East Books / Camden, Maine

Contents

CHARLES G. WAUGH

Introduction: Bright Darkness

Stories of lighthouses and horror have always been popular, and the seventeen stories in this book—written over a span of 110 years—tie these themes together in an anthology for the first time.

Lighthouses are, for the most part, esthetically pleasing—picturesque structures in dramatic settings. Most people seem to feel an affinity toward lighthouses. In Maine, I've seen countless tourists pose by them and reach to touch their rugged walls. And Freud, it is claimed, never met a lighthouse he didn't like.

For the immigrant, turning hopeful eyes toward a new shore, or for mariners and fishermen pursuing their often perilous livelihoods, an outlying lighthouse can be a welcome beacon—the first promise of dry land and homecoming. Lighthouses represent selfless service. As Philip Conkling, director of the Island Institute, writes: "It is a hard person who has no soft place in his or her heart for lighthouses. Their physical presence speaks of absolute service to mankind, and their lights, beaming across a dark wilderness of sea, are widely recognized as beacons of care, integrity, and perseverance."*

* From the introduction to *Lighthouse in My Life,* by Philmore Wass. Down East Books, 1987.

Today, when all the U.S. Lighthouses have been automated (*unmanned* is the official term), the sight of a historic light tower and keeper's house evokes nostalgia for simpler and more adventurous times. We cannot help but wonder what life was like for the hardy men (and sometimes their families as well) who stayed there. A solitary lightkeeper, we realize, would have to face not only external dangers but also his own internal demons. Lightkeepers at larger stations had to learn to accommodate themselves to the other crew members, no matter how eccentric or antagonistic they might be.

And even on a bright, calm day, a visit to a lighthouse reminds us of how vast and potentially dangerous the ocean is—after all, the lighthouse would not be there if those waters were not treacherous. In one sense, a lighthouse is a testament of lives and treasures lost.

Lighthouses have existed since ancient times, indeed, since well before the birth of Christ. The first known lighthouse, the Pharos of Alexandria, exceeded 350 feet and was considered by some to be one of the seven wonders of the ancient world.

As waterborne commerce grew from the sixteenth century on, so too did the importance of lighthouses, with their golden age beginning around 1820 and concluding in 1945, at the end of World War II. In 1820, about 250 major lighthouses existed worldwide, by 1945 there were more than thirty thousand. The invention of a powerful new type of lens led to a dramatic building boom. First used in 1822, Augustin Jean Fresnel's new lens design focused and intensified the beam of light cast by the oil-fired lanterns.

But in the twentieth century the development of electronic navigation aids—first radio direction finding, radar, sonar, and loran, and then inertial guidance and satellite navigation—reduced the need for lighthouses. Virtually all that still function are now fully automated and unmanned, and many have been replaced by utilitarian, and totally automatic, electronic buoys.

Horror stories are even more popular than lighthouses,

and considerably more ancient. Ghost (spirit) stories were told around the campfires of primitive tribes way back when, and today horror writer Stephen King is the best selling author of all time.

The explanation is simple: scaring ourselves can be fun. Adaptation Level Theory holds that we seek an optimum level of stimulation. Too much, and we cut down—by taking vacations or less demanding jobs. Too little, and we seek more—by finding adventures or reading thrilling stories. For her Ph.D. dissertation, the late science fiction writer Alice H. Sheldon (who wrote under the pen name James T. Tiptree, Jr.) devised an experiment that illustrates this point. Her research showed that rats in familiar environments investigated new objects, but those in unfamiliar surroundings avoided strange objects. Presumably, the former wanted more excitement. Optimum stimulation levels for individuals vary widely, but, at times, all of us crave more excitement.

Horror stories may also offer therapy for personal upsets (assuming awful things haven't happened to us directly). Studies have shown that when there is no obvious, immediate threat to explain a sense of unease we are experiencing, we tend to imagine causes for those feelings. Rumors of impending disaster can justify these vague fears, and horror stories may fill similar emotional needs. They may also reduce anxiety by comparison; after reading about protagonists who encounter terrifying or inexplicable creatures, our own problems seem smaller. We begin to realize things are not so bad that they couldn't be worse.

Despite the popularity and abundance of horror tales, just four basic variations exist. *Material stories* reveal the horrors to be something natural, such as madmen or criminals. Material lighthouse horror stories include struggles with the elements, known animals (such as the rats in "Three Skeleton Key), one's self, or others. *Weird stories* depict the horrors as something fantastic (not currently known to exist) and supernatural (unexplainable by natural laws). Ghosts are most common, but werewolves, vampires, zombies, and other similar beings also qualify. *Janus stories* usually emphasize the psychological approach, and leave the nature of the horrors unresolved. For example, in "Land's End" are ghosts and fate really involved, or is it just imagination and coincidence? We may choose an interpretation, but we never really know whether the story is material or fantastic, for the author does not say. Finally, *science fictional stories* depict the horrors as something fantastic (not currently known to exist) but natural (explainable, or believed to be explainable, by natural laws). Obvious examples are aliens, robots, mutants, death rays, animals previously unknown or thought to be extinct, and new poisons. However, it is also possible to argue, as Lord Bulwer-Lytton once did, that if ghosts exist (and the same could be said for other traditional monsters), they must be explainable by natural laws. In other words, holographic images would have been supernatural to Sumerians, but to us, who have more knowledge, they are not.

This anthology contains all four types of horror story, and you might enjoy trying to categorize each yarn as you read. But if that doesn't interest you, the stories themselves will. Many are by extremely talented authors such as Ray Bradbury, Edgar Allen Poe, Rudyard Kipling, Robert Bloch, and Wilbur Daniel Steele. Five have never been included in any other anthologies. And I guarantee that everyone who reads these "lighthouse horrors" will find more than one of the stories to be unforgettable.

RUDYARD KIPLING

The Disturber of Traffic

Britain's greatest literary exponent of colonialism, Rudyard Kipling, was born in Bombay, India, on December 30, 1865, but was sent to England at the age of six because of his delicate constitution. In 1883 he returned to India to work for the Lahore Civil and Military Gazette. *The short stories he began contributing to his paper were collected in* Plain Tales from the Hills *(1888) and made his reputation. In 1889, the* Allahabad Pioneer *returned him to London as a correspondent. During the next decade he reached the height of his powers, traveling frequently and publishing such classics as* Barrack-Room Ballads *(1892),* The Jungle Books *(1894–95),* Captains Courageous *(1897), and* Kim *(1901).*

Kipling received the Nobel Prize for Literature in 1907, but as enthusiasm for war, imperialism, and chauvinism declined, so too did his literary reputation. On January 18, 1936, he died in London.

"The Disturber of Traffic," which first appeared in Atlantic *in September 1891, was written on the Isle of Wight. It is a powerful story of a man's inability to handle physical loneliness.*

⌑

> From the wheel and the drift of Things
> Deliver us, good Lord,
> And we will meet the wrath of kings,
> The faggot, and the sword.

Lay not Thy toil before our eyes,
Nor vex us with Thy wars,
Lest we should feel the straining skies
O'ertrod by trampling stars.

A veil 'twixt us and Thee, dread Lord,
A veil 'twixt us and Thee:
Lest we should hear too clear, too clear,
And unto madness see!

Miriam Cohen

The Brothers of the Trinity order that none unconnected with their service shall be found in or on one of their Lights during the hours of darkness; but their servants can be led to think otherwise. If you are fair-spoken and take an interest in their duties, they will allow you to sit with them through the long night and help to scare the ships into mid-channel.

Of the English south-coast Lights, that of St. Cecilia-under-the-Cliff is the most powerful, for it guards a very foggy coast. When the sea-mist veils all, St. Cecilia turns a hooded head to the sea and sings a song of two words once every minute. From the land that song resembles the bellowing of a brazen bull; but off-shore they understand, and the steamers grunt gratefully in answer.

Fenwick, who was on duty one night, lent me a pair of black glass spectacles, without which no man can look at the Light unblinded, and busied himself in last touches to the lenses before twilight fell. The width of the English Channel beneath us lay as smooth and as many-coloured as the inside of an oyster shell. A little Sunderland cargo-boat had made her signal to Lloyd's Agency, half a mile up the coast, and was lumbering down to the sunset; her wake lying white behind her. One star came out over the cliffs, the waters turned lead-colour, and St. Cecilia's Light shot out across the sea in eight long pencils that wheeled slowly from right to left, melted into one beam of solid light laid down directly in front of the tower, dissolved again into eight, and passed away. The light-frame of the thousand lenses circled on its rollers, and the compressed-air engine that drove it hummed like a blue-bottle under a glass. The hand of the indicator on the wall pulsed from mark to mark. Eight pulse-beats timed one half-revolution of the Light; neither more nor less.

Fenwick checked the first few revolutions carefully; he opened the engine's feed-pipe a trifle, looked at the racing governor, and again at the indicator, and said: "She'll do for the next few hours. We've just sent our regular engine to London, and this spare one's not by any manner so accurate."

"And what would happen if the compressed air gave out?" I asked, from curiosity.

"We'd have to turn the flash by hand, keeping an eye on the indicator. There's a regular crank for that. But it hasn't happened yet. We'll need all our compressed air to-night."

"Why?" said I. I had been watching him for not more than a minute.

"Look," he answered, and I saw that the dead sea-mist had risen out of the lifeless sea and wrapped us while my back had been turned. The pencils of the Light marched staggeringly across tilted floors of white cloud. From the balcony round the light-room the white walls of the lighthouse ran down into swirling, smoking space. The noise of the tide coming in very lazily over the rocks was choked down to a thick drawl.

"That's the way our sea-fogs come," said Fenwick, with an air of ownership. "Hark, now, to that little fool calling out 'fore he's hurt."

Something in the mist was bleating like an indignant calf; it might have been half a mile or half a hundred miles away.

"Does he suppose we've gone to bed?" continued Fenwick. "You'll hear us talk to him in a minute. He knows puffickly where he is, and he's carrying on to be told like if he was insured."

"Who is 'he'?"

"That Sunderland boat, o' course. Ah!"

I could hear a steam-engine hiss down below in the mist where the dynamos that fed the Light were clacking together. Then there came a roar that split the fog and shook the lighthouse.

"Git-toot!" blared the foghorn of St. Cecilia. The bleating ceased.

"Little fool!" Fenwick repeated. Then, listening: "Blest if that aren't another of them! Well, well, they always say that a fog do draw the ships of the sea together. They'll be calling all night, and so'll the siren. We're expecting some tea ships up-Channel. . . . If you put my coat on that chair, you'll feel more so fash, sir."

It is no pleasant thing to thrust your company upon a man for the night. I looked at Fenwick, and Fenwick looked at me; each gauging the other's capacities for boring and being bored. Fenwick was an old, clean-shaven, gray-haired man who had followed the sea for thirty years, and knew nothing of the land except the lighthouse in which he served. He fenced cautiously to find out the little that I knew, and talked down to my level till it came out that I had met a captain in the merchant service who had once commanded a ship in which Fenwick's son had served; and further, that I had seen some places that Fenwick had touched at. He began with a dissertation on pilotage in the Hugli. I had been privileged to know a Hugli pilot intimately. Fenwick had only seen the imposing and masterful breed from a ship's chains, and his intercourse had been cut down to "Quarter less five," and remarks of a strictly business-like nature. Hereupon he ceased to talk down to me, and became so amazingly technical that I was forced to beg him to explain every other sentence. This set him fully at his ease; and then we spoke as men together, each too interested to think of anything except the subject in hand. And that subject was wrecks, and voyages, and old-time trading, and ships cast away in desolate seas, steamers we both had known, their merits and demerits, lading, Lloyd's, and, above all, Lights. The talk always came back to Lights: Lights of the Channel; Lights on forgotten islands, and men forgotten on them; Light-ships—two months' duty and one month's leave—tossing on kinked cables in ever-troubled tideways; and Lights that men had seen where never lighthouse was marked on the charts.

Omitting all those stories, and omitting also the wonderful ways by which he arrived at them, I tell here, from Fenwick's mouth, one that was not the least amazing. It was delivered in pieces between the roller-skate rattle of the revolving lenses, the bellowing of the fog-horn below, the answering calls from the sea, and the sharp tap of reckless night-birds that flung themselves at the glasses. It concerned a man called Dowse, once an intimate friend of Fenwick, now a waterman at Portsmouth, believing that the guilt of blood is on his head, and finding no rest either at Portsmouth or Gosport Hard.

. . . "And if anybody was to come to you and say, 'I know the Javva currents,' don't you listen to him; for those currents is never yet known to mortal man. Sometimes they're here, sometimes they're there, but they never runs less than five knots an hour through and among those islands of the Eastern Archipelagus. There's reverse currents in the Gulf of Boni— and that's up north in Celebes—that no man can explain; and through all those Javva passages from the Bali Narrows, Dutch Gut, and Ombay, which I take it is the safest, they chop and they change, and they banks the tides fust on one shore and then on another, till your ship's tore in two. I've come through the Bali Narrows, stern first, in the heart o' the south-east monsoon, with a sou'-sou'-west wind blowing atop of the northerly flood, and our skipper said he wouldn't do it again, not for all Jamrach's. You've heard o' Jamrach's, sir?"

"Yes; and was Dowse stationed in the Bali Narrows?" I said.

"No, he was at Bali, but much more east o' them passages, and that's Flores Strait, at the east end o'Flores. It's all on the way south to Australia when you're running through that Eastern Archipelagus. Sometimes you go through Bali Narrows if you're full-powered, and sometimes through Flores Strait, so as to stand south at once, and fetch round Timor, keeping well clear o' the Sahul Bank. Else-ways, if you aren't full-powered, why it stands to reason you go round by the Ombay Passage, keeping careful to the north side. You understand that, sir?"

I was not full-powered, and judged it safer to keep to the north side—of Silence.

"And on Flores Strait, in the fairway between Adonare Island and the mainland, they put Dowse in charge of a screw-

pile Light called the Wurlee Light. It's less than a mile across
the head of Flores Strait. Then it opens out to ten or twelve
mile for Solor Strait, and then it narrows again to a three-mile
gut, with a topplin' flamin' volcano by it. That's old Loby Toby
by Loby Toby Strait, and if you keep his Light and the Wurlee
Light in a line you won't take much harm, not on the darkest
night. That's what Dowse told me, and I can well believe him,
knowing these seas myself; but you must ever be mindful of
the currents. And there they put Dowse, since he was the only
man that the Dutch government, which owns Flores could
find that would go to Wurlee and tend a fixed Light. Mostly
they uses Dutch and Italians; Englishmen being said to drink
when alone. I never could rightly find out what made Dowse
accept of that position, but accept he did, and used to sit for to
watch the tigers come out of the forests to hunt for crabs and
such like round about the lighthouse at low tide. The water
was always warm in those parts, as I know well, and uncommon sticky, and it ran with the tides as thick and smooth as
hogwash in a trough. There was another man along with
Dowse in the Light, but he wasn't rightly a man. He was a
Kling. No, nor yet a Kling he wasn't, but his skin was in little
flakes and cracks all over, from living so much in the salt water
as was his usual custom. His hands was all webby-foot, too.
He was called, I remember Dowse saying now, an Orange-
Lord, on account of his habits. You've heard of an Orange-
Lord, sir?"

"Orang-Laut?" I suggested.

"That's the name," said Fenwick, smacking his knee. "An
Orang-Laut, of course, and his name was Challong; what they
call a sea-gypsy. Dowse told me that that man, long hair and
all, would go swimming up and down the straits just for
something to do; running down on one tide and back again
with the other, swimming side-stroke, and the tides going
tremenjus strong. Elseways he'd be skipping about the beach
along with the tigers at low tide, for he was most part a beast;
or he'd sit in a little boat praying to old Loby Toby of an
evening when the volcano was spitting red at the south end of
the strait. Dowse told me that he wasn't a companionable man,
like you and me might have been to Dowse.

"Now I can never rightly come at what it was that began to ail Dowse after he had been there a year or something less. He was saving of all his pay and tending to his Light, and now and again he'd have a fight with Challong and tip him off the Light into the sea. Then, he told me, his head began to feel streaky from looking at the tide so long. He said there was long streaks of white running inside it; like wall paper that hadn't been properly pasted up, he said. The streaks, they would run with the tides, north and south, twice a day, accordin' to them currents, and he'd lie down on the planking—it was a screw-pile Light—with his eye to a crack and watch the water streaking through the piles just so quiet as hogwash. He said the only comfort he got was at slack water. Then the streaks in his head went round and round like a sampan in a tide-rip; but that was heaven, he said, to the other kind of streaks,—the straight ones that looked like arrows on a wind-chart, but much more regular, and that was the trouble of it. No more he couldn't ever keep his eyes off the tides that ran up and down so strong, but as soon as ever he looked at the high hills standing all along Flores Strait for rest and comfort his eyes would be pulled down like to the nesty streaky water; and when they once got there he couldn't pull them away again till the tide changed. He told me all this himself, speaking just as though he was talking of somebody else."

"Where did you meet him?" I asked.

"In Portsmouth harbour, a-cleaning the brasses of a Ryde boat, but I'd known him off and on through following the sea for many years. Yes, he spoke about himself very curious, and all as if he was in the next room laying there dead. Those streaks, they preyed upon his intellecks, he said; and he made up his mind, every time that the Dutch gunboat that attends to the Lights in those parts come along, that he'd ask to be took off. But as soon as she did come, something went click in his throat, and he was so took up with watching her masts, because they ran longways, in the contrary direction to his streaks, that he could never say a word until she was gone away and her masts was under sea again. Then, he said, he'd cry by the hour; and Challong swum round and round the Light, laughin' at him and splashin' water with his webby-foot hands. At last he took it into his pore sick head that the ships, and particularly the steamers that came by,—there wasn't many of them,—made the streaks, instead of the tides as was natural. He used to sit, he told me, cursing every boat that come along,—sometimes a junk, sometimes a Dutch brig, and now and again a steamer rounding Flores Head and poking about in the mouth of the strait. Or there'd come a boat from Australia running north past old Loby Toby hunting for a fair current, but never throwing out any papers that Challong might pick up for Dowse to read. Generally speaking, the steamers kept more westerly, but now and again they came looking for Timor and the west coast of Australia. Dowse used to shout to them to go round by the Ombay Passage, and not to come streaking past him, making the water all streaky, but it wasn't likely they'd hear. He says to himself after a month, 'I'll give them one more chance,' he says. 'If the next boat don't attend to my just representations,'—he says he remembers using those very words to Challong,—'I'll stop the fairway.'

"The next boat was a Two-streak cargo-boat very anxious to make her northing. She waddled through under old Loby Toby at the south end of the strait, and she passed within a quarter of a mile of the Wurlee Light at the north end, in seventeen fathom o' water, the tide against her. Dowse took the trouble to come out with Challong in a little prow that they had,—all bamboos and leakage,—and he lay in the fairway waving a palm branch, and, so he told me, wondering why and what for he was making this fool of himself. Up come the Two-streak boat, and Dowse shouts: 'Don't you come this way again, making my head all streaky! Go round by Ombay, and leave me alone.' Some one looks over the port bulwarks and shies a banana at Dowse, and that's all. Dowse sits down in the bottom of the boat and cries fit to break his heart. Then he says, 'Challong, what am I a-crying for?' and they fetch up by the Wurlee Light on the half flood.

" 'Challong,' he says, 'there's too much traffic here, and that's why the water's so streaky as it is. It's the junks and the brigs and the steamers that do it,' he says; and all the time he was speaking he was thinking, 'Lord, Lord, what a crazy fool

I am!' Challong said nothing, because he couldn't speak a word of English except say 'dam,' and he said that where you or me would say 'yes.' Dowse lay down on the planking of the Light with his eye to the crack, and he saw the muddy water streaking below, and he never said a word till slack water, because the streaks kept him tongue-tied at such times. At slack water he says, 'Challong, we must buoy this fairway for wrecks,' and he holds up his hands several times, showing that dozens of wrecks had come about in the fairway; and Challong says, 'Dam.'

"That very afternoon he and Challong goes to Wurlee, the village in the woods that the Light was named after, and buys canes,—stacks and stacks of canes, and coir rope thick and fine, all sorts,—and they sets to work making square floats by lashing of the canes together. Dowse said he took longer over those floats than might have been needed, because he rejoiced in the corners, they being square, and the streaks in his head all running longways. He lashed the canes together, criss-cross and thwart-ways,—any way but longways,—and they made up twelve-foot-square floats, like rafts. Then he stepped a twelve-foot bamboo or a bundle of canes in the centre, and to the head of that he lashed a big six-foot W letter, all made of canes, and painted the float dark green and the W white, as a wreck-buoy should be painted. Between them two they makes a round dozen of these new kind of wreck-buoys, and it was a two months' job. There was no big traffic, owing to it being on the turn of the monsoon, but what there was, Dowse cursed at, and the streaks in his head, they ran with the tides, as usual.

"Day after day, so soon as a buoy was ready, Challong would take it out, with a big rock that half sunk the prow and a bamboo grapnel, and drop it dead in the fairway. He did this day or night, and Dowse could see him of a clear night, when the sea brimed, climbing about the buoys with the sea-fire dripping off him. They was all put into place, twelve of them, in seventeen-fathom water; not in a straight line, on account of a well-known shoal there, but slantways, and two, one behind the other, mostly in the centre of the fairway. You must keep the centre of those Javva currents, for currents at the side is different, and in narrow water, before you can turn a spoke, you get your nose took round and rubbed upon the rocks and the woods. Dowse knew that just as well as any skipper. Likeways he knew that no skipper daren't run through uncharted wrecks in a six-knot current. He told me he used to lie outside the Light watching his buoys ducking and dipping so friendly with the tide; and the motion was comforting to him on account of its being different from the run of the streaks in his head.

"Three weeks after he'd done his business up comes a steamer through Loby Toby Straits, thinking she'd run into Flores Sea before night. He saw her slow down; then she backed. Then one man and another came up on the bridge, and he could see there was a regular powwow, and the flood was driving her right on to Dowse's wreck-buoys. After that she spun round and went back south, and Dowse nearly killed himself with laughing. But a few weeks after that a couple of junks came shouldering through from the north, arm in arm, like junks go. It takes a good deal to make a Chinaman understand danger. They junks set well in the current and went down the fairway, right among the buoys, ten knots an hour, blowing horns and banging tin pots all the time. That made Dowse very angry; he having taken so much trouble to stop the fairway. No boats run Flores Straits by night, but it seemed to Dowse that if junks'd do that in the day, the Lord knew but what a steamer might trip over his buoys at night; and he sent Challong to run a coir rope between three of the buoys in the middle of the fairway, and he fixed naked lights of coir steeped in oil to that rope. The tides was the only things that moved in those seas, for the airs was dead still till they began to blow, and then they would blow your hair off. Challong tended those lights every night after the junks had been so impident,—four lights in about a quarter of a mile hung up in iron skillets on the rope; and when they was alight,—and coir burns well, most like a lamp wick,—the fairway seemed more madder than anything else in the world. Fust there was the Wurlee Light, then these four queer lights, that couldn't be riding-lights, almost flush with the water, and behind them, twenty mile off, but the biggest light of all, there was the red top of old Loby Toby volcano. Dowse told me that he used to go out in the prow and look at his handiwork, and it made him scared, being like no lights that ever was fixed.

"By and by some more steamers came along, snorting and snifting at the buoys, but never going through, and Dowse says to himself: 'Thank goodness I've taught them not to come streaking through my water. Ombay Passage is good enough for them and the like of them.' But he didn't remember how quick that sort of news spreads among the shipping. Every steamer that fetched up by those buoys told another steamer and all the port officers concerned in those seas that there was something wrong with Flores Straits that hadn't been charted yet. It was block-buoyed for weeks in the fairway, they said, and no sort of passage to use. Well, the Dutch, of course they didn't know anything about it. They thought our Admiralty Survey had been there, and they thought it very queer but neighbourly. You understand us English are always looking up marks and lighting sea-ways all the world over, never asking with your leave or by your leave, seeing that the sea concerns us more than any one else. So the news went to and back from Flores to Bali, and Bali to Probolingo, where the railway is that runs to Batavia. All through the Javva seas everybody got the word to keep clear o' Flores Straits, and Dowse, he was left alone except for such steamers and small craft as didn't know. They'd come up and look at the straits like a bull over a gate, but those nodding wreck-buoys scared them away. By and by the Admiralty Survey ship—the *Britomarte* I think she was—lay in Macassar Roads off Fort Rotterdam, alongside of the *Amboina,* a dirty little Dutch gunboat that used to clean there; and the Dutch captain says to our captain, 'What's wrong with Flores Straits?' he says.

" 'Blowed if I know,' says our captain, who'd just come up from the Angelica Shoal.

" 'Then why did you go and buoy it?' says the Dutchman.

" 'Blowed if I have,' says our captain. 'That's your look-out.'

" 'Buoyed it is,' said the Dutch captain, 'according to what they tell me; and a whole fleet of wreck-buoys, too.'

" 'Gummy!' says our captain. 'It's a dorg's life at sea, any way. I must have a look at this. You come along after me as soon as you can;' and down he skimmed that very night, round the heel of Celebes, three days' steam to Flores Head, and he met a Two-streak liner, very angry, backing out of the head of the strait; and the merchant captain gave our Survey ship something of his mind for leaving wrecks uncharted in those narrow waters and wasting his company's coal.

" 'It's no fault o' mine,' says our captain.

" 'I don't care whose fault it is,' says the merchant captain, who had come aboard to speak to him just at dusk. 'The fairway's choked with wreck enough to knock a hole through a dock-gate. I saw their big ugly masts sticking up just under my forefoot. Lord ha' mercy on us!' he says, spinning round. 'The place is like Regent Street of a hot summer night.'

"And so it was. They two looked at Flores Straits, and they saw lights one after the other stringing across the fairway. Dowse, he had seen the steamers hanging there before dark, and he said to Challong: 'We'll give 'em something to remember. Get all the skillets and iron pots you can and hang them up alongside o' the regular four lights. We must teach 'em to go round by the Ombay Passage, or they'll be streaking up our water again!' Challong took a header off the lighthouse, got aboard the little leaking prow, with his coir soaked in oil and all the skillets he could muster, and he began to show his lights, four regulation ones and half a dozen new lights hung on that rope which was a little above the water. Then he went to all the spare buoys with all his spare coir, and hung a skillet-flare on every pole that he could get at,—about seven poles. So you see, taking one with another, there was the Wurlee Light, four lights on the rope between the three centre fairway wreck-buoys that was hung out as a usual custom, six or eight extry ones that Challong had hung up on the same rope, and seven dancing flares that belonged to seven wreck-buoys,—eighteen or twenty lights in all crowded into a mile of seventeen-fathom water, where no tide 'd ever let a wreck rest for three weeks, let alone ten or twelve wrecks, as the flares showed.

"The Admiralty captain, he saw the lights come out one

after another, same as the merchant skipper did who was standing at his side, and he said:—

" 'There's been an international catastrophe here or else-ways,' and then he whistled. 'I'm going to stand on and off all night till the Dutchman comes,' he says.

" 'I'm off,' says the merchant skipper. 'My owners don't wish for me to watch illuminations. That strait's choked with wreck, and I shouldn't wonder if a typhoon hadn't driven half the junks o' China there.' With that he went away; but the Survey ship, she stayed all night at the head o' Flores Strait, and the men admired the lights till the lights was burning out, and then they admired more than ever.

"A little bit before morning the Dutch gunboat come flustering up, and the two ships stood together watching the lights burn out and out, till there was nothing left 'cept Flores Straits, all green and wet, and a dozen wreck-buoys, and Wurlee Light.

"Dowse had slept very quiet that night, and got rid of his streaks by means of thinking of the angry steamers outside. Challong was busy, and didn't come back to his bunk till late. In the very early morning Dowse looked out to sea, being, as he said, in torment, and saw all the navies of the world riding outside Flores Straits fairway in a half-moon, seven miles from wing to wing, most wonderful to behold. Those were the words he used to me time and again in telling the tale.

"Then, he says, he heard a gun fired with a most tremenjus explosion, and all them great navies crumbled to little pieces of clouds, and there was only two ships remaining, and a man-o'-war's boat rowing to the Light, with the oars going side-ways instead o' longways as the morning tides, ebb or flow, would continually run.

" 'What the devil's wrong with this strait?' says a man in the boat as soon as they was in hailing distance. 'Has the whole English Navy sunk here, or what?'

"There's nothing wrong,' says Dowse, sitting on the plat-form outside the Light, and keeping one eye very watchful on the streakiness of the tide, which he always hated, 'specially in the morning. 'You leave me alone and I'll leave you alone.

Go round by the Ombay Passage, and don't cut up my water. You're making it streaky.' All the time he was saying that he kept on thinking to himself, 'Now that's foolishness,—now that's nothing but foolishness,' and all the time he was holding tight to the edge of the platform in case the streakiness of the tide should carry him away.

"Somebody answers from the boat, very soft and quiet, 'We're going round by Ombay in a minute, if you'll just come and speak to our captain and give him his bearings.'

"Dowse, he felt very highly flattered, and he slipped into the boat, not paying any attention to Challong. But Challong swum along to the ship after the boat. When Dowse was in the boat, he found, so he says, he couldn't speak to the sailors 'cept to call them 'white mice with chains about their neck,' and Lord knows he hadn't seen or thought o' white mice since he was a little bit of a boy and kept 'em in his handkerchief. So he kept himself quiet, and so they come to the Survey ship; and the man in the boat hails the quarter-deck with something that Dowse could not rightly understand, but there was one word he spelt out again and again,—m-a-d, mad,—and he heard some one behind him saying it backwards. So he had two words,—m-a-d, mad, d-a-m, dam; and he put those two words together as he come on the quarter-deck, and he says to the captain very slowly, 'I be damned if I am mad,' but all the time his eye was held like by the coils of rope on the belaying pins, and he followed those ropes up and up with his eye till he was quite lost and comfortable among the rigging, which ran criss-cross, and slopeways, and up and down, and any way but straight along under his feet north and south. The deck-seams, they ran that way, and Dowse daresn't look at them. They was the same as the streaks of the water under the planking of the lighthouse.

"Then he heard the captain talking to him very kindly, and for the life of him he couldn't tell why; and what he wanted to tell the captain was that Flores Strait was too streaky, like bacon, and the steamers only made it worse; but all he could do was to keep his eye very careful on the rigging and sing:—

'I saw a ship a-sailing,
A-sailing on the sea;
And oh, it was all lading
With pretty things for me!'

Then he remembered that was foolishness, and he started off to say about the Ombay Passage, but all he said was: 'The captain was a duck,—meaning no offence to you, sir,—but there was something on his back that I've forgotten.

'And when the ship began to move
The captain says, "Quack-quack." '

"He noticed the captain turn very red and angry, and he says to himself, 'My foolish tongue's run away with me again. I'll go forward'; and he went forward, and catched the reflection of himself in the binnacle brasses; and he saw that he was standing there and talking mother-naked in front of all them sailors, and he ran into the fo'c's'le howling most grievous. He must ha' gone naked for weeks on the Light, and Challong o' course never noticed it. Challong was swimmin' round and round the ship, sayin' 'dam' for to please the men and to be took aboard, because he didn't know any better.

"Dowse didn't tell what happened after this, but seemingly our Survey ship lowered two boats and went over to Dowse's buoys. The took one sounding, and then finding it was all correct they cut the buoys that Dowse and Challong had made, and let the tide carry 'em out through the Loby Toby end of the strait; and the Dutch gunboat, she sent two men ashore to take care o' the Wurlee Light, and the *Britomarte,* she went away with Dowse, leaving Challong to try to follow them, a-calling 'dam—dam' all among the wake of the screw, and half heaving himself out of water and joining his webby-foot hands together. He dropped astern in five minutes, and I suppose he went back to the Wurlee Light. You can't drown an Orange-Lord, not even in Flores Strait on flood-tide.

"Dowse come across me when he came to England with the Survey ship, after being more than six months in her, and cured of his streaks by working hard and not looking over the side more than he could help. He told me what I've told you, sir, and he was very much ashamed of himself: but the trouble on his mind was to know whether he hadn't sent something or other to the bottom with his buoyings and his lightings and such like. He put it to me many times, and each time more and more sure he was that something had happened in the straits because of him. I think that distructed him, because I found him up at Fratton one day, in a red jersey, a-praying before the Salvation Army, which had produced him in their papers as a Reformed Pirate. They knew from his mouth that he had committed evil on the deep waters,—that was what he told them,—and piracy, which no one does now except Chineses, was all they knew of. I says to him: 'Dowse, don't be a fool. Take off that jersey and come along with me.' He says: 'Fenwick, I'm a-saving of my soul; for I do believe that I have killed more men in Flores Strait than Trafalgar.' I says: 'A man that thought he'd seen all the navies of the earth standing round in a ring to watch his foolish false wreck-buoys' (those was my very words I used) 'ain't fit to have a soul, and if he did he couldn't kill a flea with it. John Dowse, you was mad then, but you are a damn sight madder now. Take off that there jersey.'

"He took it off and come along with me, but he never got rid o' that suspicion that he'd sunk some ships a-cause of his foolishness at Flores Straits; and now he's a wherryman from Portsmouth to Gosport, where the tides run crossways and you can't row straight for ten strokes together. . . . So late as all this! Look!"

Fenwick left his chair, passed to the Light, touched something that clicked, and the glare ceased with a suddenness that was pain. Day had come, and the Channel needed St. Cecilia no longer. The sea-fog rolled back from the cliffs in trailed wreaths and dragged patches, as the sun rose and made the dead sea alive and splendid. The stillness of the morning held us both silent as we stepped on the balcony. A lark went up from the cliffs behind St. Cecilia, and we smelt a smell of cows in the lighthouse pastures below.

So you see we were both at liberty to thank the Lord for another day of clean and wholesome life.

ANONYMOUS

The Lighthouse Keeper's Secret

"My man, do you want a berth?" said he.

"Aye, aye, cappen," said I. "I want one badly. I'm half-starved and half-frozen."

He made no answer but just a sign to follow him. He stalked away towards Casco Bay and I pegged after him. He kept close along the shore as we walked, and for a while he said nothing. At last he turned and pointed seaward.

He indicated a lighthouse on a lonely rock. "I'm the keeper," said he. "I want you to cook my meals and keep my bachelor's hall for me. Now and then I shall want you to row in and buy provisions. The work won't be hard. I think the pay will suit you. Do you know why I chose you?"

"No, Cappen," said I.

"Because I saw that hope was at an end with you," he said. "It's only a man who had come to that who could live with me in a lighthouse."

I'd been in a lighthouse before; it was no new thing to me, but after I'd been there for a few hours I wondered what my master hired me for. It was like being pensioned off; there was nothing to do. But, mark ye, when it came night, and the wind began to moan about the lighthouse, and the lamps were lit and all outside was black as pitch, and all the sound

we heard was the swash, swash, swash of the waves, my
master mixed some grog and called me to sit along with him.
That looked sociable, but I can't say he did. He sat glowering
over his glass for a while, and opening his mouth as if to
speak, and shutting it again. Then said he:

"What's your name?"

"Ben Dare," said I.

"Would you mind calling yourself Brace?"

"I've no reason to be ashamed of my name," said I.

"Look here," said he, "I am a gentleman born and bred. I
never came to earning my bread before. I'm ashamed of it.
This is what I mean: If any strangers come out here and ask for
William Brace, why, you can say you are the man. You claim
to be lighthouse keeper. It's easy. I don't suppose much
company will call, but I choose not to see them if they do.
That's what I hired you for."

"Oh," said I.

"You see," said he, "I got this place through a rich man
who had influence. Those who gave it to me never saw me. If
I die some day, why, here you are in the place. If I go off, and
I may, here you are still."

"Well, it's shamming," said I, "but, after all, what does
any one care what my name is; and what shall I call you?"

"Call me nothing," said he. "Call me Captain."

Gentleman or no, he wasn't lazy. He didn't care how he
worked. The lamps were as bright as jewels. There wasn't a
speck of dirt in the whole tower. But let any boat come nigh
us, away he went and hid himself, and came out with a white,
scared face and a shaking hand. At night he was afraid to go
up to the lamps alone, and he'd look over his shoulder and
turn white as we stood together. At last he took a new turn.
He stood staring for awhile. Then he spoke to me in a low
voice: "Brace, do you believe in ghosts?"

"I hadn't considered the question," I answered.

"Well," he said, softlier than before, "look into that corner," and he pointed. I looked.

"Don't you see anything?" he asked.

"No," said I; "no, Cappen."

But that wasn't nothing to what happened the very next night. We slept in two bunks nigh each other, and naturally when he woke up with a yell I woke too. He was shrieking and shaking and wringing his hands.

"The woman! The woman!" he said. "She stood here just now, all red with blood. It dripped down the white ruffles. It dripped on her hands. Stop her! She has gone to call them. Stop her! Stop her!"

"Where did she go?" I asked.

He stared at me with his wide-open eyes.

"She couldn't have been here," said he. "It was a dream." So we went asleep. But I heard of the woman so often after that that I grew used to her. The Cappen, as I called him, got to be worse and worse every day. I wanted to go ashore and fetch the doctor, but he would not hear to it.

At last there came a hot, hot night in June. It was burning hot all day, and a dead calm at night. About dark the Cappen went to sleep, and I went and sat where I could see the water and hear the sailors in a Spanish ship moored not far away singing in their foreign lingo. And I was sort of quiet and dreamy-like, when something happened that waked me mighty wide and sudden. Something was standing on the steps below me, something white. Something came toward me.

It was a little, slender figure, with long hair all about its shoulders. I couldn't see its face. I don't think I really saw it plainly at all. But it went past me softly while I looked, and I knew it was a woman in a white, ruffled gown, and that she had gone to the room where my master lay. I shook too hard for a moment to move; but as soon as I could I started to go to him. Just then a voice cried: "Lighthouse, ahoy!"

I answered, "Aye, aye," and stopped a bit.

A boat lay at the foot of the steps, and four men jumped out of it.

"We want William Brace, keeper of this lighthouse," said one, a big man in a linen overcoat.

"I'm one that answers to the name," says I. He swung a lantern over my head.

"Search the place, my men," said he.

"I've got a sick friend aloft," says I. "Don't disturb him. I'm afraid the woman will skeer him, anyhow, he's so low."

"No woman came with us," he snarled.

"Sand aside. Men, do your duty."

Then went upstairs. I followed. I saw them walk into the Cappen's room. I heard them cry out and stand still. When I got to the door they stood in a row looking down on the bed. I looked, too. Man nor woman couldn't frighten the Cappen more. He was dead.

"What had he done?" I asked the officer.

"Killed his wife," said he, "that's all. No doubt she deserved it; but it's not allowed by law when they do."

"God help him," said I.

T. JENKINS HAINS

The End of the Reef

A tragically flawed figure, Thornton Jenkins Hains was born in Washington, D.C., on November 14, 1866, and spent much of his early life at sea. He later settled in New York City and became a successful writer of short stories and novels about the sea, placing stories in Atlantic, Century, *and* Harper's. *In 1908, he was charged with helping to murder the lover of his brother's wife, but was acquitted on the grounds of temporary insanity, but the sensational trial—as well as the revelation that he had killed another man, possibly over a woman, in 1891— destroyed his career. (The many* New York Times *articles covering the murder case are listed listed on page 160 of the paper's index for 1908.) For a few more years, Hains published pseudonymously under the name of Mayn Clew Garnett, but after claiming to have been challenged to a duel in 1912, he drifted out of sight, never to be seen again.*

"The End of the Reef" seems to provide an eerie forshadowing of Hains's later legal defense. It was first published in Century *in August 1905.*

◻

The old keeper of the Fowey Rocks lighthouse came out upon the gallery to take the morning air. The sun was shining and the warm wind from the Gulf Stream blew lazily through the doorway into the lantern-room. The blue sea sparkled in

31

the sunshine, and the long, easy roll of the swell told of calm weather offshore. It was a perfect day, a day of peace and quiet, upon the end of the great Florida Reef, which stretched away for miles to the southward. Eastward nothing rose above the blue rim which compassed all. To the northward the low line of hummocks showed where Virgina Key and Key Biscayne rose above the water some ten miles distant. To the westward the little lump of Soldier Key showed where there might be a solitary human within a dozen miles. And all about the blue sea sparkled in the bright light, taking on the varicolored hues found above the coral banks. Near the lighthouse, in three feet of water, the coral showed distinctly even from the height of the tower. Old man Enau gazed down at it, watching the bright green tinge melt to deeper color until, in three fathoms, the pure limpid blue of the great stream flowed past uncolored and undefiled. Fish were swimming around the iron piles of the lighthouse; great big bonito, sinuous barracuda, and now and then a shark would drift up to the iron pillars and bask a moment in the shade of the tall structure which rose above the coral bank to the height of a hundred feet and more, standing like a huge long-legged spider upon its iron feet in the shallow water.

The quiet of the morning was oppressive to the keeper. Not a sound rose from the reef save the low roll of the sea as it broke upon the edge of the bank, not the cry of a single seabird to break the great stillness and beautiful quiet of the day. The old man had been in the light for three years. He was the head keeper, and his assistant had taken the small boat and gone to the distant village of Miami for the mail, which was due with the quarterly salaries. The assistant would be gone for several days, and the old man would be alone until he came back. Perhaps the younger man would take his vacation of three weeks to spend his money, for he was not supposed to remain forever upon the tower like a prisoner. Old Enau had not set foot upon the shore for nearly two years. To him the world was that eternal sea bounded by the blue rim and spotted in one or two places by the distant Keys. Whatever he had seen of human life he left behind him when he took the position as keeper. He had tried to forget. And now, as the years passed, his memories were fading. The human struggle was over. The thought of what he had seen and done was dimmed in the glare of the tropic sunshine, and the shadow of his past had faded to nothing.

He had a fine old face. Rugged and burned from the weather on the reef, his features still bore traces of culture. His nose was straight and small, and his eyes were bright and blue, the deep blue of the surrounding sea, which had kept him apart from his fellow-men so long.

He leaned out over the rail and looked down. The heat and stillness oppressed him, and as he gazed below at the white and green formations he seemed to see again the inside of a court-room. The quiet and heat were there, and the stillness was strained and intense, as he waited for the word which meant his ruin. The faces of the jury who were trying a murder case were before him, the man on the right looking hard at him, and the foreman bowing his head gravely in that moment of utter silence before he spoke the words which meant his end. It had been a peculiar case, a case of great brutality and cruelty, apparently, from the evidence produced. He, the master of a large square-rigged ship, had been accused of a horrible crime, and the evidence of two witnesses was there to prove it. He remembered the man whose evidence was the strongest against him, a sailor whom he had be-friended, and he could see the look of pious resignation upon the fellow's face. He also remembered the furtive gleam that came now and again from the corner of his eye as he sat near the witness-box and waited his turn to tell of the horror.

Why was it? Was it the heat that brought back those scenes which were fading, or was it the ominous silence of the torrid sunshine upon the reef? The lines in the face of the old man grew rigid and drawn, and he gazed stolidly into the blue water until the coral banks took on new shapes. He saw a ship's deck with the long plank strakes stretching hundreds of feet fore and aft; the low white deck-house, with the galley smoke-pipe stretching across it and the boats upon the strong-backs or booms atop of it; the solid combings of the hatchways, with the battened hatches as strong as the sides of the vessel itself; the high topgallant-rail which shut off the view to windward, and the rows of belaying-pins stuck beneath with the neatly coiled braces upon them; the high head of the topgallant-forecastle and the long jibboom pointing out over the sea; and, above all, the long, tapering spars lifting upward into the blue above, with the white canvas bellying in the breath of the tradewind. It was all plain before him again. Then it changed—the pampero off the River Plate, the great hurricane sea which swept the ship and smashed her up, leaving her a wreck, leaking and settling, six hundred miles from shore. The fracas was there before him—the men struggling, trying to save her, until, tired out with exertion and suffering, the man with the furtive eyes had refused to do duty and managed to get the rest to back him.

Then the days following, full of desperate endeavor: the fellow who refused duty shirking and endangering the lives of all; the measures he took, hanging the man by the hands and flogging him until he fell in a faint; how he staggered to his feet and looked at the master—one long look full of a purpose implacable, unrelenting, and then the quiet manner he had when he obeyed. He had picked the fellow up starving upon the streets, an outcast from some country and of a social sphere above his own, taking him aboard his ship and providing food and clothing with a fair wage—and this had been the outcome.

They had left her in the one remaining boat two days after, crowding the craft almost to the gunwales; but the sea was now smooth and the wind gone, leaving a quiet strangely like that of the beautiful day about him. The row westward over that oily, heaving ocean, day after day, day after day!

One by one they had dropped off, overboard, to float astern, and all the time the *rip, rip, rip* of a triangular fin above a great shadow below the surface.

He had done what he could, taking no more of the meager food than the rest. Then the last days—four of them left, the men who witnessed against him and another, a stout fellow who had kept up better than the rest. How he had discovered that the fellow had stolen the scant store of food steadily and divided it with the man he had flogged. How, when they had taken all, they had set upon him, and he had killed the stout thief and wounded the other. There was nothing left to eat,— absolutely nothing for five days,—and they had—ugh!—it was too horrible; and upon the seventh day they had been picked up with the evidences of the horror too plain for their rescuers to make a mistake in the matter, even without the two men, who openly accused him of the whole wrong— accused him of not only killing his men, but—ugh!

The trial had lasted a week and the evidence was most horrible. The jury had convicted him upon that of the fellow who sat there with a pious look and furtive glance; the other fellow had merely corroborated his story, and, as it was two against him, his own tale was not believed. He had received a life sentence for the crime, for he had admitted killing the stout man who had stolen the last of the food. He explained that it was his duty as captain to protect his life from their combined assault. The jury had not believed him, for the man who was against him was ready to show the falsity of his tale; he had been sentenced for life. He had served seven years and had escaped by cutting the bars of his cell and gaining a vessel which was wrecked on the coast of Africa, letting him get ashore unmolested. After drifting about for a time he had come back to America and taken the position as keeper in the tower, where his past was not open to inspection, for no one knew him or whence he came.

The sunshine was as quiet as before, but the blue Gulf Stream showed a darkening far away on the horizon, where a breeze ruffled the surface. He turned and gazed over the sea toward Florida, and a tiny black speck showed upon the waters of the reef. It looked like a small boat coming out through the Hawk's Channel, and he looked at it steadily for a long time, trying to see if it might be Johnson, the assistant keeper, returning.

The sunshine was very hot on this side of the tower, and it dazzled him for a little while as he gazed over the sparkling sea. The speck drew nearer, and he saw that it was a boat. It came very slowly, sailing with the light air, the bit of white canvas looking no larger than a handkerchief in the distance. Soon the figure of a man could be seen lying easily in the stern-sheets of the craft, and the old keeper saw that the man's legs were bare and brown. Then the tiny shallop took more definite form and showed to be a canoe, its occupant an Indian from the Everglades, coming out to fish upon the reef.

Indians seldom came so far away from land, and as the craft drew nearer and nearer Enau watched it carefully. The Seminoles were friendly. They were an unconquered tribe of Indians who had managed to evade all efforts made by the United States to subdue them. They had retired into the fastnesses of the great swamps, where no white soldier could pursue with any hope to capture, and after years of peace had come to the coast again with the understanding that they should not be molested. The old man had heard of them from Johnson, the assistant, and he had once or twice seen canoes skirting the edge of the great bay in the distance, but he had never seen an Indian close enough to recognize him. The canoe had now come within half a mile of the tower, and was still heading straight for it.

The breeze died away again and the sun shone straight down with an intense heat. The tower cast no shadow either to east or west, and the ship's clock in the kitchen struck off eight bells. Enau mopped his streaming forehead and was about to turn into the galley to get a drink of water. The heat made him reel with dizziness, but the man in the boat made a movement, and he held his gaze fixed upon him. The canoe was coming close to the tower, and it was evident that the Indian would land there if the keeper allowed him. There was no way of getting up to the light except by way of the long iron ladder which reached from the gallery to the sea, a hundred feet below. It was an easy path to dispute with any number of men, especially as they must come through the heavy trap-door in the gallery at the top. There was no way of getting up over the outside, unless one could climb the long, smooth iron rods for a great distance and then reach out under the sill to get a hand-grip upon the edge of the floor and swing out over the gulf below. It would be a mere finger-grip at most, and a tap upon the bare knuckles would send the fellow to his death below. A good sailor might climb the smooth iron rods with great difficulty, but no one could climb up a hundred feet and swing out on that finger-tip hold with the hope of climbing to the rail above. The trap-door worked with a five-hundred-pound weight, and if any one tried to come up the thin iron ladder the keeper could simply lower the door and the stout three-inch planks would drop easily into place at will. Enau studied it all out while he gazed below, and it amused him to think what a surprised Indian it would be when he climbed up there to find the door drop fast in his face. No; the keeper was as much his own master in regard to human visitors as though he were a resident of some other planet. A thousand men could not approach him if he did not wish it. He could be all alone for an indefinite time, for he had provisions for half a year and water enough for a lifetime.

While he gazed at the approaching boat the man in her looked up. It was but a glance, a mere look at the head upon the rail above. Enau gasped. That one glance upward was enough for him. The fellow was not an Indian, after all. The suntanned face, burned to a dark mahogany color, belonged to one he had not forgotten. That glance, furtive, half shrinking, animal-like, without the movement of a single feature, belonged to—yes, there was no mistake. It was Robledo, the sailor who had witnessed against him, the survivor of the horror, the man who had encompassed his ruin.

Enau drew his breath quickly and stood up straight. The place seemed to swing about in the sunshine, the tower to rock like a ship in a seaway. Then he peered over again just as the craft came alongside one of the iron pillars. He did not show his face,—just his eyes,—for fear the fellow might recognize him and not come up the ladder. He would have the trapdoor ready for him, for it would never do to let that human devil know he was upon the light. Yes; perhaps he would let him come up, inside the gallery, but never go back. The sea would tell no tales. There would be no marks of a struggle, no evidence of a fight—a quick crack upon the head, and over the side, down a hundred feet to the waters of the reef, where the sharks lay waiting. That would be all. He could do it easily. But, then, the fellow might be missed, after all. Some one might know he had gone out to the light, and then there would be the investigation. This was what he did not want. There must be no inquiries, no questions asked him about his past. He was an old man now, and the memory of his terrible wrongs was fading. Let them die out. He would let the enemy go as he came. The fellow could not know he was in the tower, and there was no possibility of his recognizing him, as he had not shown his whole face over the rail. Even if he had, the hair and the beard of three years' growth would hide anything of Captain William Jacobs that still existed in him. No; he would let no one come up that ladder. He would live the rest of his life in peace and quiet. He loved the bright sunshine and the beautiful sea, and he could be satisfied where he was. His wife and daughter he had long given up. They had bade him farewell at the end of that trial, holding away from him, yet with tears streaming down their faces in the agony and horror of it all. He must be alone. There must be no one to tell him about them.

He looked down again, and saw the man below drawing on his trousers preparatory to climbing the ladder. Enau could see into the bottom of the boat beneath, and he noticed a harpoon used for spearing crawfish. Would the fellow take it with him? If so, it would be well not to let him come too near, for it could be thrown and might be dangerous. The man gave no hail, but turned his smooth-shaved face upward and began to mount the ladder. Enau went to the trap-door and loosed the weight softly. It creaked upon its hinges and settled slowly down until only a crack remained. Here he stopped it, with the bolts in readiness to shoot if necessary. He would watch the fellow and see if he showed signs of recognition. Ten years was a long time; the end of the Florida Reef was many thousand miles from where he had last seen him.

The man climbed slowly up the iron ladder, stopping now and then to look seaward. The current had swept his canoe to the northward of the lighthouse, where it trailed at the end of a long line. There was now nothing under him but the blue water. When he reached the first platform he climbed on to it and rested. It was very hot, and the climb made his mahogany-colored face darker than before. His hair was freshly parted, and looked as though it had been oiled or moistened. His coat he had left in his boat below, and his shirt was open at the neck, showing the strong, corded muscles of his throat and chest. His hands were brown and powerful, and the keeper noticed how his fingers closed with a light but certain grip upon the irons of the ladder.

In a moment he came on again, and when within a few feet of the door he looked upward and hailed. At that instant the old man closed the door and shot the bolts. He was now cut off as completely as though he had gone to the moon. The heat and excitement made his head whirl. He staggered away from the closed door and went back to the gallery. The sunshine danced upon the sea and all was quiet. Then he peered over the rail. A string of muttered curses floated up to him and a drunken voice called him many foul names, but he only smiled and stood gazing out to sea. He could not see the man below now, for the fellow was too high up under the platform, and he made his way to the kitchen and from there higher up into the lantern, where the man's voice could not be heard distinctly.

Hours passed, and the sunshine began to slant sharply. The tower cast a long shadow to the eastward, but the canoe was still swinging to her painter, and the voice of the fellow below was still heard calling forth curses upon him. The keeper was evidently not recognized, for he heard the name "Enau" repeated over and over again, and this was his name as lightkeeper—Robert Enau, head keeper of the Fowey Rocks lighthouse. If the fellow had recognized him he would have called him Jacobs, and then he would have tried to kill him. It grew dark, but he forgot to light his lantern, his whole mind taken with the one thought of how to get rid of his visitor. If the lantern was not lighted, the fellow might think that there was no one in the tower, after all, and would go away. The idea flashed through his brain for an instant, and then he centered his thoughts again on the fellow below and forgot the darkness and quiet of the tropic night. Suddenly he thought of the fellow's boat. If he could endanger it, the man might leave. He seized a heavy piece of iron and dropped it at the dark shadow floating at the end of the line. A dull crash told of the accuracy of his aim. Then the shadow faded out, and he knew the boat had sunk. There was no sound from the man upon the ladder below. Evidently he had gone down to the first landing and gone to sleep or was waiting, not knowing the damage done his craft. He could now neither go away nor come up, and the idea worried the keeper greatly. He was very dizzy with the heat and excitement, and his thoughts went again and again over the scenes of that last voyage and the trial following. In the gray of the early morning he was still sitting in the lantern, gazing out to sea, waiting for the sun to rise and show him his enemy below. The day dawned beautiful and clear, and the quiet heat continued. In a little while a noise upon the ladder attracted the old man's attention. He listened. What was the fellow saying?

"For God's sake let me up!"

Not he. No! Had the fellow shown him any mercy when he was at the end of his liberty? Why should he show him any now? All he wanted was for him to go away and let him be. He did not want to see the man. Go away!

The pitiless sunshine streamed through the iron piling and upon the man. His boat was gone. It had sunk during the night from the weight Enau had thrown into it, and the current had torn it loose. There was no way for the man to get off the light without swimming. He must stay or die. He might cling for a long time to the iron ladder and rest upon the landing, but he could not swim ten miles in that current with sharks abounding.

The day passed slowly, and the man upon the ladder raved and swore, begged and cajoled, but Enau was silent and implacable. He went back into the lantern, taking some bread with him. He was not hungry, but the heat made his head swim, and he must eat something. The day drew to a close and silence reigned below. The man had given up talking. Enau lay prone upon his stomach and peeped over the edge of the platform. He could see the man crouching upon the landing, lashed fast, to keep from falling, by a line made of his clothes. Darkness came and the heat abated a little, but no wind ruffled the surface of the Gulf Stream.

With a heavy bar in his hand the keeper sat and waited for any signs of fingers showing upon the edge of the platform. He would not let the fellow up—no, not for anything. If he died there, it was not his fault. He did not want him to come out to the light. He would not have him know that he, Captain Jacobs, was keeper.

The lantern remained unlighted. Now Enau was afraid to leave the platform an instant, for fear the fellow, desperate from his position, would climb over and kill him. He sat there during the hours of darkness and waited.

About three in the morning Enau saw two eyes staring at him. They were far away in the Hawk's Channel, but as the moments flew by they drew nearer. Soon a great shadow loomed up through the night, coming straight for the light-house. Then there was a sudden crash close aboard, the rattle and banging of ship's gear, followed by hoarse cries and curses. Enau went inside to the trap-door in the gallery, and sat there watching the bolts until daylight.

In the early morning there was a great noise below. Men shouted and called him by name, but he refused to answer. He peered over the edge of the platform, and he no sooner had done so than a perfect storm of voices greeted him. Two ship's boats were tied to the piling of the tower, and many men were crowding up the ladder. More were upon the deck of the vessel, which had rammed her nose high and dry upon the reef close to the light. They were coming to take possession of the tower by force, and he saw that he must now be inter-viewed, perhaps taken away bodily, for the fellow on the ladder had joined the rest, and they were calling to him to open that door.

The day passed without a disturbance. The men of the four-masted schooner upon the reef spent their time rigging gear to heave the vessel off, and the man had joined them. At dark Enau, seeing that no one was upon the ironwork, lighted the lantern and then came back to his post at the trap-door, holding his club in readiness to prevent any trespassing. He sat there hour after hour, but there was no sign of an attack from below.

About midnight there was a slight noise upon the plat-form of the gallery near the rail. The old man noticed it, but waited. Then some one rapped sharply upon the door at his feet, and he stood ready for the attack. Then all was quiet as before.

The heat was intense inside the gallery, and Enau mopped his forehead again and again. The whole lighthouse seemed to stagger, and the room went round and round. He was dizzy and failed to see the fingers which grasped the edge of the outside platform, or the form that swung out over the gulf below. A man drew himself up until his head was level with the floor. Then he put one foot up on the landing. He could not get back. It was a sheer hundred feet and over to the sea below, and the water was only three or four feet deep over the coral. He must gain the platform or go down to his death. Gradually he drew his weight upon the landing, clutching the rail with powerful fingers. Then he quickly stood upright and sprang over. He was in the light.

Enau saw him instantly and sprang at him. It was the same hated face, the furtive eyes he had reason to hate with all his soul. They clinched, and then began a struggle for life. And while they struggled the old man's mind could no longer hold his pent-up despair. He called out upon the scoundrel who had ruined him:

"You villain! you have pursued me for revenge—I'll give you all you want," he cried. "I know you; don't think I'll let you go." And, snarling like a wild beast, he strove with enormous power to crush the other against the rail, and so over into the sea. But the younger man was powerful. His strong fingers clutched at the old keeper's throat and closed upon it.

"I know you—I know you—I know your look—you pious-faced scoundrel!" gasped the old man. Then they fought on in silence. Suddenly those below heard a heavy fall. There was a moment's pause.

The room seemed to reel about the old keeper. He struggled wildly in that frightful grip. His breath came in bits of gasps and finally stopped under the awful pressure of those fingers. The scenes of his earlier life flitted through his mind. He saw the life boat again riding the oily sea in the South Atlantic; the starving men, their strained faces pinched and lined, their eager eyes staring about the eternal horizon for a sight of a sail; the last few days and the last survivors, the man with that look he would never forget—stars shot through his brain and fire flared before his vision. Then came blackness—a blank.

Those below, hearing the sounds of struggle dying away, called loudly to be let in. The man released his hold of the keeper's throat and shot back the bolts in the trap-door, letting a crowd of seamen come streaming into the light.

"Get some water, quick!" called Johnson, the assistant keeper, standing back and panting after the struggle. He was nearly exhausted, but still kept his gaze fixed upon the fallen old man.

"It's a touch of the sun," said the captain of the wrecked vessel, bending over the old keeper. "We must get him cooled off and ice to his head. Quick, John! jump aboard and tell the doctor to get a lump of ice and bring it here—git!"

"It's pretty bad," said Johnson; "I've been hanging on to the irons for two days, and you lose your ship, on account of a poor devil giving way under that sun; but it can't be helped."

"If you hadn't shaved and changed yourself so, and had come back in your own boat, he might have recognized you in time," said the captain; "but of course you didn't know."

"I think I did all I could," said Johnson, thinking of his climb over that outer rail.

"Yes, yes; I don't mean to find fault," said the captain; "but I lose my ship by it."

JOHN FLEMING WILSON

Ghost Island Light

Virtually forgotten today, John Fleming Wilson was born in Erie, Pennsylvania, on February 22, 1877, and received his A.B. degree from Princeton University in 1900. He taught for two years in Portland, Oregon, then turned to journalistic and literary work with newspapers and magazines such as the San Francisco Argonaut, The Oregonian, Pacific Monthly, *and the* Honolulu Advertiser. *Turning to the sea, he worked also as a lighthouse keeper, drydock worker, and deck officer on a seagoing tug—and the best of his hundred or so short stories often incorporate these experiences. He died in Santa Monica, California, on March 5, 1922, as a result of a freakish accident: as he began to shave that morning, a gas heater set fire to his robe, and he burned to death.*

His "Ghost Island Light" is a starkly realistic story first published in Harper's Weekly *on February 25, 1911.*

◻

When the commander of the Fortieth Light-house District assigned Thomas Sedgwick as assistant keeper of Ghost Island Light, he gazed at that young man contemplatively; his eyes then met the shy glance of Mrs. Sedgwick, who stood beside her slim husband. "I understand from Congressman Matthews that you haven't been married long, and that you think a stay in the north would be—would be *nice*." The last word the commander emphasized gently, as though to intimate that he had borrowed it for the moment from the girl who faced him so charmingly. "So I've assigned you to Ghost Island. Mr. Mason is the keeper, and after he has instructed you in your duties he will go off on three months' leave. It is a lonely post, but very likely you and Mrs. Sedgwick will enjoy it—sort of—ah—honeymoon." He smiled faintly, and then his manner became more brusque.

"You understand, Mr. Sedgwick, that in this Establishment the *light* is the important thing, and nothing must interfere with the complete and careful execution of our rigid rules. You will proceed to your station on the next steamer, the *Falcon*, which sails hence to-morrow. I have given your wife permission to accompany you and remain with you on the island until the return of Keeper Mason." He dismissed them with a pleasant nod. When they were gone, slim man and shapely woman, he leaned back in his official chair, and said to himself: "Now, I hope Matthews will help the Establishment to get that appropriation for those new lights and beacons. And we need—" But the commander's soliloquy has nothing more to do with the friend of a politician.

Sedgwick stared at his new station for the first time through a clinging mist. He leaned over the rail of the *Falcon*, and followed the mate's extended arm. That officer's grim glance scanned the assistant keeper, and caught the look of dismay. "It *is* lonely," he admitted. "And you won't see much shipping. Most of the time this mist hangs in the strait, and besides the *Falcon* no vessels at all take this passage except during the summer season when the tourist travel is heavy. You'll see us once a month going up, and eight days later coming down."

They, both of them, stared at the high, shrouded figure of Ghost Island, mere pinnacle of dripping rock rising out of the sullen sea. To the mate it stood a landmark: to the assistant keeper it meant nothing except the gentle touch on his arm that he knew expressed his wife's sudden comprehension of what Ghost Island was.

The mate went his way, and Mrs. Sedgwick whispered: "Is that our place, Tom? It's—it's only a rock—and wet—and it's so far away!"

"Only twenty miles from Metchnikan, Edie," he said, comfortingly.

That twenty miles they made the following day in a swinging launch, which plunged and snorted across the foamy strait, to land them on a damp noon in a crevice of the islet up which the slow waves hissed and sucked. The keeper met them, rubber-booted and flannel-shirted. He caught Mrs. Sedgwick out of the shallows, and lifted her to the concrete steps that led to the tower. Then he shook hands awkwardly with his new assistant. Sedgwick, in his unsoiled uniform, suddenly felt out of place before this rugged man, but managed to smile boyishly. Keeper Mason returned the glimmer of a smile, took the bundle of mail tossed him from the launch, shouldered a gunny-sack of provisions, and led the way up to the slim, white-painted tower. On the little landing before the door he turned and bellowed to the departing launch. "Take me off next week!" The launchman waved an assenting hand, and snorted off into the mist toward the hidden town twenty miles across.

In the bare entry to the light Edith Sedgwick's heart sank. Unadorned walls, heavy doors, thick window-glasses, and uncarpeted floors smelled of the salt mist, though the eye saw that everything had been cleaned and polished. The keeper gruffly said, "Here you are, ma'am." And with this became silent.

A week later the three of them stood on the railing about the lantern, and their attitudes showed that the days had altered their first strained relations. Edith Sedgwick, poised over the ledge, had one light hand on the keeper's jacket sleeve, and her husband was smiling across at him. "We'll do our best, Mr. Mason. Don't worry!"

Mason's tones came hoarsely from his throat. "I hope you won't get lonely," he rumbled. "It's an awfully lonesome rock, Mrs. Sedgwick. But then—law! the two of you will be company for each other."

"And I'll clean the lenses before I wash the dishes," she assured him.

The launch suddenly appeared, a speck in the gray fog. Mason turned abruptly and went down to the foot of the tower. There he waited till the other two caught up with him. "This is September," he remarked. "I'll be back Christmastime and let you two go over to Metchnikan for a holiday, ma'am."

Edith Sedgwick's face flushed warmly, and she turned shy eyes to her husband. "He mustn't be late!" she breathed.

Mason's face took on a ruddy hue. "I sha'n't be late, ma'am. Good-by!" He ran down the steps and to the shallow where the launch was swinging. Sedgwick followed him, and came back with a bundle of papers and some provisions.

"Now we're all alone, and you can sew for dear life, Edie," he laughed.

"Mr. Mason caught me with my sewing the other afternoon," she said, smiling softly. "And he nearly died, poor fellow. He was red as a beet all the rest of the day."

Sedgwick's face grew tense. "If he isn't back in time, I'll send you across in the launch, anyway," he told her.

"You might row me across in that boat you have all wrapped up out there," was the laughing rejoinder.

For two weeks after the keeper was gone they found their new duties fully occupying. Ghost Island, lying in a tortuous strait, had no fog signal, but the labor needed to keep lenses shining and lamp trimmed, with all their puzzlings over the sunset and sunrise hours in the almanac, and their deliberations as how to vary their menu, and bright hopings for Christmas sped the time. Then, with October's shrill winds, the fog lifted and the strait spread before them day and night in shimmering blue, rimmed with snow peaks, swept by black squalls from the far entrance to the nestled roofs of Metchnikan. When the full moon paled their bright lamp into a mere glow, the two of them would stand on the ledge and talk the intimate speech of lovers. Under that pallid splendor past life seemed almost tasteless and colorless. Their plans swept onward out of their solitude into a gorgeous world where he was to achieve fame and fortune in the great Establishment, and she, mother of strength and beauty, would bring up for the government a sturdy son to take his father's place when age overtook him.

In the last good days came the long straggling procession of cannery tenders, deep laden with salmon, top heavy with rollicking, singing men, free of the season's toil, bound down for the south and rude revelry. Their songs, rising to the gallery of Ghost Island Light, seemed prophetic of happiness and prosperity, and when the night finally came when the mist settled down once more behind the last south-bound craft, Edith crept into her husband's arms and shivered. "I hope Mr. Mason won't be late!" she whispered.

November flung its angry cloak about them, and for three weeks not a glimpse was to be had of far Metchnikan. Edith no longer flew up and down the iron stairs in the tower, and Sedgwick tended the lamp alone. And in his solitude, watching the gleam of the faithful lamp over the desolate waters, or its dart piercing into the whirling fog, the grim reality of his calling bore in on him. He no longer wore his uniform. Instead, he made his rounds in working clothes, cap tied under his chin. Once he heard some steamer making its way up the straits with odd, irregular whistle blasts that told of a pilot feeling his way through perils. That night he trimmed the great wick more carefully and more often. He pored over the instructions painfully, trying to assure himself that he was doing his best. To Edith he appeared as cheerful as ever, but when by himself his compressed lips and anxious eyes told of the maturing of manhood in him. He continually recalled Mason's brief remark: "A steamer coming through the pass expects to find this light burning, fog or no fog. That's what the light is here for. If the skippers weren't sure it was burning all the time, it would be worse than useless to 'em."

More and more this passing statement of the great fact of duty dug into his inner heart. Responsibility lightly entered upon became the plan of life. But he didn't open his mind to Edith till one night he came down on tiptoe to find her watching him wide-eyed. "Tom, you ought to get more sleep."

Forced heartiness was in his tones. "Sleep yourself, Edie. You ought to sleep too. I must keep good watch."

She stared at him out the dusky shadow of her bed. "I was thinking," she said, slowly. "This isn't fun, Tom. This is work."

"Work," he repeated, dully. "Yes. Just think—"

She caught the quick stoppage of his speech and took up the unspoken word. "I hear the sea down there on the rocks, and I think, too—what if some ship should come up here at night trying to find its way to safety, and the light wasn't lit?"

"It will always be lit," he said, confidently.

Her gentle thoughts went farther. "You must never forget the light on account of me," she murmured. "You 'member what the nice man in the office told us? He said we weren't here just on a honeymoon, but to tend to the light."

"Don't worry, dear heart," he whispered in her ear. "I'll not forget."

"And when I go ashore and you come back, and you know I'm sick, Tom, you won't neglect anything?"

"What makes you think I might?"

She thought for a while, and then turned her head sleepily on the pillow. "I think of so many things, Tom dear!"

The next night she slipped in on him in the lantern. So slowly and quietly did she come up the winding stairs and enter the full blast of the light that he started when he saw her.

"Are you sick?" he cried.

"Afraid!" she whispered, shrilly. "Afraid!"

Something in her tone stirred into action the dread that had lain crouched in his heart since they had come to Ghost Island. Together they sat on the iron plates under the lamp, huddled in each other's arms, dully hearing the roar of the wind and the thunder of the angry sea. At first he could not still her alarm. Each breaker crashing far below them seemed to shake her very soul. Every shriek of the wind made her wince. But gradually the warmth of his arms flowed into her chill veins, and when she slept he still held her closely.

In the dawn he carried her down the steps. She looked

back over his shoulder and murmured, drowsily, "I'll never go up there again—except in dreams, Tom."

Such foolish, fond fancies did she torture him with till December's gloom brought the day for Mason's return nearer. And as if to atone for weeks of tempest, the skies brightened and the wind died. But the launch, dancing over crested seas, brought evil news. The *Falcon* had been stormbound six hundred miles to the south, according to wireless reports. Mason could not arrive until three days later. "But I'll bring him over, fair or foul," the boatman assured Sedgwick. And when he was gone the assistant keeper realized too late his mistake. Edith should have gone off that day. But she accepted the situation gayly.

"I wouldn't think of going away without you," she cried. "And Mr. Mason promised us a holiday. And if it's stormy, maybe you can't get back, and then you will be near me when—" She hid her face on his shoulder.

For the next two days they watched the end of the strait for the smoke that should announce the coming of the *Falcon*. But the pass remained empty, apart from little clouds that sailed through between the peaks. And the second night Edith slipped on the iron stairs and fell to the cement-paved entry. When he picked her up, she smiled at him tremulously. "It is all right, Tom," she whispered through her white lips.

He would not take her assurance, sweet as it was. And his miserable persistence earned due reward. Tenderly wrought bravado fell away. Her sob pierced him to the heart as he bent over her. "He is dead!" she wailed.

Toiling to stay her ebbing spirit, he would have forgot the light burning above had she not time and again urged him with startled vehemence. "You haven't forgot the light, Tom! Please don't forget the light!" And he would rush up the steps, see that all was well, and rush down again. The last time he was just in time to know that she had spoken truth when motherhood had cried, "He is dead!" He wrapped the child in his jacket and laid it, at her anguished bidding, under the hollow of her arm. "I'll take him with me!" she breathed, and died.

At noon he halted about his automatic rounds and stared down into the peaceful, fair face. "She was afraid of the sea," he muttered, hoarsely. Later he came back to stoop over and whisper into the deaf ear: "I'll take you to the land, Edie. You sha'n't ever see the sea again!"

But the next day's violence tore the calmness from the straits, and morning showed him that all prospect of a vessel was beyond question. The barometer, consulted with aching eyes, offered no hope. And the *Falcon* was not yet in sight. He spent the afternoon in making a shroud of canvas into which he gently wrapped her, her babe under her protecting arm. Then he lit the great lamp, and paced the narrow gallery till dawn.

When the sunless day showed him only driving mist and a seething sea, and his attuned ear could not catch the sound of the *Falcon*'s whistle, he doggedly took his last look at his bride and babe, and carefully weighted the foot of the heavy shroud with rocks broken from the dripping cliff. Then, at the foot of the steps, bracing himself against the hurtling spray, he consigned his burden to the sweep of the tide. And dark, unseen fingers clutched at it and drew it down. He could have leaped after it in one last effort to reclaim this precious cargo had not the clock inside rung out the hour at which he must prepare the lamp, for now sunset and sunrise were but a few short hours apart. He turned and went up the steps, and shut the door on happiness and hope.

That night some flow in the tide drove against the wind, and Ghost Island's feet stood in a tide-rip that stretched in sinuous cruelty far out into the strait. Sedgwick stared down at it now and then. "If that should catch the *Falcon*, and the light were out, it would be all off with ship and passengers." So he trimmed the light assiduously and repeated to himself Edith's injunctions. Hoarse grief broke his dry-eyed calm at times, but each time he controlled its expression, till just before the dawn he looked down to the foot of the cliff and saw his wife's face staring up at him. He ran sobbing down the steps and snatched her from the waters, dragging her weight up the concrete steps till she lay once more on her own bed. The weights were gone from the foot of the shroud and some sharp rock's edge had cut the canvas back from her face. All that day he ate nothing, though he mechanically made his rounds.

When night was settled down and the lamp was burning brightly, Sedgwick carefully brought the body up into the lantern and laid it down under the warm glow of it. "I'll never leave you again alone," he told the pallid face, and sat by her till morning came again. As the belated sun drove the fog before it, his eyes caught a plume of smoke entering Metchnikan harbor. The *Falcon* had at last arrived. But the sweeping wind forebade hope of launch or keeper, and he contemplated the appearance bitterly before the mist once more engulfed it.

But the next day offered a slight hope. The wind had declined and the waves ran with no dangerous cresting: but no launch drove through the gray expanse. That evening Sedgwick glowered at the great lantern and cursed it. But a notice pinned on the wall forced him back to his duties, for that notice announced that the *Falcon* would repass the third night on her southward journey. And if the light were not shining? Sedgwick kissed the woman's frozen cheek and drove his arm against the resistance of the oil-pump.

Then he lost track of time. Day dawned and he extinguished the lamp. Night came and he lit it. Betweenwhiles he wandered from oil-house to lantern praying for strength to forget duty. That was the sole cry of his agonizing body and heart; that he might for an hour forget the great Establishment, whose bond servant he was, and enjoy the luxury of grief. But the shadow of authority lay over him, even when the *Falcon* had gone her lit way and the sun came out for a short hour. The dazed man stared into the sky and moaned, "I must never forget the light!"

But at last the frozen cheek of the dead woman took on a curious flush. Sedgwick saw that rising color and gazed down at the surf below him. "I can't send her down there again," he whispered, dry-lipped. And under the strain of that awful moment, confronting gross mortality, he ceased to be a servant of the government. He went and carefully undid the lashings of the boat that swung high in the shelter of the oil-house against emergency. When it was lowered (how, he did not know, himself) and rode in the sheltered shallows under the cliff, he went up the stairs for the last time and brought down his burden. A first trip had seen him carefully stop the oil flow in the font and put up the shutters to protect the lenses. Now he thrust the boat off, leaped in, and took the oars.

All the daylight hours he pulled weakly at the oars through the sullen sea, watching the ruddy flush creep up and up in the dead woman's face. And when the darkness came he watched for the loom of the land ahead of him, that vast shadow gained, followed it toward Metchnikan.

Father Francis was wakened at dawn by a cold hand on his arm. Accustomed to sudden wakings, he opened his eyes and saw the drawn face of a man exhausted by toil. Recognizing the signs, by the light of his candle, he rose and silently donned clothes and cassock. Then he came in, holding to glazed eyes the flickering light. "My son, what is the matter?" Sedgwick rose and went out.

One glance satisfied the priest, and himself he lifted the burden from the brine that filled the boat. And together, with a sleepy Indian to help, they buried Edith Sedgwick and her child far up among the low pines, out of sight of the sea. Then Sedgwick stonily turned back to his boat, notwithstanding entreaties.

But at the boat newly awakened men held him back. "You can't go back to-day," they told him, roughly.

"The light must be kept burning," he huskily explained.

Then the word passed that the light on Ghost Island had not been lit the night before, and they let him go: for Mason was not returned, owing to an accident, and the very launchman, properly sympathetic, refused even for pity's sake to risk his craft in the straits. Father Francis gave him a parting blessing. "Better to perform duty, my son," he said, wet-eyed, seeing the young man's sodden and stony face, "than to live wretchedly. *Abi in pacem!*"

That night the watchers in Metchnikan saw a flicker of

light twenty miles to the eastward, and went home. Father Francis, picking Ghost Island's slender gleam out of the increasing darkness, returned to his chapel and his prayers.

A month later Congressman Matthews entered the office of the Inspector of the Fortieth Light-house District. He greeted the commander and sat down in a chair close by him. "Look here," he said curiously, "I understand that youngster I was interested in—Sedgwick—didn't pan out well. What was the matter? Why did you discharge him?"

The commander's eyes met the Congressman's. "He did pretty well," he said, "but he left his light out one night."

"And you fired him?"

"It is against the rules," was the quiet answer. "You know, Congressman, the Establishment always expects its men to do their duty."

"But—"

The commander reached over and opened a magazine before his visitor's eye. "Read that," he said, gently.

Congressman Matthews read aloud, word by word: "'LIGHT-HOUSE—A tall building on the seashore in which the government maintains a lamp and the friend of a politician.'"

There ensued a silence. Then the Congressman met the commander's eye. "That poor boy went ashore to bury his wife!" he protested.

The commander smiled faintly. "I've transferred him to another light," he mentioned. They faced each other, man to man.

The Congressman was the first to speak, reaching for his hat. "I'm much obliged," he said, quietly. "I know your Establishment doesn't—"

"It didn't this time," came the clear official voice. "It appeared, from my investigation, that Assistant-Keeper Sedgwick, before leaving his station, carefully shut off his oil and *did not light his lamp*."

The politician stared. "Didn't light his lamp! Why, I should think—"

"Second-order lamps burn only eighteen hours on one

filling," said the commander, slowly. "And if he had lit his light before leaving the station, it would have burned down to the wick and very likely have set fire to the tower, and the government would have been out many thousands of dollars, and shipping would have lacked a beacon for a year."

The Congressman was thoughtful. He took his hat firmly in one hand. "Then he did his best?"

"All the men in the Establishment do their best," was the brief reply.

The Congressman held out his hand. "I'm glad Sedgwick was my friend," he said, simply.

HENRY VAN DYKE

Messengers
at the Window

A man who used stories to inspire and teach values, Henry Van Dyke was born in Germantown, Pennsylvania, on November 10, 1852. He received his baccalaureate in 1873 and a degree in Theology in 1874 from Princeton. In 1899 he returned to Princeton as a professor of literature after achieving fame as a pastor and writer. He remained at Princeton—with time out for government and military service—for the rest of his life. He died on April 10, 1933, two days after his golden wedding anniversary.

Perhaps best known for his Christmas classic, "The Story of the Other Wise Man," Van Dyke also wrote fantasies such as our choice for this anthology. "Messengers at the Window," a ghost story, first appeared in American, *October 1911. (Another story, "The Keeper of the Light," despite its similar setting, is a mostly unrelated prequel.)*

◻

The lighthouse on the Isle of the Wise Virgin—formerly called the Isle of Birds—still looks out over the blue waters of the Gulf of Saint Lawrence; its white tower motionless through the day, like a seagull sleeping on the rock; its great yellow eye wide-open and winking, winking steadily once a minute, all through the night. And the birds visit the island,—not in great flocks as formerly, but still plenty of them,—long-winged

57

waterbirds in the summer, and in the spring and fall short-winged landbirds passing in their migrations—the children and grandchildren, no doubt, of the same flying families that used to pass there fifty years ago, in the days when Nataline Fortin was "The Keeper of the Light." And she herself, that brave girl who said that the light was her "law of God," and who kept it, though it nearly broke her heart—Nataline is still guardian of the island and its flashing beacon of safety.

Not in her own person, you understand, for her dark curly hair long since turned white, and her brown eyes were closed, and she was laid at rest beside her father in the little grave-yard behind the chapel at Dead Men's Point. But her spirit still inhabits the island and keeps the light. The son whom she bore to Marcel Thibault was called Baptiste, after her father, and he is now the lighthouse-keeper; and her grand-daughter, Nataline, is her living image; a brown darling of a girl, merry and fearless, who plays the fife bravely all along the march of life.

It is good to have some duties in the world which do not change, and some spirits who meet them with a proud cheer-fulness, and some families who pass on the duty and the cheer from generation to generation—aristocrats, first families, the best blood.

Nataline the second was bustling about the kitchen of the lighthouse, humming a little song, as I sat there with my friend Baptiste, snugly sheltered from the night fury of the first September storm. The sticks of sprucewood snapped and crackled in the range; the kettle purred a soft accompaniment to the girl's low voice; the wind and the rain beat against the seaward window. I was glad that I had given up the trout fishing, and left my camp on the Sainte-Marguérite-en-bas, and come to pass a couple of days with the Thibaults at the lighthouse.

Suddenly there was a quick blow on the window behind me, as if someone had thrown a ball of wet seaweed or sand against it. I leaped to my feet and turned quickly, but saw nothing in the darkness.

"It is a bird, m'sieu'," said Baptiste, "only a little bird. The light draws them, and then it blinds them. Most times they fly against the big lantern above. But now and then one comes to this window. In the morning sometimes after a big storm we find a hundred dead ones around the tower."

"But, oh," cried Nataline, "the pity of it! I can't get over the pity of it. The poor little one,—how it must be deceived,—to seek light and to find death! Let me go out and look for it. Perhaps it is not dead."

She came back in a minute, the rain-drops shining on her cheeks and in her hair. In the hollow of her firm hands she held a feathery brown little body, limp and warm. We examined it carefully. It was stunned, but not killed, and apparently neither leg nor wing was broken.

"It is a white-throat sparrow," I said to Nataline, "you know the tiny bird that sings all day in the bushes, *sweet-sweet-Canada, Canada, Canada*?"

"But yes!" she cried, "he is the dearest of them all. He seems to speak to you,—to say, 'be happy.' We call him the *rossignol*. Perhaps if we take care of him, he will get well, and be able to fly to-morrow—and to sing again."

So we made a nest in a box for the little creature, which breathed lightly, and covered him over with a cloth so that he should not fly about and hurt himself. Then Nataline went singing up to bed, for she must rise at two in the morning to take her watch with the light. Baptiste and I drew our chairs up to the range, and lit our pipes for a good talk.

"Those small birds, m'sieu'," he began, puffing slowly at his pipe, "you think, without doubt, that it is all an affair of chance, the way they come,—that it means nothing,—that it serves no purpose for them to die?"

Certain words in an old book, about a sparrow falling to the ground, came into my mind, and I answered him carefully, hoping, perhaps, that he might be led on into one of those mystical legends which still linger among the exiled children of Britanny in the new world.

"From our side, my friend, it looks like chance—and from

the birds' side, certainly, like a very bad chance. But we do
not know all. Perhaps there is some meaning or purpose
beyond us. Who can tell?"

"I will tell you," he replied gravely, laying down his pipe,
and leaning forward with his knotted hands on his knees. "I
will tell you that those little birds are sometimes the messengers of God. They can bring a word or a warning from Him.
That is what we Bretons have believed for many centuries at
home in France. Why should it not be true here? Is He not
here also? Those birds are God's *coureurs des bois*. They do His
errands. Would you like to hear a thing that happened in this
house?"

This is what he told me.

My father, Marcel Thibault, was an honest man, strong in
the heart, strong in the arms, but, in the conscience,—well, he
had his little weaknesses, like the rest of us. You see his
father, the old Thibault lived in the days when there was no
lighthouse here, and wrecking was the chief trade of this
coast.

It is a cruel trade, m'sieu'—to live by the misfortune of
others. No one can be really happy who lives by such a trade
as that. But my father—he was born under that influence; and
all the time he was a boy he heard always people talking of
what the sea might bring to them, clothes and furniture, and
all kinds of precious things—and never a thought of what the
sea might take away from the other people who were ship-
wrecked and drowned. So what wonder is it that my father
grew up with weak places and holes in his conscience?

But my mother, Nataline Fortin—ah, m'sieu', she was a
straight soul, for sure—clean white, like a wild swan! I suppose she was not a saint. She was too fond of singing and
dancing for that. But she was a good woman, and nothing
could make her happy that came from the misery of another
person. Her idea of goodness was like this light in the lantern
above us—something faithful and steady that warns people
away from shipwreck and danger.

Well, it happened one day, about this time forty-eight

years ago, just before I was ready to be born, my father had to go up to the village of La Trinité on a matter of business. He was coming back in his boat at evening, with his sail up, and perfectly easy in his mind—though it was after sunset—because he knew that my mother was entirely capable of kindling the light and taking care of it in his absence. The wind was moderate, and the sea gentle. He had passed the Point du Caribou about two miles, when suddenly he felt his boat strike against something in the shadow.

He knew it could not be a rock. There was no hardness, no grating sound. He supposed it might be a tree floating in the water. But when he looked over the side of the boat, he saw it was the body of a dead man.

The face was bloated and blue, as if the man had been drowned for some days. The clothing was fine, showing that he must have been a person of quality; but it was disarranged and torn, as if he had passed through a struggle to his death. The hands, puffed and shapeless, floated on the water, as if to balance the body. They seemed almost to move in an effort to keep the body afloat. And on the little finger of the left hand there was a great ring of gold with a red stone set in it, like a live coal of fire.

When my father saw this ring a passion of covetousness leaped upon him.

"It is a thing of price," he said, "and the sea has brought it to me for the heritage of my unborn child. What good is a ring to a dead man? But for my baby it will be a fortune."

So he luffed the boat, and reached out with his oar, and pulled the body near to him, and took the cold, stiff hand into his own. He tugged at the ring, but it would not come off. The finger was swollen and hard, and no effort that he could make served to dislodge the ring.

Then my father grew angry, because the dead man seemed to withhold from him the bounty of the sea. He laid the hand across the gunwale of the boat, and, taking up the axe that lay beside him, with a single blow he chopped the little finger from the hand.

The body of the dead man swung away from the boat,

turned on its side, lifting its crippled left hand into the air, and sank beneath the water. My father laid the finger with the ring upon it under the thwart, and sailed on, wishing that the boat would go faster. But the wind was light, and before he came to the island it was already dark, and a white creeping fog, very thin and full of moonlight, was spread over the sea like a shroud.

As he went up the path to the house he was trying to pull off the ring. At last it came loose in his hand; and the red stone was as bright as a big star on the edge of the sky, and the gold was heavy in his palm. So he hid the ring in his vest.

But the finger he dropped in a cluster of blueberry bushes not far from the path. And he came into the house with a load of joy and trouble on his soul; for he knew that it is wicked to maim the dead, but he thought also of the value of the ring.

My mother Nataline was able to tell when people's souls had changed, without needing to wait for them to speak. So she knew that something great had happened to my father, and the first word she said when she brought him his supper was this:

"How did it happen?"

"What has happened?" said he, a little surprised, and putting down his head over his cup of tea to hide his face.

"Well," she said in her joking way, "that is just what you haven't told me, so how can I tell you? But it was something very bad or very good, I know. Now which was it?"

"It was good," said he, reaching out his hand to cut a piece from the loaf, "it was as good—as good as bread."

"Was it by land," she said, "or was it by sea?"

He was sitting at the table just opposite that window, so that he looked straight into it as he lifted his head to answer her.

"It was by sea," he said smiling, "a true treasure of the deep."

Just then there came a sharp stroke and a splash on the window, and something struggled and scrabbled there against the darkness. He saw a hand with the little finger cut off spread out against the pane.

"My God," he cried, "what is that?"

But my mother, when she turned, saw only a splotch of wet on the outside of the glass.

"It is only a bird," she said, "one of God's messengers. What are you afraid of? I will go out and get it."

She came back with a cedar-bird in her hand—one of those brown birds that we call *recollets* because they look like a monk with a hood. Her face was very grave.

"Look," she cried, "it is a *recollet*. He is only stunned a little. Look, he flutters his wings, we will let him go—like that! But he was sent to this house because there is something here to be confessed. What is it?"

By this time my father was disturbed, and the trouble was getting on top of the joy in his soul. So he pulled the ring out of his vest and laid it on the table under the lamp. The gold glittered, and the stone sparkled, and he saw that her eyes grew large as she looked at it.

"See," he said, "this is the good fortune that the waves brought me on the way home from La Trinité. It is a heritage for our baby that is coming."

"The waves!" she cried, shrinking back a little. "How could the waves bring a heavy thing like that? It would sink."

"It was floating," he answered, casting about in his mind for a good lie; "it was floating—about two miles this side of the Point du Caribou—it was floating on a piece of—"

At that point there was another blow on the window, and something pounded and scratched against the glass. Both of them were looking this time, and again my father saw the hand without the little finger—but my mother could see only a blur and a movement.

He was terrified, and fell on his knees praying. She trembled a little, but stood over him brave and stern.

"What is it that you have seen," said she; "tell me, what has made you afraid?"

"A hand," he answered, very low, "a hand on the window."

"A hand!" she cried, "then there must be some one waiting outside. You must go and let him in."

"Not I," whispered he, "I dare not."

Then she looked at him hard, and waited a minute. She opened the door, peered out, trembled again, crossed the threshold, and returned with the body of a blackbird.

"Look," she cried, "another messenger of God—his heart is beating a little. I will put him here where it is warm— perhaps he will get well again. But there is a curse coming upon this house. Confess. What is this about hands?"

So he was moved and terrified to open his secret half-way.

"On the rocks this side of the point," he stammered, "as I was sailing very slowly—there was something white—the arm and hand of a man—this ring on one of the fingers. Where was the man? Drowned and lost. What did he want of the ring? It was easy to pull it—"

As he said this, there was a crash at the window. The broken pane tinkled upon the floor. In the opening they both saw, for a moment, a hand with the little finger cut off and the blood dripping from it.

When it faded, my mother Nataline went to the window, and there on the floor, in a little red pool, she found the body of a dead cross-bill, all torn and wounded by the glass through which it had crashed.

She took it up and fondled it. Then she gave a great sigh, and went to my father Marcel and kneeled beside him.

(You understand, m'sieu', it was he who narrated all this to me. He said he never should forget a word or a look of it until he died—and perhaps not even then.)

So she kneeled beside him and put one hand over his shoulder, the dead cross-bill in the other.

"Marcel," she said, "thou and I love each other so much that we must always go together—whether to heaven or to hell—and very soon our little baby is to be born. Wilt thou keep a secret from me now? Look, this is the last messenger at the window—the blessed bird whose bill is twisted because he tried to pull out the nail from the Saviour's hand on the cross, and whose feathers are always red because the blood of

Jesus fell upon them. It is a message of pardon that he brings us, if we repent. Come, tell the whole of the sin."

At this the heart of my father Marcel was melted within him, as a block of ice is melted when it floats into the warmer sea, and he told her all of the shameful thing that he had done.

She stood up and took the ring from the table with the ends of her fingers, as if she did not like to touch it.

"Where hast thou put it," she asked, "the finger of the hand from which this thing was stolen?"

"It is among the bushes," he answered, "beside the path to the landing."

"Thou canst find it," said she, "as we go to the boat, for the moon is shining and the night is still. Then thou shalt put the ring where it belongs, and we will row to the place where the hand is—dost thou remember it?"

So they did as she commanded. The sea was very quiet and the moon was full. They rowed together until they came about two miles from the Point du Caribou, at a place which Marcel remembered because there was a broken cliff on the shore.

When he dropped the finger, with the great ring glittering upon it, over the edge of the boat, he groaned. But the water received the jewel in silence, with smooth ripples, and a circle of light spread away from it under the moon, and my mother Nataline smiled like one who is well content.

"Now," she said, "we have done what the messengers at the window told us. We have given back what the poor man wanted. God is not angry with us now. But I am very tired—row me home, for I think my time is near at hand."

The next day, just before sunset, was the day of my birth. My mother Nataline told me, when I was a little boy, that I was born to good fortune. And, you see, m'sieu', it was true, for I am the keeper of her light.

WILBUR DANIEL STEELE

The Woman at Seven Brothers

Superb prose stylist Wilbur Daniel Steele was born in Greensboro, North Carolina, on March 17, 1886. He received an A.B. degree from the University of Denver in 1907 and an honorary doctorate from the same institution in 1932. A writers' writer, he was primarily known for his many excellent short stories. Indeed, the O. Henry Award Committee presented him with a special award in 1921 "for maintaining the highest level of merit for three years among American short story writers." Later they awarded him three first prizes for best American short story of the year in 1925, 1926, and 1931. On May 26, 1970, Steele died in Essex, Connecticut.

"The Woman at Seven Brothers" first appeared in Harper's *in December 1917. It is one of an early series of stories he wrote about Massachusetts fishermen—particularly the ones of Portuguese background—and the sea.*

⌑

I tell you sir, I was innocent. I didn't know any more about the world at twenty-two than some do at twelve. My uncle and aunt in Duxbury brought me up strict; I studied hard in high school, I worked hard after hours, and I went to church twice on Sundays, and I can't see it's right to put me in a place like this, with crazy people. Oh yes, I know they're crazy—

you can't tell *me*. As for what they said in court about finding her with her husband, that's the inspector's lie, sir, because he's down on me, and wants to make it look like my fault.

No, sir, I can't say as I thought she was handsome—not at first. For one thing, her lips were too thin and white, and her color was bad. I'll tell you a fact, sir; that first day I came off to the light I was sitting on my cot in the storeroom (that's where the assistant keeper sleeps at the Seven Brothers), as lone-some as I could be, away from home for the first time and the water all around me, and, even though it was a calm day, pounding enough on the ledge to send a kind of a *woom-woom-woom* whining up through all that solid rock of the tower. And when old Fedderson poked his head down from the living room, with the sunshine above making a kind of bright frame around his hair and whiskers, to give me a cheery, "Make yourself to home, son!" I remember I said to myself: "*He's* all right. I'll get along with *him*. But his wife's enough to sour milk." That was queer, because she was so much under him in age—'long about twenty-eight or so, and him nearer fifty. But that's what I said, sir.

Of course that feeling wore off, same as any feeling will wear off sooner or later in a place like the Seven Brothers. Cooped up in a place like that you come to know folks so well that you forget what they *do* look like. There was a long time I never noticed her, any more than you'd notice the cat. We used to sit of an evening around the table, as if you were Fedderson there, and me here, and her somewhere back there, in the rocker, knitting. Fedderson would be working on his Jacob's ladder, and I'd be reading. He'd been working on that Jacob's ladder a year, I guess, and every time the inspector came off with the tender he was so astonished to see how good that ladder was that the old man would go to work and make it better. That's all he lived for.

If I was reading, as I say, I daren't take my eyes off the book, or Fedderson had me. And then he'd begin—what the inspector said about him. How surprised the member of the board had been, that time, to see everything so clean about the light. What the inspector had said about Fedderson's being stuck here in a second-class light—best keeper on the coast. And so on and so on, till either he or I had to go aloft and have a look at the wicks.

He'd been there twenty-three years, all told, and he'd got used to the feeling that he was kept down unfair—so used to it, I guess, that he fed on it and told himself how folks ashore would talk when he was dead and gone—best keeper on the coast—kept down unfair. Not that he said that to me. No, he was far too loyal and humble, and respectful, doing his duty without complaint, as anybody could see.

And all the time, night after night, hardly ever a word out of the woman. As I remember it, she seemed more like a piece of furniture than anything else—not even a very good cook, nor over and above tidy. One day, when he and I were trimming the lamp, he passed the remark that his *first* wife used to dust the lens and take a pride in it. Not that he said a word against Anna, though. He never said a word against any living mortal; he was too upright.

I don't know how it came about; or, rather, I *do* know, but it was so sudden, and so far away from my thoughts, that it shocked me, like the world turned over. It was at prayers. That night I remember Fedderson was uncommon long-winded. We'd had a batch of newspapers out by the tender, and at such times the old man always made a long watch of it, getting the world straightened out. For one thing, the United States minister to Turkey was dead. Well, from him and his soul, Fedderson got on to Turkey and the Presbyterian college there, and from that to heathen in general. He rambled on and on, like the surf on the ledge, *woom-woom-woom,* never coming to an end.

You know how you'll be at prayers sometimes. My mind strayed. I counted the canes in the chair seat where I was kneeling; I plaited a corner of the tablecloth between my fingers for a spell, and by and by my eyes went wandering up the back of the chair.

The woman, sir, was looking at me. Her chair was back to mine, close, and both our heads were down in the shadow under the edge of the table, with Fedderson clear over on the other side by the stove. And there was her two eyes hunting mine between the spindles in the shadow. You won't believe me, sir, but I tell you I felt like jumping to my feet and running out of the room—it was so queer.

I don't know what her husband was praying about after that. His voice didn't mean anything, no more than the seas on the ledge away down there. I went to work to count the canes in the seat again, but all my eyes were in the top of my head. It got so I couldn't stand it. We were at the Lord's Prayer, saying it singsong together, when I had to look up again. And there her two eyes were, between the spindles, hunting mine. Just then all of us were saying, "Forgive us our trespasses . . ." I thought of it afterward.

When we got up she was turned the other way, but I couldn't help seeing her cheeks were red. It was terrible. I wondered if Fedderson would notice, though I might have known he wouldn't—not him. He was in too much of a hurry to get at his Jacob's ladder, and then he had to tell me for the tenth time what the inspector'd said that day about getting him another light—Kingdom Come, maybe, he said.

I made some excuse or other and got away. Once in the storeroom, I sat down on my cot and stayed there a long time, feeling queerer than anything. I read a chapter in the Bible, I don't know why. After I'd got my boots off I sat with them in my hands for as much as an hour, I guess, staring at the oil tank and its lopsided shadow on the wall. I tell you, sir, I was shocked. I was only twenty-two, remember, and I was shocked and horrified.

And when I did turn in, I didn't sleep at all well. Two or three times I came to, sitting straight up in bed. Once I got up and opened the outer door to have a look. The water was like glass, dim, without a breath of wind, and the moon was going down. Over on the black shore I made out two lights in a village, like a pair of eyes watching. Lonely? My, yes! Lonely and nervous. I had a horror of her, sir. The dinghy boat hung on its davits just there in front of the door, and for a minute I had an awful hankering to climb into it, lower away, and row off, no matter where. It sounds foolish.

Well, it seemed foolish next morning, with the sun shining and everything as usual—Fedderson sucking his pen and wagging his head over his eternal "log," and his wife down in the rocker with her head in the newspaper, and her breakfast work still waiting. I guess that jarred it out of me more than anything else—sight of her slouched down there, with her stringy, yellow hair and her dusty apron and the pale back of her neck, reading the society notes. *Society notes!* Think of it! For the first time since I came to Seven Brothers I wanted to laugh.

I guess I did laugh when I went aloft to clean the lamp and found everything so free and breezy, gulls flying high and little whitecaps making under a westerly. It was like feeling a big load dropped off your shoulders. Fedderson came up with his dust rag and cocked his head at me.

"What's the matter, Ray?" said he.

"Nothing," said I. And then I couldn't help it. "Seems kind of out of place for society notes," said I, "out here at Seven Brothers."

He was the other side of the lens, and when he looked at me he had a thousand eyes, all sober. For a minute I thought he was going on dusting, but then he came out and sat down on a sill.

"Sometimes," said he, "I get to thinking if may be a mite dull for her out here. She's pretty young, Ray. Not much more'n a girl, hardly."

"Not much more'n a *girl!*" It gave me a turn, sir, as though I'd seen my aunt in short dresses.

"It's a good home for her, though," he went on slow. "I've seen a lot worse ashore, Ray. Of course if I could get a shore light—"

"Kingdom Come's a shore light."

He looked at me out of his deep-set eyes, and then he turned them around the lightroom, where he'd been so long.

"No," said he, wagging his head. "It ain't for such as me."

I never saw so humble a man.

"But look here," he went on, more cheerful. "As I was telling her just now, a month from yesterday's our fourth anniversary, and I'm going to take her ashore for the day and give her a holiday—new hat and everything. A girl wants a mite of excitement now and then, Ray."

There it was again, that "girl." It gave me the fidgets, sir. I had to do something about it. It's close quarters for last names in a light, and I'd taken to calling him Uncle Matt soon after I came. Now, when I was at table that noon, I spoke over to where she was standing by the stove, getting him another help of chowder.

"I guess I'll have some, too, *Aunt* Anna," said I, matter-of-fact.

She never said a word nor gave a sign—just stood there kind of round-shouldered, dipping the chowder. And that night at prayers I hitched my chair around the table, with its back the other way.

You get awful lazy in a lighthouse, some ways. No matter how much tinkering you've got, there's still a lot of time and there's such a thing as too much reading. The changes in weather get monotonous, too, by and by; the light burns the same on a thick night as it does on a fair one. Of course there's the ships, northbound, southbound—windjammers, freighters, passenger boats full of people. In the watches at night you can see their lights go by and wonder what they are, how they're laden, where they'll fetch up, and all. I used to do that almost every evening when it was my first watch, sitting out on the walk-around up there with my legs hanging over the edge and my chin propped on the railing—lazy. The Boston boat was the prettiest to see, with her three tiers of portholes lit, like a string of pearls wrapped round and round a woman's neck—well away, too, for the ledge must have made a couple of hundred fathoms off the light, like a white dogtooth of a breaker, even on the darkest night.

Well, I was lolling there one night, as I say, watching the Boston boat go by, not thinking of anything special, when I heard the door on the other side of the tower open and footsteps coming around to me.

By and by I nodded toward the boat and passed the remark that she was fetching in uncommon close tonight. No answer. I made nothing of that, for oftentimes Fedderson wouldn't answer, and after I'd watched the lights crawling on through the dark a spell, just to make conversation I said I guessed there'd be a bit of weather before long.

"I've noticed," said I, "when there's weather coming on, and the wind in the northeast, you can hear the orchestra playing aboard of her just over there. I make it out now. Do you?"

"Yes. Oh—yes! I hear it all right!"

You can imagine I started. It wasn't him, but her. And there was something in the way she said that speech, sir—something—well—unnatural. Like a hungry animal snapping at a person's hand.

I turned and looked at her sidewise. She was standing by the railing, leaning a little outward, the top of her from the waist picked out bright by the lens behind her. I didn't know what in the world to say, and yet I had a feeling I ought not to sit there mum.

"I wonder," said I, "what that captain's thinking of, fetching in so handy tonight. It's no way. I tell you, if 'twasn't for this light, she'd go to work and pile up on the ledge some thick night——"

She turned at that and stared straight into the lens. I didn't like the look of her face. Somehow, with its edges cut hard all around, and its two eyes closed down to slits, like a cat's, it made a kind of mask.

"And then," I went on, uneasy enough, "—and then where'd all their music be of a sudden, and their goings on and their singing——"

"And dancing!" She clipped me off so quick it took my breath.

"D-d-dancing?" said I.

"That's dance music," said she. She was looking at the boat again.

"How do you know?" I felt I had to keep on talking.

Well, sir—she laughed. I looked at her. She had on a shawl of some stuff or other that shined in the light; she had it pulled tight around her with her two hands in front at her breast, and I saw her shoulders swaying in tune.

"How do I *know*?" she cried. Then she laughed again, the

same kind of a laugh. It was queer, sir, to see her, and to hear her. She turned, as quick as that, and leaned toward me. "Don't you know how to dance, Ray?" said she.

"N-no," I managed, and I was going to say "Aunt Anna," but the thing choked in my throat. I tell you she was looking square at me all the time with her two eyes and moving with the music as if she didn't know it. By heavens, sir, it came over me of a sudden that she wasn't so bad-looking, after all. I guess I must have sounded like a fool.

"You—you see," said I, "she's cleared the rip there now, and the music's gone. You—you—hear?"

"Yes," said she, turning back slow. "That's where it stops every night—night after night—it stops just there—at the rip."

When she spoke again her voice was different. I never heard the like of it, thin and taut as a thread. It made me shiver, sir.

"I hate 'em!" That's what she said. "I hate 'em all. I'd like to see 'em dead. I'd love to see 'em torn apart on the rocks, night after night. I could bathe my hands in their blood, night after night."

And do you know, sir, I saw it with my own eyes, her hands moving in each other above the rail. But it was her voice, though. I didn't know what to do or what to say, so I poked my head through the railing and looked down at the water. I don't think I'm a coward, sir, but it was like a cold—ice-cold—hand, taking hold of my beating heart.

When I looked up finally, she was gone. By and by I went in and had a look at the lamp, hardly knowing what I was about. Then, seeing by my watch it was time for the old man to come on duty, I started to go below. In the Seven Brothers, you understand, the stair goes down in a spiral through a well against the south wall, and first there's the door to the keeper's room, and then you come to another, and that's the living room, and then down to the storeroom. And at night, if you don't carry a lantern, it's as black as the pit.

Well, down I went, sliding my hand along the rail, and as usual I stopped to give a rap on the keeper's door, in case he was taking a nap after supper. Sometimes he did.

I stood there, blind as a bat, with my mind still up on the walk-around. There was no answer to my knock. I hadn't expected any. Just from habit, and with my right foot already hanging down for the next step, I reached out to give the door one more tap for luck.

Do you know, sir, my hand didn't fetch up on anything. The door had been there a second before, and now the door wasn't there. My hand just went on going through the dark, on and on, and I didn't seem to have sense or power enough to stop it. There didn't seem any air in the well to breathe, and my ears were drumming to the surf—that's how scared I was. And then my hand touched the flesh of a face, and something in the dark said, "Oh!" no louder than a sigh.

Next thing I knew, sir, I was down in the living room, warm and yellow-lit, with Fedderson cocking his head at me across the table, where he was at that eternal Jacob's ladder of his.

"What's the matter, Ray?" said he. "Lord's sake, Ray!"

"Nothing," said I. Then I think I told him I was sick. That night I wrote a letter to A.L. Peters, the grain dealer in Dux-bury, asking for a job—even though it wouldn't go ashore for a couple of weeks, just the writing of it made me feel better.

It's hard to tell you how those two weeks went by. I don't know why, but I felt like hiding in a corner all the time. I had to come to meals. But I didn't look at her, though, not once, unless it was by accident. Fedderson thought I was still ailing and nagged me to death with advice and so on. One thing I took care not to do, I can tell you, and that was to knock on his door till I'd made certain he wasn't below in the living room—though I was tempted to.

Yes, sir; that's a queer thing, and I wouldn't tell you if I hadn't set out to give you the truth. Night after night, stopping there on the landing in that black pit, the air gone out of my lungs and the surf drumming in my ears and sweat standing cold on my neck—and one hand lifting up in the air—God forgive me, sir! Maybe I did wrong not to look at her more, drooping about her work in her gingham apron, with her hair stringing.

When the inspector came off with the tender, that time, I told him I was through. That's when he took the dislike to me, I guess, for he looked at me kind of sneering and said, soft as I was, I'd have to put up with it till next relief. And then, said he, there'd be a whole house-cleaning at Seven Brothers, because he'd gotten Fedderson the berth at Kingdom Come. And with that he slapped the old man on the back.

I wish you could have seen Fedderson, sir. He sat down on my cot as if his knees had given way. Happy? You'd think he'd be happy, with all his dreams come true. Yes, he was happy, beaming all over—for a minute. Then, sir, he began to shrivel up. It was like seeing a man cut down in his prime before your eyes. He began to wag his head.

"No," said he. "No, no; it's not for such as me. I'm good enough for Seven Brothers, and that's all, Mr. Bayliss. That's all."

And for all the inspector could say, that's what he stuck to. He'd figured himself a martyr so many years, nursed that injustice like a mother with her first-born, sir; and now in his old age, so to speak, they weren't going to rob him of it. Fedderson was going to wear out his life in a second-class light, and folks would talk—that was his idea. I heard him hailing down as the tender was casting off:

"See you tomorrow, Mr. Bayliss. Yep. Coming shore with the wife for a spree. Anniversary. Yep."

But he didn't sound much like a spree. They *had* robbed him, partly, after all. I wondered what she thought about it. I didn't know till night. She didn't show up to supper, which Fedderson and I got ourselves—had a headache, he said. It was my early watch. I went and lit up and came back to read a spell. He was finishing off the Jacob's ladder, and thoughtful, like a man that's lost a treasure. Once or twice I caught him looking about the room on the sly. It was pathetic, sir.

Going up the second time, I stepped out on the walk-around to have a look at things. She was there on the seaward side, wrapped in that silky thing. A fair sea was running across the ledge, and it was coming on a little thick—not too thick. Off to the right the Boston boat was blowing, *whroom-*

whroom! Creeping up on us, quarter-speed. There was another fellow behind her, and a fisherman's conch farther offshore.

I don't know why, but I stopped beside her and leaned on the rail. She didn't appear to notice me, one way or another. We stood and we stood, listening to the whistles, and the longer we stood the more it got on my nerves, her not noticing me. I suppose she'd been too much on my mind lately. I began to be put out. I scraped my feet. I coughed. By and by I said out loud:

"Look here, I guess I better get out the foghorn and give those fellows a toot."

"Why?" said she, without moving her head—calm as that.

Why? It gave me a turn, sir. For a minute I stared at her. "Why? Because if she don't pick up this light before very many minutes she'll be too close in to wear—tide'll have her on the rocks—that's why!"

I couldn't see her face, but I could see one of her silk shoulders lift a little, like a shrug. And there I kept on staring at her, a dumb one, sure enough. I know what brought me to was hearing the Boston boat's three sharp toots as she picked up the light—mad as anything—and swung her helm aport. I turned away from her, sweat dripping down my face, and walked around to the door. It was just as well, too, for the feed pipe was plugged in the lamp and the wicks were popping. She'd have been out in another five minutes, sir.

When I'd finished, I saw that woman standing in the doorway. Her eyes were bright. I had a horror of her, sir, a living horror.

"If only the light had been out," said she, low and sweet.

"God forgive you," said I. "You don't know what you're saying."

She went down the stair into the well, winding out of sight, and as long as I could see her, her eyes were watching mine. When I went myself, after a few minutes, she was waiting for me on that first landing, standing still in the dark. She took hold of my hand, though I tried to get it away.

"Good-by," said she in my ear.

"Good-by?" said I. I didn't understand.

"You heard what he said today—about Kingdom Come? Be it so—on his own head. I'll never come back here. Once I set foot ashore—I've got friends in the Brightonboro, Ray."

I got away from her and started on down. But I stopped. "Brightonboro?" I whispered back. "Why do you tell *me*?" My throat was raw to the words, like a sore.

"So you'd know," said she.

Well, sir, I saw them off next morning, down that new Jacob's ladder into the dinghy boat, her in a dress of blue velvet and him in his best cutaway and derby—rowing away, smaller and smaller, the two of them. And then I went back and sat on my cot, leaving the door open and the ladder still hanging down the wall, along with the boat falls.

I don't know whether it was relief, or what. I suppose I must have been worked up even more than I'd thought those past weeks, for now it was all over I was like a rag. I got down on my knees, sir, and prayed to God for the salvation of my soul, and when I got up and climbed to the living room it was half past twelve by the clock. There was rain on the windows and the sea was running blue-black under the sun. I'd sat there all that time not knowing there was a squall.

It was funny; the glass stood high, but those black squalls kept coming and going all afternoon, while I was at work up in the light-room. And I worked hard, to keep myself busy. First thing I knew it was five, and no sign of the boat yet. It began to get dim and kind of purplish gray over the land. The sun was down. I lit up, made everything snug, and got out the night glasses to have another look for that boat. He'd said he intended to get back before five. No sign. And then, standing there, it came over me that of course he wouldn't be coming off—he be hunting *her*, poor old fool. It looked like I had to stand two men's watches that night.

Never mind. I felt like myself again, even if I hadn't had any dinner or supper. Pride came to me that night on the walk-around, watching the boats go by—little boats, big boats, the Boston boat with all her pearls and her dance music. They couldn't see me; they didn't know who I was; but to the last of them, they depended on *me*. They say a man must be born again. Well, I was born again. I breathed deep in the wind.

Dawn broke hard and red as a dying coal. I put out the light and started to go below. Born again; yes, sir. I felt so good I whistled in the well, and when I came to that first door on the stair I reached out in the dark to give it a rap for luck. And then, sir, the hair prickled all over my scalp, when I found my hand just going on and on through the air, the same as it had gone once before, and all of a sudden I wanted to yell, because I thought I was going to touch flesh. It's funny what their just forgetting to close their door did to me, isn't it?

Well, I reached for the latch and pulled it to with a bang and ran down as if a ghost was after me. I got up some coffee and bread and bacon for breakfast. I drank the coffee. But somehow I couldn't eat, all along of that open door. The light in the room was blood. I got to thinking. I thought how she'd talked about those men, women, and children on the rocks, and how she'd made to bathe her hands over the rail. I almost jumped out of my chair then; it seemed for a wink she was there beside the stove watching me with that queer half smile—really, I seemed to see her for a flash across the red tablecloth in the red light of dawn.

"Look here!" said I to myself, sharp enough; and then I gave myself a good laugh and went below. There I took a look out of the door, which was till open, with the ladder hanging down. I made sure to see the poor old fool come pulling around the point before very long now.

My boots were hurting a little, and taking them off, I lay down on the cot to rest, and somehow I went to sleep. I had horrible dreams. I saw her again standing in that blood-red kitchen, and she seemed to be washing her hands, and the surf on the ledge was whining up the tower, louder and louder all the time, and what it whined was, "Night after night—night after night." What woke me was cold water in my face.

The storeroom was in gloom. That scared me at first; I thought night had come, and remembered the light. But then I saw the gloom was of a storm. The floor was shining wet, and the water in my face was spray, flung up through the open door. When I ran to close it, it almost made me dizzy to see the gray-and-white breakers marching past. The land was gone; the sky shut down heavy overhead; there was a piece of wreckage on the back of a swell, and the Jacob's ladder was carried clean away. How that sea had picked up so quick I can't think. I looked at my watch, and it wasn't four in the afternoon yet.

When I closed the door, sir, it was almost dark in the storeroom. I'd never been in the light before in a gale of wind. I wondered why I was shivering so, till I found it was the floor below me shivering, and the walls and stair. Horrible crunchings and grindings ran away up the tower, and now and then there was a great thud somewhere, like a cannon shot in a cave. I tell you, sir, I was alone, and I was in a mortal fright for a minute or so. And yet I had to get myself together. There was the light up there not tended to, and an early dark coming on and a heavy night and all, and I had to go. And I had to pass that door.

You'll say it's foolish, sir, and maybe it *was* foolish. Maybe it was because I hadn't eaten. But I began thinking of that door up there the minute I set foot on the stair, and all the way up through that howling dark well I dreaded to pass it. I told myself I wouldn't stop. I didn't stop. I felt the landing under-foot and I went on, four steps, five—and then I couldn't. I turned and went back. I put out my hand and it went on into nothing. That door, sir, was open again.

I left it be; I went on up to the lightroom and set to work. It was bedlam there, sir, screeching bedlam, but I took no notice. I kept my eyes down. I trimmed those seven wicks, sir, as neat as ever they were trimmed; I polished the brass till it shone, and I dusted the lens. It wasn't till that was done that I let myself look back to see who it was standing there, half out of sight in the well. It was her, sir.

"Where'd you come from?" I asked. I remember my voice was sharp.

"Up Jacob's ladder," said she, and hers was like the sirup of flowers.

I shook my head. I was savage, sir. "The ladder's carried away."

"I cast it off," said she, with a smile.

"Then," said I, "you must have come while I was asleep." Another thought came on me heavy as a ton of steel. "And where's *he*?" said I. "Where's the boat?"

"He's drowned," said she, as easy as that. "And I let the boat go adrift. You wouldn't hear me when I called."

"But look here," said I. "If you came through the store-room, why didn't you wake me up? Tell me that!" It sounds foolish enough, me standing like a lawyer in court, trying to prove she *couldn't* be there.

She didn't answer for a moment. I guess she sighed, though I couldn't hear for the gale, and her eyes grew soft, sir, so soft.

"I couldn't," said she. "You looked so peaceful—dear one."

My cheeks and neck went hot, sir, as if a warm iron was laid on them. I didn't know what to say. I began to stammer: "What do you mean——" but she was going back down the stair, out of sight. My God, sir, and I used not to think she was good-looking!

I started to follow her. I wanted to know what she meant. Then I said to myself, "If I don't go—if I wait here—she'll come back." And I went to the weather side and stood looking out of the window. Not that there was much to see. It was growing dark, and the Seven Brothers looked like the mane of a running horse, a great, vast, white horse running into the wind. The air was awelter with it. I caught one peep of a fisherman, lying down flat trying to weather the ledge, and I said, "God help them all tonight," and then I went hot at sound of that "God."

I was right about her, though. She was back again. I wanted her to speak first, before I turned, but she wouldn't. I didn't hear her go out; I didn't know what she was up to till I saw her coming outside on the walk-around, drenched wet already. I pounded on the glass for her to come in and not be a fool; if she heard, she gave no sign of it.

There she stood, and there I stood watching her. Lord, sir—was it just that I'd never had eyes to see? Or are there women who bloom? Her clothes were shining on her, like a carving, and her hair was let down like a golden curtain tossing and streaming in the gale, and there she stood with her lips half open, drinking, and her eyes half closed, gazing straight away over the Seven Brothers, and her shoulders swaying, as if in tune with the wind and water and all the ruin. And when I looked at her hands over the rail, sir, they were moving in each other as if they bathed, and then I remembered, sir.

A cold horror took me. I knew now why she had come back again. She wasn't a woman—she was a devil. I turned my back on her. I said to myself: "It's time to light up. You've got to light up"—like that, over and over, out loud. My hand was shivering so I could hardly find a match; and when I scratched it, it only flared a second and then went out in the back draft from the open door. She was standing in the doorway, looking at me. It's queer, sir, but I felt like a child caught in mischief.

"I—I—was going to light up," I managed to say, finally.

"Why?" said she. No, I can't say it as she did.

"Why?" said I. *"My God!"*

She came nearer, laughing, as if with pity, low, you know. "Your God? And who is your God? What is God? What is anything on a night like this?"

I drew back from her. All I could say anything about was the light.

"Why not the dark?" said she. "Dark is softer than light—tenderer—dearer than light. From the dark up here, away up here in the wind and storm, we can watch the ships go by, you and I. And you love me so. You've loved me so long, Ray."

"I never have!" I struck out at her. "I don't. I don't."

Her voice was lower than ever, but there was the same laughing pity in it. "Oh yes, you have." And she was near me again.

"I have?" I yelled. "I'll show you! I'll show you if I have!"

I got another match, sir, and scratched it on the brass. I gave it to the first wick, the little wick that's inside all the others. It bloomed like a yellow flower. "I *have*?" I yelled, and gave it to the next.

Then there was a shadow, and I saw she was leaning

beside me, her two elbows on the brass, her two arms stretched out above the wicks, her bare forearms and wrists and hands. I gave a gasp:

"Take care! You'll burn them! For God's sake——"

She didn't move or speak. The match burned my fingers and went out, and all I could do was stare at those arms of hers, helpless. I'd never noticed her arms before. They were rounded and graceful and covered with a soft down, like a breath of gold. Then I heard her speaking, close to my ear:

"Pretty arms!" she said. "Pretty arms!"

I turned. Her eyes were fixed on mine. They seemed heavy, as if with sleep, and yet between their lids they were two wells, deep and deep, and as if they held all the things I'd ever thought or dreamed in them. I looked away from them, at her lips. Her lips were red as poppies, heavy with redness. They moved, and I heard them speaking:

"Poor boy, you love me so, and you want to kiss me— don't you?"

"No," said I. But I couldn't turn around. I looked at her hair. I'd always thought it was stringy hair. Some hair curls naturally with damp, they say, and perhaps that was it, for there were pearls of wet on it, and it was thick and shimmering around her face, making soft shadows by the temples. There was green in it, queer strands of green like braids.

"What is it?" said I.

"Nothing but weed," said she, with that slow sleepy smile.

Somehow or other I felt calmer than I had any time. "Look here," said I. "I'm going to light this lamp." I took out a match, scratched it, and touched the third wick. The flame ran around, bigger than the other two together. But still her arms hung there. I bit my lip. "By God, I will!" said I to myself, and I lit the fourth.

It was fierce, sir, fierce! And yet those arms never trembled. I had to look around at her. Her eyes were still looking into mine, so deep and deep, and her red lips were still smiling with that queer sleepy droop; the only thing was that tears were raining down her cheeks—big, showing, jewel tears. It wasn't human, sir. It was like a dream.

"Pretty arms!" she sighed, and then, as if those words had

broken something in her heart, there came a great sob bursting from her lips. To hear it drove me mad. I reached to drag her away, but she was too quick, sir; she cringed from me and slipped out from between my hands. It was like she faded away, sir, and went down in a bundle, nursing her poor arms and mourning over them with those terrible, broken sobs.

The sound of them took the manhood out of me—you'd have been the same, sir. I knelt down beside her on the floor and covered my face.

"Please," I moaned. "Please! Please!" That's all I could say. I wanted her to forgive me. I reached out a hand, blind, for forgiveness, and I couldn't find her anywhere. I had hurt her so, and she was afraid of me, of *me*, sir, who loved her so deep it drove me crazy.

I could see her down the stair, though it was dim and my eyes were filled with tears. I stumbled after her, crying, "Please! Please" The little wicks I'd lit were blowing in the wind from the door and smoking the glass beside them black. One went out. I pleaded with them, the same as I would plead with a human being. I said I'd be back in a second. I promised. And I went on down the stair, crying like a baby because I'd hurt her, and she was afraid of me—of me, sir.

She had gone into her room. The door was closed against me and I could hear her sobbing beyond it, brokenhearted. My heart was broken too. I beat on the door with my palms. I begged her to forgive me. I told her I loved her. And all the answer was that sobbing in the dark.

And then I lifted the latch and went in, groping, pleading. "Dearest—please! Because I love you!"

I heard her speak down near the floor. There wasn't any anger in her voice; nothing but sadness and despair.

"No," she said. "You don't love me, Ray. You never have."

"I do! I have!"

"No, no," said she, as if she was tired out.

"Where are you?" I was groping for her. I thought, and lit a match. She had got to the door and was standing there as if ready to fly. I went toward her, and she made me stop. She took my breath away. "I hurt your arms," said I, in a dream.

"No," said she, hardly moving her lips. She held them out to the match's light for me to look, and there was never a scar on them—not even that soft, golden down was singed, sir. "You can't hurt my body," said she, sad as anything. "Only my heart, Ray; my poor heart."

I tell you again, she took my breath away. I lit another match. "How can you be so beautiful?" I wondered.

She answered in riddles—but oh, the sadness of her, sir. "Because," said she, "I've always so wanted to be."

"How come your eyes so heavy?" said I.

"Because I've seen so many things I never dreamed of," said she.

"How come your hair so thick?"

"It's the seaweed makes it thick," said she, smiling queer, queer.

"How come seaweed there?"

"Out of the bottom of the sea."

She talked in riddles, but it was like poetry to hear her, or a song.

"How come your lips so red?" said I.

"Because they've wanted so long to be kissed."

Fire was on me, sir. I reached out to catch her, but she was gone, out of the door and down the stair. I followed, stumbling. I must have tripped on the turn, for I remember going through the air and fetching up with a crash, and I didn't know anything for a spell—how long I can't say. When I came to, she was there, somewhere, bending over me crooning, "My love—my love—," under her breath like, a song.

But then, when I got up, she was not where my arms went; she was down the stair again, just ahead of me. I followed her. I was tottering and dizzy and full of pain. I tried to catch up with her in the dark of the storeroom, but she was too quick for me, sir, always a little too quick for me. Oh, she was cruel to me, sir. I kept bumping against things, hurting myself still worse, and it was cold and wet and a horrible noise all the while, sir; and then, sir, I found the door was open, and a sea had parted the hinges.

I don't know how it all went, sir. I'd tell you if I could, but it's all so blurred—sometimes it seems more like a dream. I couldn't find her any more; I couldn't hear her; I went all over, everywhere. Once, I remember, I found myself hanging out of that door between the davits, looking down into those big black seas and crying like a baby. It's all riddles and blur. I can't seem to tell you much, sir. It was all—all—I don't know.

I was talking to somebody else—not her. It was the inspector. I hardly knew it was the inspector. His face was as gray as a blanket, and his eyes were bloodshot, and his lips were twisted. His left wrist hung down, awkward. It was broken coming aboard the light in that sea. Yes, we were in the living room. Yes, sir, it was daylight—gray daylight. I tell you, sir, the man looked crazy to me. He was waving his good arm toward the weather windows, and what he was saying, over and over, was this:

"Look what you done, damn you! Look what you done!"

And what I was saying was this:

"I've lost her!"

I didn't pay any attention to him, nor him to me. By and by he did, though. He stopped his talking all of a sudden, and his eyes looked like the devil's eyes. He put them up close to mine. He grabbed my arm with his good hand, and I cried, I was so weak.

"Johnson," said he, "is that it? By the living God—if you got a woman out here, Johnson!"

"No," said I. "I've lost her."

"What do you mean—lost her?"

"It was dark," said I—and it's funny how my head was clearing up—"and the door was open—the storeroom door—and I was after her—and I guess she stumbled, maybe—and I lost her."

"Johnson," said he, "what do you mean? You sound crazy—downright crazy. Who?"

"Her," said I. "Fedderson's wife."

"Who?"

"Her," said I. And with that he gave my arm another jerk.

"Listen," said he, like a tiger. "Don't try that on me. It won't do any good—that kind of lies—not where you're going to. Fedderson and his wife, too—the both of 'em's drowned deader 'n a doornail."

"I know," said I, nodding my head. I was so calm it made him wild.

"You're crazy! Crazy as a loon, Johnson!" And he was chewing his lip red. "I know, because it was me that found the old man laying on Back Water Flats yesterday morning—me! And she'd been with him in the boat, too, because he had a piece of her jacket tore off, tangled in his arm."

"I know," said I, nodding again, like that.

"You know what, you *crazy, murdering fool*?" Those were his words to me, sir.

"I know," said I, "what I know."

"And *I* know," said he, "what *I* know."

And there you are sir. He's inspector. I'm nobody.

ROBERT W. SNEDDON

On the
Isle of Blue Men

Prolific writer Robert William Sneddon was born in Beith, Scotland, in 1880 and emigrated to the United States in 1910. Although he wrote three novels and several plays, it is for his more than three hundred short stories, many of which involve crime or horror, that he is remembered. On March 8, 1944, he died in New York City.

As it was first published in Ghost Stories, *April 1927, "On the Isle of Blue Men" was an atmospheric, Lovecraftian thriller with a weak and seemingly bowdlerized ending. Apparently the editor didn't think his audience could handle the idea of monsters breeding with humans. But internal evidence in the story suggests that it is the monsters' goal, as implied by Sneddon. And in an earlier, similarly plotted, Scottish story by Sneddon, "The Valley of Mystery" (*Metropolitan, *September 1919), he actually has members of a lost race kidnap a traveler for breeding purposes. In this anthology, therefore, we have restored what we believe to have been the author's original ending.*

◻

Summer had crept into fall. We had seen the heather turn purple on the hills of this remote island of the Hebrides which lies off the north of Scotland, and winter still found us lingering. The few tourists had long since gone. In the little, low stone cottage with its thatched roof held down by heavy stones, the peat fire burned night and day. Only two lovers in the divinest of sympathy could have existed as we did, so remote from human intercourse, our only visitors a shepherd or a fisherman. Sometimes they had no English, and we knew no Gaelic, but we nodded and grinned amiably at each other as we bartered for a piece of mutton or a basket of herring. A few of them spoke over each "s" or converted hard sounds into soft.

I seem to hear old Hamish, our man-of-all-work, saying: "I am thinking it was time you were going away, you and your leddy. Soon it will be blowing great gales of wind, whatever."

But Alice was content to wait, to see me cover canvas after canvas with those majestic, rocky, snowcapped peaks, sometimes sharp against a brilliant blue sky, sometimes wrapped in a misty veil. And I shivered many a day on the rocks by the sea, striving to capture the secret of the surge and swell of the tossing waters.

We had a taut little yacht, of sea-going qualities that I had tested many a time. Alice was as good a skipper as I, and we were fearless.

Twenty-five miles from the inlet in which our yacht rode at anchor, lies an outpost of civilization—the isles of the Seven Hunters. Seven little islands, hardly more than rocks they are, and beyond them is the Atlantic Ocean, the farthest surges of which beat upon the coast of my own country. On the largest of the islands stands a lighthouse which flashes its warning rays forty miles out to sea, and guides daring vessels passing around the North of Scotland to Scandinavian ports.

Now, I had heard stories of this island. On it was a ruined church, the Gaelic name of which was translated to me as the "Temple of Blessing." It had been founded by a sixteenth-century monk, still held in reverence. Until the past year, when the lighthouse had reached completion, the only visitors to the island were the fishermen who went to gather seafowl eggs and to kill birds for their feathers. Strange old customs were observed there. The men went in pairs, and did everything in unison. One could not take as much as a drink of water alone unless his comrade did likewise. On landing they took off their upper garments, laid them on a stone, and went toward the chapel, praying at intervals. No man must kill a bird with a stone, or after evening prayer.

The name of the island I cannot remember. It was always spoken of as "the Country."

Little did I know what a country of horrors unspeakable I was to find it—though I might have guessed something from the reluctance of those about me to give me any information.

The day was clear when we left the shores of Loch Roig and put out into the unknown, Alice and I, with a good store of provisions and some presents that we knew would please the lighthouse keepers. It was cold, but we were well muffled up; we laughed gaily as a couple of school-children when the wind caught our sails.

As we approached the egg-shaped rock with its gray cliffs rising sheer, and caught the glint of turf patches gleaming with frost crystals and the tall white tower of the lighthouse, its base 200 feet or so above sea level, Alice clapped her hands. Though no more than five hundred by two hundred yards in extent, the island was a spectacle of stern and menacing beauty.

Already we could see two men hastening down a zigzag stair cut in the rock, and making for the landing place visible to us. As we came in we could see the amazement on their faces, and there was amazement in the voices that hailed us. They threw us a rope, and we drew into the stone landing. I moored the boat so that it would not knock to pieces on the rocks, and then we scrambled ashore. They stood staring at us, two men sea-tanned, with wrinkled eyes under the woolen tams they wore, rather solemn looking, and saying not a word as I explained.

Could we spend the night? Any shakedown of a bed they could give us would be all right. We had provisions of our own—and would they accept the bundle of magazines and tins of tobacco we had brought?

I could see they were troubled, and especially about Alice.

"It was a rash-like thing, sir," said one of them, at length.

"There is no accommodation for visitors. But it is plain you cannot be going back the day, for there is a storm on the way."

"Then we stay," I said cheerfully.

They helped us to carry our bundles to the lighthouse, and the third man came out, Jamieson, they called him, a short, stout man with eyes which seemed to look beyond us. When he saw us, he got to his feet quickly, and seemed under the control of some strange fear. Why our presence should inspire Jamieson with fear I did not then know.

"Angus," said one of our guides, who had told us his name was Ross, "the gentleman and leddy are stopping with us over night. There will be nothing in the regulations against that, now?"

Jamieson appeared strangely troubled and looked behind him once or twice with an abrupt turn of his head.

"The woman!" he said at last in a husky voice. "*They* will not be wanting her here. The curse will fall! The curse— Is it not a fact that no woman has set foot on the Country since— since the time—" And he added something in Gaelic.

"Man," said Ross roughly, "will you ever be letting alone these old wive's tales? It's bad enough when you are glooming over the fire of a night, but here in broad daylight, what is there to fear? Put an end to it, Angus Jamieson." I could see Alice was upset by the show on ungraciousness.

"Perhaps we'd better try and get back," she suggested.

"No! No! That would be madness indeed," protested the third man, McLeod. "Would you be driving the leddy out into the night? Stay you here, and welcome, ma'am."

We had come up a narrow, winding iron stair, past the oil tanks and storage room, into a circular living room.

"We sleep above," McLeod continued; "so maybe you can be making shift here with some rugs and the like."

We told him anything would do, and so the matter was settled.

I went up with Ross into the lamp room, saw him light the wicks and set the clockwork going, and then we came down to a meal to which we were happy to contribute some dainties. Afterward we settled round the fire. Jamieson, to my surprise, busied himself knitting an enormous wool sock.

"Angus is not much for reading," said McLeod, "but there is not a woman can make a better pair of socks, whatever. It is a good thing you stayed, for hark to it now."

Indeed, the wind was battering upon the smooth pillar for raising its head in defiance, and I had a vision of the yacht grating its planking to shreds; but there was nothing to be done that night.

Suddenly Alice raised her head. I, too, heard what had attracted her attention—a steady body of sound, like some ancient religious composition, like an unknown Wagnerian opera played by some vast orchestra and taken up by other orchestras.

"Oh, how wonderful!" she said softly.

Ross laughed slyly. "The birds, ma'am," he said; "the puffins and the gulls, the divers and the cormorants. There's no counting the beasties."

The night choir of the seabirds swelled solemnly, majestically, then died away, to recur again with such awe-inspiring notes that I felt my flesh creep. Then all at once, as though stilled by a master leader's baton, the wild sea music ceased. A thin flutter of ashes ascended from the peat fire. Something made me look at Jamieson, who sat staring into blank space beyond him, his knitting needles motionless as though he heard sounds not audible to our ears.

All at once there reached us dimly through the thick walls a screeching so hellish that my blood ran cold.

"In God's name!" cried Ross, rising to his feet and looking about the room. "A year I've been stationed here, yet never heard I the like."

"Nor I," added McLeod.

"What would it be?" said Jamieson in a quick, tense tone as he set his needles in motion once more. "What but the *sluagh*?"

I caught at the word. "What's that?"

"It will be some of the old tales, sir. Be paying no heed to

Angus," said Ross slowly. "He's meaning the host of the dead that are about us."

"Aye!" said Jamieson in a strange, remote tone, "the gray, watery forms of ghosts. Maybe worse."

"Tush!" said Ross roughly. "Will you be frightening the leddy, Angus?"

Jamieson looked at us, and I fancied there was real concern in his look, and this caused vague uneasiness in my mind.

"God forbid, leddy. But I will be telling you, John Ross, and you, Donald McLeod, see to it this night that the door be locked and all shut tight and close. Something is speaking within me, and I am seeing beyond. The call is coming. Aye! The dark one is at hand, the dread one that we will be calling 'The Kindly—' "

"Peace, man," said Ross. "You and your death fancies, and we as snug here as any man could be asking! What could be the hurt of us?" He looked at his watch. "Time it is you were keeping your watch, Angus."

Jamieson rose to his feet and disappeared up the spiral stairway without another word.

"They will be saying," explained Ross, lowering his voice, "that Angus has the gift of the second-sight."

"Do you think he really can see into the future?"

"Ma'am," said Ross, with an odd expression, "I could be telling you things that are better left unsaid. Angus Jamieson is a strange lad, and whatever be his power, it is true that he sees more than the rest of us. But rest your mind. There's safety here for yourself and your gentleman this night. And now, by your leave, we'll be going upstairs and having our sleep."

We heard their heavy tread die away on the iron steps. Drawing our blankets over to the fire, we lay down.

Suddenly Alice clung to me, whispering: "I'm frightened. I never felt like this in all my life. That queer Angus—and what was that screech?"

"Some seal, probably, or the sea in a hollow cave," I said, but as I spoke I knew I lied.

All night long as I lay there my flesh tingled, and it

seemed to me that the tower of the lighthouse was beset with stealthy prowling horrors to which I could give neither shape nor name, and Alice moaned in her sleep and more than once put out an appealing hand to mine.

The morning came cold, brisk, and wild. While McLeod busied himself over the cookstove, I climbed to the lantern and looked abroad. One look was enough to tell me we could not leave the island that day. We were surrounded by a circle of tempestuous seas, rising and falling in monstrous surges.

We were sitting at breakfast when Jamieson came down to join us. Scarcely had he nodded to us than I saw a terrified light flash into his eyes, and he half rose from his seat with a hoarse exclamation:

"The red-haired woman!"

Alice looked at him with surprise in her blue eyes. Her hand went up to her hair.

"Yes, it is red," she said, smiling faintly.

"I did not notice it last night," muttered Jamieson, with his eyes still upon her, his face convulsed with an emotion which was communicated to us all. "God have mercy upon us!"

"What is the matter with red hair, my friend?" I asked abruptly. "Don't you admire it?"

Jamieson swayed in his seat.

"What is the matter?" I asked, turning to McLeod.

"I don't know, sir," he said slowly. "I never saw him act this way before. Angus, my man, will you be feeling sick this day?"

I never saw such a desperate look on any man's face as that which Jamieson turned to us.

"It is not sickness!" he cried suddenly. "It is death that is all about. Oh, it was an ill day that brought a red-haired woman to the Country. Did I not hear them crying aloud last night, licking their mouths for their victims?"

"You are *fey*, Angus Jamieson," said Ross harshly. "Cease your wild talk."

"No, there is no madness in my brain," said Jamieson with solemn sincerity. "Oh, sir"—he turned to me—"will you not be leaving us now—this very minute—you and the leddy, before They come upon us and destroy us?"

"How can we put to sea? Look for yourself, man," I shouted, losing my temper. "It's utterly impossible. I'm sorry we're so unwelcome."

Ross laid his hand on my arm.

"Wheesht, sir. There is no need to be saying that. McLeod and me will not hear of your going."

But I was determined to get to the root and bottom of the business.

"What's all this talk about destroying—what will come upon us—who are licking their mouths for victims?"

Jamieson looked as though stunned by my vehemence. Then he put his hands to his eyes as though to shut out some terrifying sight. A strange babble of sound came from his lips.

"What is he saying, Ross?" I cried. "What is *Na fir gorma*?"

Ross drew a long breath, then rolled his eyes toward heaven.

"The Blue Men, sir. . . . But never heed him. I'll see to him."

He caught Jamieson roughly by the shoulder and propelled him toward the ladder. I heard him speak soothingly in Gaelic, and then we were left alone.

McLeod sat looking at us in silence; then as the stillness weighed upon us, he cleared his throat.

"It's the lonely life here," he said as if in apology. "It would be a wonder indeed if it did not go to the head sometimes, sir and ma'am. Angus will be all right after a bit of sleep. Angus is perfectly harmless, leddy. You need not be afraid. You see, he is full of old stories . . . and it is well known no woman has ever set foot on this island."

"Why not?" asked Alice. "And why doesn't he like my red hair?"

"Well," answered McLeod with evident uneasiness, "there's an old prophecy about this part—it says 'Man's day will end when the Blue Men and the red-haired witch come together.' "

"A witch!" cried Alice, opening her pretty eyes wide. "I like that. So he thinks I'm a witch!"

"Oh, 'deed not, Ma'am," said McLeod hastily; "but there's a prejudice against the red hair among some of them that live hereabouts. Poor creatures! I come from Oban myself, where we're civilized—yes, indeed."

"But the Blue Men? What are they?" I asked. "What does he mean?"

"I don't know," said McLeod simply. "Some other old tale, no doubt."

Alice appeared comforted, but I noticed that when Ross came down again, he was stern and uncommunicative.

"You'll excuse him, leddy," he said; "and now, Donald, we'll be cleaning the lenses and trimming the wicks."

"We'll go out and get the air," I suggested.

"Very good," Ross answered with an air of relief. "A good blow will do good, but do not be going close to the water. It has a trick of heaving itself up and not a warning. A cruel, treacherous thing, the sea."

As we passed through the low iron door to the cemented square in front of it, I slipped on something.

"Why, how odd!" said Alice. "A piece of seaweed. Fancy it being up here."

"Carried up by the wind, I suppose," and I kicked it carelessly aside. "What a strange smell, though."

"Hasn't it?"

"It's a sea smell, and yet. . . . Did you ever smell a tank of seals? Like that. That's odd."

Alice laughed. "Everything's queer here. Don't you think we ought to see how the *Sprite* is?"

"Nice thing if she's knocked to pieces and we're marooned here till the Northern Lighthouse Board tender comes to relieve the men."

"I suppose they take turns."

"Yes, there're four of them, Ross tells me. Three on duty, one on shore. The tender isn't due for ten days or so."

"Oh, be careful," Alice begged as we hugged the rock in

our descent of the zigzag steps. "There's more of that weed here. Oh look, the *Sprite*'s all safe, but what is that on the landing?"

"A seal, probably. You wait here. I'll go down and see."

I came gingerly down, and as I reached the bottom step the seal slithered into the water with a loud plop. I stood there, staring, rubbing my eyes wet with the salt spray.

And then I found myself shuddering. With incredulous eyes I peered into the water. I caught a glint of a blue-black, shadowy, twisting thing—and then it was gone, melted into the waters, as though it possessed a protective coloration which blended with that of the sea.

I heard Alice shout, and in unreasoning alarm scrambled back to her.

"You scared it," she said.

"Yes," I answered curtly, clenching my jaws tight. My pulse was drumming so loudly I thought she must have heard it. I would never confess to her what I had seen or fancied I had seen—not a harmless seal, but a froglike monster such as I had never heard of, nor seen pictured in any work on natural history.

"Come along!" I said roughly. "It's perishing cold here. Let's get out of the wind."

She did not seem to wonder at my abruptness, but followed me obediently. Strive as I would, however, I could not help turning my head to look behind, but all I could see was the spray flung high into the air.

We sat huddled together in a cranny. Never had I felt Alice so close to my heart as in that hour. A strange, fatal apprehension was upon me, a mad desire to get aboard the *Sprite* and flee the island, yet cold common sense, that bondage which civilization has cast upon us, told me that to do this would be folly unspeakable. We could not hope to reach shore in that sea.

After a time we returned to the lighthouse. Alice went up to the living room, leaving me with Ross busy at work on the oil tanks.

I sat down on a box. "Ross," I said, "I imagine there's lots of strange fish in these waters."

"I dare say," he answered carelessly. "There are some will be saying they have seen the sea-serpent, and 'deed, the way the water comes plunging up sometimes, it looks like maybe he'd be kicking down at the bottom."

"I don't suppose you ever came across anything like a monstrous frog."

He stopped work to look at me.

"No, indeed. I never heard of frogs in the sea, sir. They're made for the fresh water, surely."

"So I always thought." I hesitated. "There was something like a frog—looked as big as a man—on the east landing, but it dived in before I got a look at it properly."

He shook his head at that.

"A seal, I'll be thinking. They twist that quick, you'll hardly get a look at them. But a frog— That's a good one."

He laughed easily, and somehow my memory became disconcerted. Of course the thing must have been a seal. My eyes were nipping with cold and salt, and it was natural I had not seen straight.

"Well, we'll keep the discovery to ourselves," I said, with a mockery of a laugh.

"Yes, indeed. If Angus were to get wind of this, we'd be having another mouthful of nonsense. 'Deed, company has a bad effect on him."

The sea-fog rose so high that afternoon that there was no thought of us venturing forth, so we spent the time in our several ways. Alice sewed, while Ross, McLeod, and I played endless games with a grimy deck of cards. Jamieson, apparently normal again, sat with his knitting. The beacon was lighted early, and faintly from above came the monotonous *tick-tock* of the clockwork which revolved it.

All at once McLeod raised his head. "Did you bolt that downstairs door, John?" he asked Ross.

"That I did. Why?"

McLeod stirred uneasily in his seat. "It sounded like it

was giving a bit of a squeak. I'll put the oil can to the hinges in the morning."

He appeared reassured, but I noticed his eyes turn now and then to the trapdoor in the flooring. At length he rose and went down. When he returned, he was sniffing.

"There's a queer kind of smell on the air this night," he said.

"I noticed it this morning—we both did, my wife and I," I said as I shuffled the cards for another deal.

He sat down, but made no effort to pick up his cards.

"There's times," he said slowly, "when I am thinking I would like a wee farm a long way from the sea. Yes! A long way."

"Are you married, Mr. McLeod?" Alice asked.

"Yes, ma'am. But what kind of a life is it for a married couple? Here I am six weeks on duty, then two ashore. You're fortunate, sir, to have your leddy with you all the time."

"I am, indeed, McLeod," I agreed.

I turned to smile at Alice, but to my amazement she had risen to her feet and was staring at the little window in the thick wall, her hand to her side as though it hurt.

"Why—" I started to say, and at that moment Ross uttered a startled:

"God spare us all, what's yon?"

Pressed against the thick glass was a white something, a blob of flesh in which two dead, unwinking, fishy eyes rose above an enormous gaping mouth set with jagged teeth.

McLeod took a step forward, and on that instant the thing vanished. I caught Alice to me. I saw Ross run to a wall rack and take down a double-barreled shotgun.

We heard him run hastily downstairs, heard the clang of the iron door as he flung it open. Mingled with the whiff of sea air which blew up to us, was a strangely musty, rank odor. I listened for the shot, which never came. McLeod had tumbled after Ross. In a few moments the pair came upstairs, somewhat shamefaced.

"Not a thing," said Ross, "but the fog's so thick that you cannot see your hand in front of your face."

"I'm thinking," added McLeod, with a look at Alice, "this

fog makes strange shapes on the windows. It's not the first time I've got a fright out of nothing, a gull blown against the glass, like. Put down your sock, Angus. Get your melodeon and give us a song. He's the bonny singer, is Angus."

Jamieson rose and brought out an accordion from a cupboard. I think at that moment his voice, untrained, yet with a pleasing tenderness, sounded better than that of any opera star. Somehow the music seemed to discharge the electric state of our nerves, so that when, after half an hour bed was proposed, I agreed willingly.

Twice through the night I was aroused by the hideous screeching I had heard the night of our arrival, but if any one else heard it, it excited no stir. All was quiet above me. Only Alice moaned in her sleep.

Next morning the fog still clung about us, a great stillness. For the fury of the wind we had exchanged that more exacting jailer. There was no hope of us leaving the island.

Though I said nothing to Alice. I was afraid. A vague terror was instilling its insidious venom into my heart. Perhaps I was mistaken, but I believe the other men felt it, also. Coming into the beacon chamber, I found Angus on his knees in prayer. And Ross, in the tank room, was cleaning his gun, squinting through its barrels and whistling a dismal air through puckered lips. I sat watching him in silence, and finally he spoke.

"I'll take a stroll down by the landing, and have a look at your boatie. I'll take the gun. Maybe I'll get a shot at something."

"Good idea!" I agreed. "I'll go with you." When we got outside, I came to the point. "What do you make of that thing last night, Ross?"

He sighed. "I cannot be saying, sir, unless it was some kind of bird, though I never saw its like. Did you ever see an octopus? Well, to me it had the looks of the eyes and mouth of one of them, though how it got up to the window I cannot be imagining, no indeed. Two hundred feet. . . . Stick close to me, sir, and look to your footing."

We moved slowly through the clinging fog. Indeed, it

needed all my attention to keep from falling. I had an unac-
countable fancy that on either side of us moved creatures, step
for step, just beyond our vision. But we came to the descending steps without mishap.

"We can't do anything down there," I said. "Never mind
the boat."

He would go down, however, and I saw him fade from my
sight. I heard his shout rise up to me, dulled by the fog, and
then a heavy silence blanketed all sound. I listened with
beating heart, and then began to fumble my way down.

I had gone only a few feet of the distance when something
ascending hastily ran into me.

"Ouch!" I ejaculated.

"That you, sir? Thank God!"

Ross was gasping. He sat down heavily and groaned.

"What's the matter? Boat gone?"

"No, no! She's there all right." He turned on me fiercely,
and I felt his hand grip my arm. "Man, you wouldn't be
saying I was mad?"

"Heavens, no! Why?"

"Not a word to your leddy—I got down to the landing,
and I bent down by the water to give a tug to the mooring rope
to see if all was secured, and as sure as God is my maker, sir,
the sea was full of faces staring up at me, mouthing and
gaping, hungering for my flesh—just like yon we saw last
night! The water was alive with bodies—aye, like human
bodies, but all bloated like. And the color of the water was so
blue and black you could scarce tell where they began and
where they ended."

"I saw something of the same kind yesterday as I told
you—that frog. . . ."

I stopped suddenly. Far behind us a faint cry rose on the
air, more like the thin scream of a trapped rabbit than anything.

"What's that?" I asked sharply.

We both listened intently, but no other sound followed.

"I'm only a plain man without much book knowledge,"
said Ross simply. "I've followed the sea all my life and been
in foreign ports, but this is beyond me, sir."

He pointed a shaking finger downward.

"Yon are devils, sir, devils!"

"Nonsense," I said roughly. "I can't explain it, but when you come to think of it, Ross, here's a part of the world that might as well be at the North Pole for all we know of it. It's quite natural there may be some creatures—sea-creatures flung up by some submarine upheaval—primitive things like those flying lizards and other monsters. You'd never believe there had been such things except in the imagination, unless you had seen the remains of them, as I have, in museums and the like. I don't know but what we may consider ourselves very fortunate in being able to get a look at them."

"I could well be spared the sight," he said dryly, as he nursed his gun between his knees. "Maybe you're right, and they're naught but some kind of fishy creature. But for the sake of all concerned I wish we were rid of them. We'd best be getting back. I don't like the looks of it, at all, at all whatever."

"You don't expect them to attack us surely?" I said. "They never could flounder up to the lighthouse."

"Where came that one we caught a glimpse of last night?"

"That's right," I said. "My God, that's right!"

This realization came upon me suddenly and with such force that I began to tremble.

"My wife!" I said brokenly.

"Ay!" Ross replied. "Give her the word not to go beyond the door. We may be wrong, and they may be harmless, but it is best not to take a chance. Man, I'm glad I have a good supply of shells for my gun."

"Yes. Let's be getting back. I hate to think of her there."

"McLeod and Jamieson are there."

"Yes, that's true."

But I was distraught with anxiety till we managed to reach the lighthouse, scrambling our way through the fog. I was relieved to hear Alice answer my hail. McLeod came to the trap.

"Did you no meet Angus?" he called down.

Ross started.

"No! Where is he?"

McLeod came down, his rugged face filled with surprise.

"He was sitting here, when all at once he rose up as if his mind was set on something, and he spoke to your leddy, sir, in a queer kind of a way. 'God be kind to you, ma'am, and keep you from harm of them,' and then he turns to me: 'I'll be going after them, Donald. My mind is ill at ease about the gentleman and John Ross.' And what was on his mind, I cannot be saying, but as he went out the door he turned to me: 'I am a single man, Donald, and my time is come. Maybe they that are seeking her will be satisfied with my blood'—and with that he was gone."

"The poor lad!" said Ross in a strained voice. "That was strange talk. Poor lad! He never should have taken to this work."

But I saw further. "Ross, Ross, don't you see?" I said wretchedly. "He knew more than we did—his second sight— He thought he might save us by giving himself as a sacrifice to—to—"

All I could do more was point toward the sea.

Ross thrust his face forward to mine, and our glances met. "The blue men Angus was talking about"—he said abruptly, tensely. "If I was thinking he had done that. . . . Bide you here, Donald, with the leddy. And you, sir, take that crowbar and come with me."

I followed, leaving McLeod agape at the door.

"That cry!" I stammered. "That cry!"

I clenched my hand on the cold bar of iron I carried.

"God help him," muttered Ross as we hurried forward. He raised his voice in a shout of "Angus! Angus, are you there?" But no response was heard.

Suddenly I stumbled.

"Ross!" I said sharply, and we stooped to look.

For a long moment neither of us touched the thing which lay at our feet.

Then Ross gave a choked sob.

"The poor lad!" he said again and again. "Poor Angus!"

I am sure no thought of our own terrible danger was in our minds.

"His arm!" I said in a whisper. "Torn from his shoulder!"

"Aye!" muttered Ross as he bent lower.

All at once he raised himself to his full height. His heavy chest swelled. He threw the gun to his shoulder and a furious bellow came from his lips:

"Come out o' the fog, you skulking things! Angus, where are you? Say the word, and I'll let hell loose. Angus! For the sake of Heaven give us a shout. Angus, my poor lad, speak!"

But both challenge and plea went without answer.

"They must have caught him nearby," said Ross, more calmly. "Devil's work. Oh, my heart is sore for that poor lad. He had neither kith nor kin, wife nor mother, to mourn him. Rest his soul in peace if he be dead, and I'm praying he may be soon if there is life left in him, wherever he be lying."

"If this fog would only lift for a minute!"

"Fog or no fog, I'm going to get them that maimed him," said Ross between clenched teeth. "Bide you here, sir."

Before I could say a word, he was lost in the fog. I stood there, every nerve atingle, filled with a strange awe and reverence. Angus undoubtedly had laid down his life for us, and yet I felt with strange intuition his sacrifice had been in vain, and the end was not yet.

Suddenly I saw something move upon the ground. I took a step forward, and then my heart stood still. My nostrils were full of the musky stench. Something had caught my ankle in a strong, tenacious grip. I did not stop to look down, but with my bar struck repeatedly on some flabby substance, and the clutch upon the ankle gave way. I was conscious of a bulk scrambling past me, blundering with a rush that knocked me on the flat of my back. Then I was up and shouting, "Ross!—Ross!"

"Sir!" came an answering hail. Never was voice so welcome. Ross was at my side in a few seconds, breathless.

"One of them caught me by the ankle," I told him excitedly.

"So!" he said and bent to the ground. "The arm's gone!" he cried, his voice rising to an inhuman screech. "Back to the lighthouse, sir, back this minute. We can do nothing for the dead. It's the living, now, the living."

He caught me by the arm, and guided by him, we came to the lighthouse. He pulled open the door, thrust me in, then slammed the iron barrier in place.

McLeod came down. "Did you find Angus?" he inquired anxiously.

"No," said Ross; "but no doubt he'll be back soon, Donald. It's grey and thick out."

He thrust his mouth to my ear.

"I'll tell him when I get the chance, but not a word to your leddy. D'ye hear me? Swallow your food down. Put a good face on it. We need all our strength against yon, whatever they be."

"Is there any hope of help—if we need it?"

"God spare us," he said solemnly. "None. The tender's not due for another seven days."

"If you were to fail to light the beacon, wouldn't they think something was wrong?"

"Never!" he said fiercely. "I'd sooner die than fail in my duty. No mention of that, sir."

"I beg your pardon, Ross," I said, gripping his hand.

"Oh, I understand, sir," he said brokenly. "Your wife— but I have a wife too on shore. We can only do our best. Ech, sir, I should be writing up the slate, but I haven't the heart to do it today."

"The slate?" I queried.

"Ay! The log. We keep a log like on board ship, but it can wait. What can I say about Angus—what, that they would believe?"

When we gathered about the table for lunch, I knew by McLeod's face that he sensed the truth, though he tried to preserve something of his usual easy manner.

"Isn't Mr. Jamieson coming?" asked Alice innocently.

"We're looking for him any minute, ma'am," said Ross, avoiding her glance. "He'll be down by the crane splicing a rope, no doubt."

"What made him act so strangely?" she continued.

"Och, just his way of talking," suggested McLeod. "Yes, that will be it. He is very religious, ma'am."

Ross took the first chance he had to tell me he had run up a distress signal, but he feared there was little likelihood of its being seen in the fog. And so we settled for the day, besieged, set about by an unseen army of devils, whose power we had no way of reckoning.

Darkness fell early. By the time the lamps were lit, Alice had begun to worry about Angus and to question us all, until Ross could stand it no longer.

"Ma'am," he said simply, "I'm thinking we'll never be seeing Angus Jamieson again. He met with an accident going down the steps, and fell into the water. He was carried away at once surely, for your good man and me could find no trace of him. Aye, you may let the tears fall, ma'am. Yon was a good lad, none better."

Under pretense of getting my help to do some slight repair to the mechanism of the beacon, Ross took me up the iron steps to the lamp room. In that narrower chamber with McLeod, we considered what was to be done.

"I'm thinking," said Ross, "if you and your leddy were to get away early in the morn, you could make the land and get a message to the board."

"What!" I said. "Leave you two here? That's out of the question. You'd better come with us if we're going. You can come back." But he shook his head.

"It cannot be done, sir." He hesitated. "You'll forgive me—there's just a thought in my mind. Maybe there was sense in what Angus said. We've been here close on a year now, and never saw nor heard of yon hellish things till—till your leddy came. There never was a woman set foot on the island here. It might be—it was the woman—that they had got the wind of—and's drawing them out from their lurking places."

I looked at him in silence, at his honest, rugged face, the blue eyes which sought mine so earnestly.

"I mean no offense, God knows that," he added hastily.

"So you think if my wife and I went," I said, "there would be an end to this business?"

"Just that, sir."

"Very well, Ross," I said at last. "We'll make a dash for it tomorrow morning, at dawn. But I swear I'll be back with help just as soon as I can gather it together. A few charges of dynamite dropped in would make short work of these things."

"Donald and myself will see you off. I wonder how the weather is. It looks like clearing."

We went out onto the gallery, and as we did so I clung to the rail in a spasm of loathing.

About the base of the lighthouse crawled groups of the creatures so closely massed that their shapes were indeterminate. They moved with a strange undulation, and for the moment I had the impression I looked down on waves. There was a flickering movement on their surface, and after a little I was able to see that their upper limbs terminated in a bunch of whipping tentacles.

"The devils! The foul sea-devils!" muttered McLeod seeing them for the first time. "So yon's them, is it? Oh, my heart is sore for Angus."

Ross vanished and came up with his gun. Leaning over the rail, he took aim and sent a scatter of shot into the midst of the vile mass. At the sound, I think, more than the hail of lead, there was an agitated stirring, and with incredible rapidity the patches began to slither. In a couple of minutes the neighborhood of the lighthouse was free of them.

Alice came running up.

"A gannet," explained Ross hastily; "but I missed the old bird."

"I heard you fire. I couldn't think what was up."

"It's like to clear, ma'am," said McLeod quickly, "so you and the gentleman can be leaving us in the morn."

"Yes, we're going Alice," I assured her. "We can't impose on our friends here any longer. And they want us to notify the Lighthouse Board to send another man right away."

"I think I'll be glad to go," said Alice, "though you have been wonderfully kind to us. Mr. Ross and Mr. McLeod."

"It's nothing," said Ross. "Common hospitality."

Such an evening! The eve of a criminal lying in the death-house awaiting the last summons! Three silent men about the card table, a wondering woman by our side—ears tense to catch the slightest sound, muscles taut to spring instantly from our hard wooden chairs; the air heavy with unspoken apprehension. We were in terror of—what?

And when finally we got to bed, it was not to sleep. The ticking of the clockwork was magnified to the stroke of some vast machine that drove spikes into my tortured brain. It seemed to me I could hear through the thick stone wall the stealthy flicker of these ghastly tentacles which could tear a man limb from limb, and so adhesive they could elevate those bloated bodies up the side of the lighthouse. What if they managed to reach the lantern, to break the glass and pour in upon us? I put my arm about the sleeping body of my dear one.

The morning came. We rose. Ross moved silently among his pots and pans. We ate something—what, I can't remember; and then McLeod, orderly as ever, washed the pans and dishes and set them in their places. The fog had gone. The dawn was cold, gray, clear. There would be no danger in our trip, I felt.

We opened the door, and Ross looked about him anxiously. Then he nodded to me and we four set out on our way. We reached the steps and began to descend them. As we passed the crane, I noticed a box of tools had been torn from the fastenings and broken open. We reached the landing; I got aboard the *Sprite*. I hoisted her anchor, and McLeod held the aft mooring ready to let go. Ross shifted his gun to shake hands with us both. We shook hands with McLeod, then Alice scrambled past me and went forward. The waters washed about us, swelling and subsiding. There was no sign of danger.

And then I happened to look at the steps, and I heard someone—was it I or another devil—cry in a harsh screech of warning:

"Behind you—look—they come!"

In one long undulating current the sea-devils poured down the steps. It was like a stream of turbulent water in which tossed the branches of submerged trees. Horrid, tentacled arms rose and fell.

They came on irresistibly. The two men turned to face

them, and McLeod let fall the mooring rope. The wind crept into my sails. Ross' gun went up. He fired, but he might as well have been armed with a child's pop gun.

The *Sprite* rocked. I felt the thud of heavy objects beneath her keel, and then in a twinkling the sea was alive. The landing and the sea alike were masses of scrambling things. I saw the two men on shore being overwhelmed by this blue-black wave of glistening slimy bodies.

The *Sprite* was moving. To attempt rescue was suicide.

Then abruptly one of the things reared itself out of the water. Its beastly eyes peered into mine, its obscene mouth gaped. Over the thwart of the boat its slimy suckers crept upon me. They leaped to my leg.

I shouted to Alice: "Loose that sheet!"

She made no reply, and I saw she had fainted. Above her reared the dead, unwinking eyes of a froglike monster as it scrambled over the thwart. What I saw seared my brain—its slimy tentacles fluttering around her skirt, encircling her hands, clutching her to its horridly masculine body. Then, the hellish thing turned away and sprang into the sea with its burden, giving me a last brief impression of Alice's unconscious face as their bodies shot spray high into the air.

Captured by the tentacles, I could not move. But my eye fell on the axe I kept in the boat, and with a madman's fury I struck at them. I felt the pressure slack, and, axe in hand, I stooped right into the swinging boom . . . and felt a crushing blow on my head.

I remember opening my eyes to a watery sun. I was lying in the bottom of the boat, alone—alone. I raised myself on my elbow. I was in mid-ocean. . . .

Once more my senses left me.

They tell me I was cast ashore here on this remote island close by Portugal. How I came, I know not. I know only that I had been robbed of all—of love, of hope, of reason.

Would to God, I had never conceived the wild fancy which assailed me, to attempt the voyage to the Seven Hunters when others less adventurous and foolhardy were snug in cities thinking of Christmas, or gifts and lighted stores and goodwill toward men. And once on that accursed Isle of the Blue Men, after seeing what the danger was, I should have taken Ross' gun and risked damnation by shooting Alice—my darling wife—dead, rather than let those terrible monsters get her. But we are all children who learn our lesson too late. So I have ended up an unkempt castaway, scarce human, whom the local fishermen regard with pity and compassion—as a hopeless madman.

A madman driven mad by obsessive thoughts and self-analysis.

I try to believe that Alice drowned on her way to the bottom and that the Blue Men hungered just for food. But I am obsessed with the foul prophecy of that island, with the thought that she lives beneath it in the secret darkness of some dank and musky chamber, forced to breed monstrous hybrids who will one day emerge to revenge themselves against mankind.

Had I the courage, I'd try to find my answers by returning to the Isle of the Blue Men. But, God forgive me, I cannot. The fear of what I might find is greater than the constant ache of uncertainty. So instead, with untold heart burnings, a cankerous remorse, and a grief only death can assuage, I have written these things down to alert fishermen and sailors to the emerging danger they may soon be facing and to save all other red-headed women from visiting that terrible spot.

CHARLES FRANCIS COE

Madhouse Light

Multi-talented Charles Francis Coe was born in Buffalo, New York, on November 25, 1890. He joined the navy at seventeen, became welter- weight boxing champion of his fleet, and then spent five years as a professional fighter. He later became a radio sports announcer and virtually invented ringside coverage. He also took up writing, earning $37,000 his first year. His specialties were boxing and crime stories, and he eventually published twelve novels and coauthored Jack Dempsey's autobiography. Coe went to Hollywood as a screenwriter, turned law- yer, and became the general counsel for the Motion Picture Producers and Distributors of America from 1940 to 1943. Then he shifted his practice to Florida and also took on the job as editor and publisher of the Palm Beach Post. *The editorials he wrote for the paper won the Freedom Foundation's first three annual awards. (Then they decided that Coe was unbeatable and barred him from further competition.) On December 28, 1956, he died in Palm Beach.*

"Madhouse Light," a psychological thriller, first appeared in Mun- sey's *in July 1929.*

⌑

Handsome young Will Kelsey knew the tragic story of Sand- ers before he accepted the assistant's post at the lighthouse, but he shut his eyes to the facts. What that madman had done

113

was one thing; what he himself might do was totally another.

Kelsey also knew that Pedersen, keeper of the light, could talk the very barnacles off the bottom of a ship. The fisher people said in all seriousness that Sanders went mad listening to the old man's eternal *blah-blah-blah*. Well, Will would shut him up like a clam.

That lighthouse job appealed to the young man; he wanted isolation, time to think, and opportunity to purge his soul of the faith he once had boasted in womankind. The girl was Alice Reid.

Village gossip never was unanimous that Will Kelsey would marry her. He was so good looking that it would have been no surprise if one of the summer flappers from the city had run away with him. Alice was nice, and proud, as befitted a school-teacher with her first class; but she never would learn how to vamp a man.

She didn't even know how to handle the boy to whom she was engaged. Here is the way she lost him, while they were strolling on a sunny, windswept beach:

"I sometimes wonder if we are suited to each other, Billy," she said, merely angling for a protestation of love. "We both have youth, but do we realize our shortcomings?"

"Meaning which?" Kelsey idly inquired.

"Well, you are headstrong, and I am rather determined myself. It would be easy for us to start a battle! Also, you squander your money—and I am of a saving disposition."

"So?" Billy retorted. "You've met some one who hasn't my handicaps, haven't you?"

Alice Reid lied like a lady. She had just returned from a brief visit to an inland city.

"Yes, I have!" she replied. "But you notice that I'm still wearing your ring, Billy."

"That can be remedied!" the young man observed darkly, and the little quarrel should have ended there. It was merely a skirmish to learn the beloved enemy's strength.

As if hypnotized, the girl removed the ring and handed it to him. It had a small diamond as its decoration, and it flashed bravely in the sun.

"I should have bought a blue-white stone as large as a soup plate," Billy remarked scathingly, "if I wanted to hold a girl like you!"

He turned away and hurled the ring far out into the sea. Then he spun about on one heel and went striding down the beach alone.

Alice put a hand to her throat, choking back a faint cry of anguish. Her ring had vanished, and there out of her life went the youth who had dreamed with her of a cottage by the sea.

"What have I done?" she asked herself numbly. "But he ought to *know* there is no other man."

Her head went up, and she, too, turned on one heel.

Three days later Sanders was brought in from the distant lighthouse. He was as mad as a March hare, stricken dumb with fear of the unknown. He had been more than six years on the job out there.

Some one had to take his place, to share watches with Pedersen and cherish the light that flashed across the sea. That some one had to be a young man, because two oldsters get on each other's nerves in that service. Will Kelsey volunteered, and his neighbors shook their heads when he closed the cottage his parents had left him.

"He'll never get on with old Pedersen," Luke Reid declared to Alice, his daughter.

"Bill Kelsey, of all people!" Mrs. Reid exclaimed. "Pedersen won't like him. Billy is a lad with ideas and imagination, and he's liable to follow poor Sanders to the insane asylum."

It was then that their only child hurriedly left the house and was absent for hours in the family motor boat.

Before she returned, the villagers had gathered at the pier to see Kelsey off for the lighthouse. Mrs. Reid was there with the others, but Billy appeared not to see the mother of the girl he had loved.

When the tender pointed her dancing prow toward the lighthouse, he sat in the bow and gazed steadily seaward. He would show them all that he could stand garrulous old Pedersen and the solitude of the long watches.

There was money in the lighthouse job, and nothing to do

out there but save the pay. In two years, three at the utmost, he could come ashore permanently and invest his capital. He could laugh at Alice Reid then—and her boy friend in the inland city who was not headstrong and did not squander his money.

Old Pedersen was a huge man, and, although in his fifties, strong. His shoulders squared like the corner of a building. He wore luxuriant blond mustaches, and he spent much time in combing them with his big, blunt fingers.

His nose stood out with no little character of its own. One nostril was noticeably larger than the other, and it gave observers the curious impression that the man carried his head at an angle.

The rest of his face was broad and flat, the eyes lusterless and bland, the whole countenance lethargic. It was somehow a shock to listeners when the mouth opened and speech fairly gushed forth.

For seven years Pedersen had been at the lighthouse, and in all that time he had only once displayed the "call" flag. That was when he signaled for the authorities to take away the mad Sanders.

Will Kelsey had never particularly noticed Pedersen on the latter's brief visits ashore. He had accepted him, as had the rest of the fishing village, as an institution.

To the best of the public knowledge, the old lighthouse keeper had neither kith nor kin, and his job exactly suited him. Lacking a listener, he would sit for hours at his indolent task, a huge, curved pipe drooping over his chin, his fingers caressing his mustaches.

He watched the same old sea, the same old rocks at the base of the lighthouse tower, the same old sky, day in and day out. When the gales blew he made simple preparations, and let them blow their heads off. When the weather calmed he opened hatches to dry out his quarters.

Every day he shaved himself, wiped the later on a piece of newspaper, and walked the twenty yards to the end of the island to throw the paper into the sea. He never hurried at any task. Time was his servant.

Into this life, and with Pedersen at his elbow, young Kelsey cast his lot. The older man had not been ashore for three months. Very good; neither would his assistant leave the lighthouse for the same period.

Within the first hour of his service Billy met a great surprise. Aside from grunting "yah" and "nay" for yes and no, Pedersen was tongue-tied.

"Well, I never dreamed you'd turn into a dumb Isaac," Kelsey remarked cheerfully.

"Yah."

"Are you doing it on an election bet?"

"Nay."

Every fifth day the tender came to the island with supplies and was available to take a man back to the mainland if he cared to go, for the purpose of stretching his legs and talking with other humans.

"How's the old codger making it now?" the skipper would ask Kelsey. And each time his reply ran: "Pedersen? Oh, great! He's a fine man, Pedersen."

Kelsey did not know that the skipper also asked Pedersen about his assistant's condition. Casual reports went back to the beach that the handsome youth had become neglectful of his daily shaving. He had forgotten to shine his boots. His shirts were worn a week or more without change. He had ceased to wear a tie, even on Sundays! But what was there to dress up for, anyhow, on the outskirts of civilization?

For the first two weeks Billy had gone out on the little island and exercised vigorously each morning. He did this no more, and resented the ease of the older man who sat around quietly and kept in excellent health.

Kelsey caught himself one day imitating Pedersen's gesture toward an upper lip. After that he began to cultivate a mustache, but Pedersen never acknowledged it with even a glance.

Once Kelsey forgot to wash his dishes, and when mealtime came Pedersen silently loaned him some clean ones. That night Billy had a dishwashing bee, and in a mild exuberance threw a plate far out into the heaving water.

He looked up to the light tower to see if Pedersen had

noted his ridiculous display of temper. The older man had followed the parabola of the dish until it cut into the sea. He did not speak or turn his head. From that moment Kelsey hated him.

Again Kelsey forgot to fill the fuel tanks for the light, and Pedersen uncomplainingly did it for him. For that kindness Kelsey hated him all the more. If he would only talk, and argue, and grow angry!

Pedersen ate a bread that came in large sheets and looked like dried waffles. At first Kelsey had eaten some of it with relish, and laughed at Pedersen's enjoyment of the stuff. He had admired to see the magnificent mustaches rise and fall as the big teeth crunched the hard food.

But after a time the sound palled upon him. It seemed as if Pedersen were catching between those teeth every raw nerve in Kelsey's body and munching them into a pulp.

The young man never spoke to the men on the tender about any one ashore. He drew within himself, learned to hide his feelings, and cultivated a canniness of behavior. He found little ways to punish Pedersen for eating hard bread, for his stolidity, and his obvious contentment in watching that damnable sea.

When three months had passed and the relationship between the two men settled into concrete form, Pedersen suddenly changed. Kelsey watched closely for several days, convinced that the old man was going mad.

He was glad that the solitude and the friction between them had finally triumphed. Pedersen now had been on the little island six full months without going to the mainland. That was too much for any man.

Therefore Pedersen was going the way of poor Sanders. What would the villagers have to say about that? What would Alice Reid think?

He desired very much that Pedersen should go mad. He wished to watch the tender take him away as Pedersen had watched it take Sanders.

When next the tender came Kelsey eyed the skipper closely to see if he detected the change in Pedersen. Apparently he did not. Kelsey was glad. Another five days might do the trick.

He did not know just what course Pedersen's insanity would take. Sanders had become violent and attacked Pedersen, and the two had fought within the lonely tower until finally Pedersen had triumphed. The old man was a powerful fighter or he could not have subdued Sanders.

So Kelsey prepared for trouble. From the kitchen he carried to his bunk a large bread knife. It gave him a feeling of security at night; he could feel it under the blankets and he pressed against it gratefully.

Kelsey could lie in his bunk and look across the black curling water. At intervals of twenty seconds there would flash out the white finger of the light over his head. He knew that Pedersen was sitting there beside the light, holding his big curved pipe or fumbling at his great blond mustache.

His bland eyes would be trained steadily out into the night. The fool! There was nothing out there that he could see, only the flash of the light over the black water every twenty seconds.

But what was the older man thinking? Behind those eyes what was there? Were the fires of insanity burning higher? That was the thing that Kelsey must learn.

Insane impulses, he knew, were like the waves of the sea about him. They writhed and twisted and arose too high, and then burst into the foam of madness.

The light was a revolving one, and the gears upon which it turned had a voice as steady and as distinctive as the roar of the sea. That voice blended with everyday sounds until it became akin to silence. But now it had a note of premonition, Kelsey thought, similar to his own feeling of impending disaster.

So he lay and watched, while near at hand the sea whispered and the gears chanted and the mysterious night winds wrapped their unquiet arms about the tower. Aloft he could see Pedersen, and now and then he caught glimpses of the slow-drifting smoke clouds that seeped from the old man's pipe.

How many times had Kelsey sat through the weary hours

of his watch beside that light! He knew just what Pedersen was now seeing. The tower was inclosed in heavy glass, and the rays of the light as it turned swept across the sill in which this glass was set.

When he was on watch Kelsey had often tried closing his eyes and counting the seconds until the light flashed directly over his head. He would detect the sudden brilliance through closed lids. He could count so accurately that just as his lips formed a silent "twenty," the light would flash.

The light was a majestic thing. You sat there in the tower and gazed outward at a black sea. Suddenly the gears clicked and radiance swept out over your head. Like a great white knife it cut through the black and under it, momentarily, the water heaved and danced and sparkled. Just as your eyes became accustomed to the miracle, the curtain of black fell again.

But these things, Kelsey knew, were lost upon the stolid Pedersen. The old fellow never had a thought. The ticking of a clock was important to him; it passed the time satisfactorily enough. While on watch his fool pipe with its foul odor and the things he did with his heavy mustaches were enough to occupy his mind.

"Small wonder," Kelsey whispered as he lay there watching the big man, "that he is going crazy!"

Leading up to the light was a circular steel stairway. The treads shone from the friction of sole leather, and the brass railing along its side always caught a reflection of the big light and flashed a vague answer. Those flashes were twenty seconds apart. Everything, Kelsey felt, was twenty seconds. The world traveled on a schedule of one-third of a minute.

But there was another flight of time that also was exacting. It was the six-hour watches he shared with Pedersen. The light operated twelve hours each night, and they divided the time equally between them.

When Pedersen stood the first watch at night he waked Kelsey by the ringing of a bell which he kept on the light platform. The young man grew to hate that sound when it roused him, and to love it when it jangled Pedersen from his blankets.

But Pedersen did not mind. He was a methodical man, and placed his pipe, filled and ready for use, beside his bunk as he turned in. When Kelsey rang the bell with ferocious delight, the old man would blink once or twice, run his fingers caressingly over his mustaches, swing his feet to the steel floor, and reach with one hand for his clothes and with the other for his pipe. Soon he would come tramping up the steel steps, his breath whistling through his big nostril.

Even when the fog crept close about the lighthouse, and everything was dripping gray, the whole world no bigger than their own little horizon, Pedersen was imperturbable. He would adjust the fog horn and appear not to hear, every twenty seconds, the blast that ripped through the air like an agonized bellow from some prehistoric monster. He puffed, and stroked, and gazed at the blank wall of fog as he did at the heaving sea.

But at last a change had come. Kelsey saw it as he lay there in his bunk one night and looked upward.

There was a droop to Pedersen's shoulders and a furtive glisten in his ordinarily bland eyes. Each time the light flashed Kelsey saw in the old man a tensity, an unrest. He smiled to himself, and fondly pressed the handle of the heavy knife.

He knew it must soon be time for Pedersen to reach for that bell and rattle its tormenting call through the tower. It was raining. When the rays flashed, he could see past Pedersen to the shield of glass by which the light was surrounded. The glass was streaked with heavy raindrops, and they were not crisscrossed, as would have been the case were the wind high.

A quiet night, but a wet one that might merge into the gray of fog banks rather than the brightness of sunshine when day broke. He hoped the fog would come, because that would let him start the horn, and so might bother Pedersen in his new disquietude.

Then Pedersen leaned over the rail, an arm stretched forth and the call bell glistened faintly in his hand. A wisp of smoke drifted from his pipe and he leaned over to knock the dottle into the sand box kept on the platform. He appeared in no hurry to ring the bell. That in itself was a sign.

After a while he leaned forward again and replaced the

bell without ringing it. Kelsey was all eyes after that. What trick was Pedersen's insane cunning up to now? He watched closely, slipped his fingers under his blankets and clutched the heavy knife.

Pedersen was coming down the steel stairs. His big feet fell softly on the steel treads. Kelsey's throat dried.

Pedersen looked weird in the faint, intermittent light. What would he do? Would he creep to Kelsey's bunk and attempt to throttle him? Well, the knife was ready!

The old man, instead, got down his oilskins and silently left the tower. Instantly Kelsey leaped up and dressed. Just as he finished the fog horn blared forth its first note. So that explained Pedersen's trip! He had gone out to start the mechanism.

But, no! Why should he do that? It was after midnight, and Kelsey himself should have faced the storm to do that job; it was his watch. There must be something else that Pedersen was scheming; perhaps he had used the fog horn as a trick.

Kelsey felt certain that this was the night when Pedersen would let his madness run away with him. The horror of his position assailed him with terrific force. He had been a fool not to tell the men of the tender about Pedersen, and have them take the madman to the beach. Kelsey promised himself that he would signal for help in the morning.

Pedersen was returning. Kelsey could hear the sloshing of his shoes in the rain as he came along the path. The younger man slipped the heavy knife under his jacket and went to the foot of the circular stairs.

Pedersen came in, and his brows raised in moderate surprise at finding Kelsey up, but he did not speak. He merely glanced upward to signify that the light was turned over to his assistant.

Kelsey went aloft, his head twisted over one shoulder so that he might watch every move of the old man. He saw that he was being watched in turn. But Pedersen shrugged finally, hung his oilskins on the pegs and went out of sight toward his bunk.

Kelsey sighed with relief. Before this night he had gleefully looked forward to the final breaking of the old man's mind. When those ashore heard that Pedersen, the stolid, unimaginative man, had gone mad, they would have a changed opinion of Billy Kelsey. Especially would Alice Reid come to her senses!

But now that feeling was gone. Kelsey was, he admitted to himself, a little afraid of Pedersen. His big, square hands had suddenly become busier, and they reflected an alertness that was the gift of insanity.

But Kelsey would not be caught unawares. He sat there on the platform, hating more and more the rain on the glass, the clicking of the gears, the flashing of the light, and the bellow of the fog horn. He did not relax, because even with Pedersen in bed there was no telling what would come next.

The madman's starting of the horn was a sly trick to make Kelsey unsuspicious. The way his eyes followed Kelsey aloft to the platform was a symptom.

Pedersen's bunk creaked, and Kelsey felt a tightening of his throat muscles. His heart started to pound.

He heard the old man fussing about the galley. That was another trick. Pedersen never ate at midnight. Kelsey gripped the big knife.

The old man appeared at the foot of the stairs. He was clad only in a long nightshirt, and he looked like a ghost. He did not speak, but he stood there gazing upward.

"Go to bed," Kelsey called out. "Everything is all right."

His voice croaked, and he paused to clear his throat.

Pedersen did not answer. He stood a moment, then his foot struck the lower steel tread and he started upward.

Kelsey muttered a curse and brandished the knife.

"I'll kill you, Pedersen," he warned him, "if you come up here. Go back! Go to bed—everything is all right!"

He had changed suddenly from threat to entreaty in the hope of reassuring the crazy man, but Pedersen kept coming steadily up the circular stairs. His ridiculous nightshirt was flapping about his sturdy legs.

Kelsey dashed to the head of the stairs, the one entrance to the platform. But the old man came closer and closer, and his steps were unhurried.

"Nay," he said at last; "nay."

He was close now, and Kelsey slashed at him with the knife. Pedersen drew back ever so slightly, like a trained fighter, and let the murderous thrust go by. The force of his effort dragged Kelsey onto the stairs, and he gripped the rail with his free hand.

Pedersen was not slow now. He leaped forward and caught Kelsey's knife arm. The younger man fought with ferocity, but the big hand could not be shaken off.

Kelsey twisted suddenly and drove his foot hard into Pedersen's stomach. The old man grunted with pain, and lost his hold.

"Nay," he moaned heavily; "nay."

"You would have it!" Kelsey shouted. "Damn you, take it!"

He swung the heavy knife upward. Pedersen grunted again and his nightshirt turned red where the point had caught.

The knife glistened again in the flashing of the big light; but the old man caught the sharp blade, and naked flesh battled with steel. Kelsey felt the hot blood spurt from Pedersen's mutilated hand. It seeped down his wrist as they struggled.

Then the knife was wrenched from Kelsey's grip and sent clattering down the stairs. He fought with all his strength, but Pedersen did not hit and rip and tear in return. He encircled the young man's body with relentless arms and squeezed like a boa constrictor.

Black spots appeared before Kelsey's eyes. Pedersen had him, was going to squeeze him to death. Locked in that fearful embrace, the two men fell to the stairway, Kelsey underneath.

Suddenly the old man changed his tactics. His right arm loosed its grip and the fingers of the square hand, wet with its own blood, clenched into a maul-like fist. The fist raised and dropped onto Kelsey's head.

The blow dazed him. Before his mind had cleared the mighty fist had risen again.

"Yah," Pedersen growled in satisfaction; "yah."

Kelsey knew he was done for. Pedersen's maniacal strength, mad perseverance, and immunity to wounds, had been too much.

Overhead the great light flashed, and through its radiance that red fist loomed. Kelsey saw it descending.

The light of the tower went out, and the hot breath of the madman was gone from his face, and the agony departed from his muscles. The horn on the island had suddenly quieted, and Pedersen was not there torturing him.

Consciousness came back slowly to Will Kelsey. He discovered that he was on the lower floor of the lighthouse and was supine. He was on his own bunk, lashed there firmly with ropes.

He saw that the fog had cleared and the rain ceased. Overhead the light was out and the gears did not click. Day had come.

Above him, Pedersen was at work with an oil can, his right hand thick with bandages and his blood-stained nightshirt discarded for dungarees. He appeared to have lapsed into routine, which often controls madmen.

Kelsey wondered how badly Pedersen had been cut with the knife, and decided that the wounds must be superficial. His own face was bruised and swollen.

He calculated that the tender was not due at the lighthouse for twenty-four hours. In that time Pedersen could torture him to death.

A shadow played across the high panes of the tower windows. At first Kelsey attributed it to the wheeling sea gulls. But the shadow persisted.

It took the frightened young man long, puzzled moments to realize that something stationary was flying between the sun and the windows. Then he knew that it must be the signal flag.

And in that moment full understanding came to Will Kelsey. It was as if the great light overhead had suddenly penetrated to every dark cranny of his mind and dissipated the mists of madness.

"Ahoy, Pedersen, you big loafer!" he called laughingly up the echoing tower. "Haul in that flag, and come down here and cut me loose. I was coocoo last night; but I'm all right now. You certainly beat some sense into me!"

The old man brought down the flag on the run, then descended and fumblingly—because of his bandaged hand—freed his captive. And then speech literally burst from him.

"There was no sign of the tender," he said. "The skipper probably is in his bunk or still at breakfast. His wife is a grand cook, and their kitchen faces away from the sea. Also, there is a—"

"I know," Will Kelsey interrupted. "No one saw your signal and—"

"I didn't say that," Pedersen explained rapidly. "There's a motor boat headed for us. And unless I'm dead wrong in my reckoning, I'll bet a new dory against an old lobster pot that Alice Reid is coming out for you because she's—"

"Fine!" Kelsey exclaimed. "You keep right on talking to me, but I'll be too busy shaving to answer back. Alice wouldn't like my mustache!"

So, while the old man's bottled-up language gushed forth and leaped from subject to subject, Billy made himself presentable. Aside from his interesting bruises, he was soon the same fine figure of youth who had whirled on his heel in a lover's quarrel three months before.

Both men were at the landing when Alice nosed her motor boat in to the mooring. She chatted as gayly with Kelsey as if there never had been a misunderstanding; but soon contrived a private talk with the older man.

"Oh, Mr. Pedersen, what happened?" she asked. "How did Billy hurt his face? And your hand is bandaged!"

"Well, we had a little mix-up," he replied lightly. "It wasn't my fault, Miss Reid. I kept my word, and for three months all I've said to Billy was 'yah' and 'nay.' But I told you when you came out to the light that day that if you'd let me talk to him all I wanted he wouldn't last two weeks. This has been a long three months; but now I'll have another assistant, and we can chew the rag to our hearts' content!"

When the girl made ready to leave she found Kelsey at the landing with his valise packed.

"I'm mighty glad you're taking me ashore, Alice; I'm cured," he said unashamedly when the craft was under way.

"Meaning which?" she inquired, imitating his stock question.

"I'm as meek as a lamb," Billy declared. "You gave me my head, and you didn't interfere out here at the light, and I've learned my lesson."

"Oh, didn't I?" Alice murmured, half to herself.

"No; but you kept an eye out for signals, didn't you?"

"In all the daylight hours, Billy; and at night I prayed for you. Weren't you afraid of Mr. Pedersen?"

"The old codger? No! He's a fine man."

They turned to look back at the lighthouse. Pedersen was still at the landing. He pointed the fingers of his bandaged hand toward his temple and made circles with them, as if indicating the workings of a deranged mind.

"Yah," he muttered. "First Sanders, then Kelsey! I'll get the next one's goat, too!"

GEORGE G. TOUDOUZE

Three Skeleton Key

Noted scholar of art and the sea, Georges Gustave Toudouze was born in Paris on June 22, 1877. After earning a doctorate of letters from the Sorbonne, he became a professor of History and Dramatic Literature at the Paris Conservatory and also served as chief editor of The French Maritime and Colonial League. *In a literary career that spanned more than fifty years, Toudouze produced at least nineteen books about the sea, twelve plays, and nine books on art and architecture. Three of his works were awarded prizes by the French Academy, and two others were recognized by the Academy of Moral and Political Sciences.*

An absolutely unforgettable story of horror, "Three Skeleton Key" seems to be his only short story to appear in English. It was published in Esquire *in January 1937.*

◻

My most terrifying experience? Well, one does have a few in thirty-five years of service in the Lights, although it's mostly monotonous routine work—keeping the light in order, making out the reports.

When I was a young man, not very long in the service, there was an opening in a lighthouse newly built off the coast of Guiana, on a small rock twenty miles or so from the mainland. The pay was high, so in order to reach the sum I had set out to save before I married, I volunteered for service in the new light.

Three Skeleton Key, the small rock on which the light stood, bore a bad reputation. It earned its name from the story of the three convicts who, escaping from Cayenne in a stolen dugout canoe, were wrecked on the rock during the night, managed to escape the sea but eventually died of hunger and thirst. When they were discovered, nothing remained but three heaps of bones, picked clean by the birds. The story was that the three skeletons, gleaming with phosphorescent light, danced over the small rock, screaming. . . .

But there are many such stories, and I did not give the warnings of the old-timers at the Isle de Sein a second thought. I signed up, boarded ship, and in a month I was installed at the light.

Picture a grey, tapering cylinder, welded to the solid black rock by iron rods and concrete, rising from a small island twenty odd miles from land. It lay in the midst of the sea, this island, a small, bare piece of stone, about one hundred fifty feet long, perhaps forty wide. Small, barely large enough for a man to walk about and stretch his legs at low tide.

This is an advantage one doesn't find in all lights, however, for some of them rise sheer from the waves, with no room for one to move save within the light itself. Still, on our island, one must.be careful, for the rocks were treacherously smooth. One misstep and down you would fall into the sea—not that the risk of drowning was so great, but the waters about our island swarmed with huge sharks who kept an eternal patrol around the base of the light.

Still, it was a nice life there. We had enough provisions to last for months, in the event that the sea should become too rough for the supply ship to reach us on schedule. During the day we would work about the light, cleaning the rooms, polishing the metalwork and the lens and reflector of the light itself, and at night we would sit on the gallery and watch our light, a twenty thousand candle-power lantern, swinging its strong, white bar of light over the sea from the top of its hundred-twenty-foot tower. Some days, when the air would be very clear, we could see the land, a thread-like line to the west. To the east, north and south stretched the ocean. Landsmen, perhaps, would soon have tired of that kind of life, perched on a small island off the coast of South America for eighteen weeks, until one's turn for leave ashore came around. But we liked it there, my two fellow-tenders and myself—so much so that, for twenty-two months on end with the exception of shore leaves, I was greatly satisfied with the life on Three Skeleton Key.

I had just returned from my leave at the end of June, that is to say mid-winter in that latitude, and had settled down to the routine with my two fellow-keepers, a Breton by the name of Le Gleo and the head-keeper, Itchoua, a Basque some dozen years or so older than either of us.

Eight days went by as usual, then on the ninth night after my return, Itchoua, who was on night duty, called Le Gleo and me, sleeping in our rooms in the middle of the tower, at two in the morning. We rose immediately and, climbing the thirty or so steps that led to the gallery, stood beside our chief.

Itchoua pointed, and following his finger, we saw a big three-master, with all sail set, heading straight for the light. A queer course, for the vessel must have seen us, our light lit her with the glare of day each time it passed over her.

Now, ships were a rare sight in our waters, for our light was a warning of treacherous reefs, barely hidden under the surface and running far out to sea. Consequently we were always given a wide berth, especially by sailing vessels, which cannot maneuver as readily as steamers.

No wonder that we were surprised at seeing this three-master heading dead for us in the gloom of early morning. I had immediately recognized her lines, for she stood out plainly, even at the distance of a mile, when our light shone on her.

She was a beautiful ship of some four thousand tons, a fast sailor that had carried cargoes to every part of the world, plowing the seas unceasingly. By her lines she was identified as Dutch-built, which was understandable as Paramaribo and Dutch Guiana are very close to Cayenne.

Watching her sailing dead for us, a white wave boiling under her bows, Le Gleo cried out:

"What's wrong with her crew? Are they all drunk or insane? Can't they see us?"

Itchoua nodded soberly, looked at us sharply as he remarked: "See us? No doubt—if there is a crew aboard!"

"What do you mean, chief?" Le Gleo had started, turned to the Basque, "Are you saying that she's the Flying Dutchman?"

His sudden fright had been so evident that the older man laughed:

"No, old man, that's not what I meant. If I say that no one's aboard, I mean she's a derelict."

Then we understood his queer behavior. Itchoua was right. For some reason, believing her doomed, her crew had abandoned her. Then she had righted herself and sailed on, wandering with the wind.

The three of us grew tense as the ship seemed about to crash on one of our numerous reefs, but she suddenly lurched with some change of the wind, the yards swung around, and the derelict came clumsily about and sailed dead away from us.

In the light of our lantern she seemed so sound, so strong, that Itchoua exclaimed impatiently:

"But why the devil was she abandoned? Nothing is smashed, no sign of fire—and she doesn't sail as if she were taking water."

Le Gleo waved to the departing ship:

"Bon voyage!" he smiled at Itchoua and went on. "She's leaving us, chief, and now we'll never know what—"

"No she's not!" cried the Basque. "Look! She's turning!"

As if obeying his words, the derelict three-master stopped, came about and headed for us once more. And for the next four hours the vessel played around us—zigzagging, coming about, stopping, then suddenly lurching forward. No doubt some freak of current and wind, of which our island was the center, kept her near us.

Then suddenly, the tropic dawn broke, the sun rose and it was day, and the ship was plainly visible as she sailed past us. Our light extinguished, we returned to the gallery with our glasses and inspected her.

The three of us focused our glasses on her poop, saw standing out sharply, black letters on the white background of a life-ring, the stenciled name:

"*Cornelius-de-Witt*, Rotterdam."

We had read her lines correctly, she was Dutch. Just then the wind rose and the *Cornelius-de-Witt* changed course, leaned to port and headed straight for us once more. But this time she was so close that we knew she would not turn in time.

"Thunder!" cried Le Gleo, his Breton soul aching to see a fine ship doomed to smash upon a reef, "She's going to pile up! She's gone!"

I shook my head:

"Yes, and a shame to see that beautiful ship wreck herself. And we're helpless."

There was nothing we could do but watch. A ship sailing with all sail spread, creaming the sea with her forefoot as she runs before the wind, is one of the most beautiful sights in the world—but this time I could feel the tears stinging my eyes as I saw this fine ship headed for her doom.

All this time our glasses were riveted on her, and we suddenly cried out together:

"The rats!"

Now we knew why this ship, in perfect condition, was sailing without her crew aboard. They had been driven out by the rats. Not those poor specimens of rats you see ashore, barely reaching the length of one foot from their trembling noses to the tip of their skinny tails, wretched creatures that dodge and hide at the mere sound of a footfall.

No, these were ships' rats, huge, wise creatures, born on the sea, sailing all over the world on ships, transferring to other, larger ships as they multiply. There is as much difference between the rats of the land and these maritime rats as between a fishing smack and an armored cruiser.

The rats of the sea are fierce, bold animals. Large, strong and intelligent, clannish and seawise, able to put the best of mariners to shame with their knowledge of the sea, their uncanny ability to foretell the weather.

And they are brave, these rats, and vengeful. If you so much as harm one, his sharp cry will bring hordes of his fellows to swarm over you, tear you and not cease until your flesh has been stripped from the bones.

The ones on this ship, the rats of Holland, are the worst, superior to other rats of the sea as their brethren are to the land rats. There is a well-known tale about these animals.

A Dutch captain, thinking to protect his cargo, brought aboard his ship—not cats—but two terriers, dogs trained in the hunting, fighting and killing of vicious rats. By the time the ship, sailing from Rotterdam, had passed the Ostend light, the dogs were gone and never seen again. In twenty-four hours they had been overwhelmed, killed and eaten by the rats.

At times, when the cargo does not suffice, the rats attack the crew, either driving them from the ship or eating them alive. And studying the *Cornelius de Witt*, I turned sick, for her small boats were all in place. She had not been abandoned.

Over her bridge, on her deck, in the rigging, on every visible spot, the ship was a writhing mass—a starving army coming towards us aboard a vessel gone mad!

Our island was a small spot in that immense stretch of sea. The ship could have grazed us, passed to port or starboard with its ravening cargo—but no, she came for us at full speed, as if she were leading the regatta at a race, and impaled herself on a sharp point of rock.

There was a dull shock as her bottom stove in, then a horrible crackling as the three masts went overboard at once, as if cut down with one blow of some gigantic sickle. A sighing groan came as the water rushed into the ship, then she split in two and sank like a stone.

But the rats did not drown. Not these fellows! As much at home in the sea as any fish, they formed ranks in the water, heads lifted, tails stretched out, paws paddling. And half of them, those from the forepart of the ship, sprang along the masts and onto the rocks in the instant before she sank. Before we had time even to move, nothing remained of the three-master save some pieces of wreckage floating on the surface and an army of rats covering the rocks left bare by the receding tide.

Thousands of heads rose, felt the wind and we were scented, seen! To them we were fresh meat, after possible weeks of starving. There came a scream, composed of innumerable screams, sharper than the howl of a saw attacking a bar of iron, and in the one motion, every rat leaped to attack the tower!

We barely had time to leap back, close the door leading onto the gallery, descend the stairs and shut every window tightly. Luckily the door at the base of the light, which we never could have reached in time, was of bronze set in granite and was tightly closed.

The horrible band, in no measurable time, had swarmed up and over the tower as if it had been a tree, piled on the embrasures of the windows, scraped at the glass with thousands of claws, covered the lighthouse with a furry mantle and reached the top of the tower, filling the gallery and piling atop the lantern.

Their teeth grated as they pressed against the glass of the lantern-room, where they could plainly see us, though they could not reach us. A few millimeters of glass, luckily very strong, separated our faces from their gleaming, beady eyes, their sharp claws and teeth. Their odor filled the tower, poisoned our lungs and rasped our nostrils with a pestilential, nauseating smell. And there we were, sealed alive in our own light, prisoners of a horde of starving rats.

That first night, the tension was so great that we could not sleep. Every moment, we felt that some opening had been made, some window given away, and that our horrible besiegers were pouring through the breach. The rising tide, chasing those of the rats which had stayed on the bare rocks, increased the numbers clinging to the walls, piled on the balcony—so much so that clusters of rats clinging to one another hung from the lantern and the gallery.

With the coming of darkness we lit the light, and the turning beam completely maddened the beasts. As the light turned, it successively blinded thousands of rats crowded against the glass, while the dark side of the lantern-room gleamed with thousands of points of light, burning like the eyes of jungle beasts in the night.

All the while we could hear the enraged scraping of claws against the stone and glass, while the chorus of cries was so loud that we had to shout to hear one another. From time to time, some of the rats fought among themselves and a dark cluster would detach itself, falling into the sea like a ripe fruit from a tree. Then we would see phosphorescent streaks as triangular fins slashed the water—sharks, permanent guardians of our rock, feasting on our jailors.

The next day we were calmer, and amused ourselves by teasing the rats, placing our faces against the glass which separated us. They could not fathom the invisible barrier which separated them from us, and we laughed as we watched them leaping against the heavy glass.

But the day after that, we realized how serious our position was. The air was foul; even the heavy smell of oil within our stronghold could not dominate the fetid odor of the beasts massed around us, and there was no way of admitting fresh air without also admitting the rats.

The morning of the fourth day, at early dawn, I saw the wooden framework of my window, eaten away from the outside, sagging inwards. I called my comrades and the three of us fastened a sheet of tin in the opening, sealing it tightly. When we had completed the task, Itchoua turned to us and said dully:

"Well—the supply boat came thirteen days ago, and she won't be back for twenty-nine." He pointed at the white metal plate sealing the opening through the granite—"If that gives way—" he shrugged—"they can change the name of this place to Six Skeletons Key."

The next six days and seven nights, our only distraction was watching the rats whose holds were insecure fall a hundred and twenty feet into the maws of the sharks—but they were so many that we could not see any diminution in their numbers.

Thinking to calm ourselves and pass the time, we attempted to count them, but we soon gave up. They moved incessantly, never still. Then we tried identifying them, naming them.

One of them, larger than the others, who seemed to lead them in their rushes against the glass separating us, we named "Nero"; and there were several others whom we had learned to distinguish through various peculiarities.

But the thought of our bones joining those of the convicts was always in the back of our minds. And the gloom of our prison fed these thoughts, for the interior of the light was almost completely dark, as we had to seal every window in the same fashion as mine, and the only space that still admitted daylight was the glassed-in lantern-room at the very top of the tower.

Then Le Gleo became morose and had nightmares in which he would see the three skeletons dancing around him, gleaming coldly, seeking to grasp him. His maniacal, raving descriptions were so vivid that Itchoua and I began seeing them also.

It was a living nightmare, the raging cries of the rats as they swarmed over the light, mad with hunger; the sickening, strangling odor of their bodies—

True, there is a way of signaling from lighthouses. But to reach the mast on which to hang the signal we would have to go out on the gallery where the rats were.

There was only one thing left to do. After debating all of the ninth day, we decided not to light the lantern that night. This is the greatest breach of our service, never committed as long as the tenders of the light are alive; for the light is something sacred, warning ships of danger in the night. Either the light gleams, a quarter hour after sundown, or no one is left alive to light it.

Well, that night, Three Skeleton Light was dark, and all the men were alive. At the risk of causing ships to crash on our reefs, we left it unlit, for we were worn out—going mad!

At two in the morning, while Itchoua was dozing in his room, the sheet of metal sealing his window gave way. The chief had just time enough to leap to his feet and cry for help, the rats swarming over him.

But Le Gleo and I, who had been watching from the

lantern-room, got to him immediately, and the three of us battled with the horde of maddened rats which flowed through the gaping window. They bit, we struck them down with our knives—and retreated.

We locked the door of the room on them, but before we had time to bind our wounds, the door was eaten through and gave way, and we retreated up the stairs, fighting off the rats that leaped on us from the knee-deep swarm.

I do not remember, to this day, how we ever managed to escape. All I can remember is wading through them up the stairs, striking them off as they swarmed over us; and then we found ourselves, bleeding from innumerable bites, our clothes shredded, sprawled across the trapdoor in the floor of the lantern-room—without food or drink. Luckily, the trapdoor was metal set into the granite with iron bolts.

The rats occupied the entire light beneath us, and on the floor of our retreat lay some twenty of their fellows, who had gotten in with us before the trapdoor closed, and whom we had killed with our knives. Below us, in the tower, we could hear the screams of the rats as they devoured everything edible that they found. Those on the outside squealed in reply, and writhed in a horrible curtain as they stared at us through the glass of the lantern-room.

Itchoua sat up, stared silently at his blood trickling from the wounds on his limbs and body, and running in thin streams on the floor around him. Le Gleo, who was in as bad a state (and so was I, for that matter) stared at the chief and me vacantly, started as his gaze swung to the multitude of rats against the glass, then suddenly began laughing horribly:

"Hee! Hee! The Three Skeletons! Hee! Hee! The Three Skeletons are now *six* skeletons! *Six* skeletons!"

He threw his head back and howled, his eyes glazed, a trickle of saliva running from the corners of his mouth and thinning the blood flowing over his chest. I shouted to him to shut up, but he did not hear me, so I did the only thing I could to quiet him—I swung the back of my hand across his face.

The howling stopped suddenly, his eyes swung around the room, then he bowed his head and began weeping softly, like a child.

Our darkened light had been noticed from the mainland, and as dawn was breaking, the patrol was there to investigate the failure of our light. Looking through my binoculars, I could see the horrified expression on the faces of the officers and crew when, the daylight strengthening, they saw the light completely covered by a seething mass of rats. They thought, as I afterwards found out, that we had been eaten alive.

But the rats had also seen the ship, or had scented the crew. As the ship drew nearer, a solid phalanx left the light, plunged into the water and, swimming out, attempted to board her. They would have succeeded, as the ship was hove to, but the engineer connected his steam to a hose on the deck and scalded the head of the attacking column, which slowed them up long enough for the ship to get underway and leave the rats behind.

Then the sharks took part. Belly up, mouths gaping, they arrived in swarms and scooped up the rats, sweeping through them like a sickle through wheat. That was one day that sharks really served a useful purpose.

The remaining rats turned tail, swam to the shore, and emerged dripping. As they neared the light, their comrades greeted them with shrill cries, with what sounded like a derisive note predominating. They answered angrily and mingled with their fellows. From the several tussles that broke out, they resented being ridiculed for their failure to capture the ship.

But all this did nothing to get us out of our jail. The small ship could not approach, but steamed around the light at a safe distance, and the tower must have seemed fantastic, some weird, many-mouthed beast hurling defiance at them.

Finally, seeing the rats running in and out of the tower through the door and the windows, those on the ship decided that we had perished and were about to leave when Itchoua, regaining his senses, thought of using the light as a signal. He lit it and, using a plank placed and withdrawn before the beam to form the dots and dashes, quickly sent out our story to those on the vessel.

Our reply came quickly. When they understood our position—how we could not get rid of the rats, Le Gleo's mind going fast, Itchoua and myself covered with bites, cornered in the lantern-room without food or water—they had a signal-man send us their reply.

His arms, swinging like those of a windmill, he quickly spelled out:

"Don't give up. Hang on a little longer! We'll get you out of this!"

Then she turned and steamed at top speed for the coast, leaving us little reassured.

She was back at noon, accompanied by the supply ship, two small coast guard boats, and the fire boat—a small squadron. At twelve-thirty the battle was on.

After a short reconnaissance, the fire boat picked her way slowly through the reefs until she was close to us, then turned her powerful jet of water on the rats. The heavy stream tore the rats from their places, hurled them screaming into the water where the sharks gulped them down. But for every ten that were dislodged, seven swam ashore, and the stream could do nothing to the rats within the tower. Furthermore, some of them, instead of returning to the rocks, boarded the fire boat, and the men were forced to battle them hand to hand. They were true rats of Holland, fearing no man, fighting for the right to live!

Nightfall came, and it was as if nothing had been done, the rats were still in possession. One of the patrol boats stayed by the island; the rest of the flotilla departed for the coast. We had to spend another night in our prison. Le Gleo was sitting on the floor, babbling about skeletons, and as I turned to Itchoua, he fell unconscious from his wounds. I was in no better shape and could feel my blood flaming with fever.

Somehow the night dragged by, and the next afternoon I saw a tug, accompanied by the fire boat, coming from the mainland with a huge barge in tow. Through my glasses, I saw that the barge was filled with meat.

Risking the treacherous reefs, the tug dragged the barge as close to the island as possible. To the last rat, our besiegers deserted the rock, swam out and boarded the barge reeking with the scent of freshly cut meat. The tug dragged the barge about a mile from shore, where the fire boat drenched the barge with gasoline. A well placed incendiary shell from the patrol boat set her on fire.

The barge was covered with flames immediately, and the rats took to the water in swarms, but the patrol boat bombarded them with shrapnel from a safe distance, and the sharks finished off the survivors.

A whaleboat from the patrol boat took us off the island and left three men to replace us. By nightfall we were in the hospital in Cayenne.

What became of my friends? Well, Le Gleo's mind had cracked and he was raving mad. They sent him back to France and locked him up in an asylum, the poor devil; Itchoua died within a week; a rat's bite is dangerous in that hot, humid climate, and infection sets in rapidly.

As for me—when they fumigated the light and repaired the damage done by the rats, I resumed my service there. Why not? No reason why such an incident should keep me from finishing out my service there, is there?

Besides—I told you I liked the place—to be truthful, I've never had a post as pleasant as that one, and when my time came to leave it forever, I tell you that I almost wept as Three Skeleton Key disappeared below the horizon.

RAY BRADBURY

The Fog Horn

Science fiction's most famous living writer, Raymond Douglas Bradbury was born in Waukegan, Illinois, on August 22, 1920. The majority of his work is, however, actually science fantasy or horror rather than science fiction. He has written novels and plays, but it is primarily his poetic short stories—mostly written in the 1940s and 1950s—that have made him famous.

His "Beast from 20,000 Fathoms" (a.k.a. "The Foghorn"), which was originally published in the Saturday Evening Post, *June 23, 1951, served as the inspiration for the thrilling 1953 movie of the same name. But the story itself, with a darker ending, occupied only about four minutes of screen time in that film.*

◻

Out there in the cold water, far from land, we waited every night for the coming of the fog, and it came, and we oiled the brass machinery and lit the fog light up in the stone tower. Feeling like two birds in the gray sky, McDunn and I sent the light touching out, red, then white, then red again, to eye the lonely ships. And if they did not see our light, then there was always our Voice, the great deep cry of our Fog Horn shuddering through the rags of mist to startle the gulls away like decks of scattered cards and make the waves turn high and foam.

"It's a lonely life, but you're used to it now, aren't you?" asked McDunn.

"Yes," I said. "You're a good talker, thank the Lord."

"Well, it's your turn on land tomorrow," he said, smiling, "to dance the ladies and drink gin."

"What do you think, McDunn, when I leave you out here alone?"

"On the mysteries of the sea." McDunn lit his pipe. It was a quarter past seven on a cold November evening, the heat on, the light switching its tail in two hundred directions, the Fog Horn bumbling in the high throat of the tower. There wasn't a town for a hundred miles down the coast, just a road which came lonely through dead country to the sea, with few cars on it, a stretch of two miles of cold water out to our rock, and rare few ships.

"The mysteries of the sea," said McDunn thoughtfully. "You know, the ocean's the biggest damned snowflake ever? It rolls and swells a thousand shapes and colors, no two alike. Strange. One night, years ago, I was here alone, when all of the fish of the sea surfaced out there. Something made them swim in and lie in the bay, sort of trembling and staring up at the tower light going red, white, red, white across them so I could see their funny eyes. I turned cold. They were like a big peacock's tail, moving out there until midnight. Then, without so much as a sound, they slipped away, the million of them was gone. I kind of think maybe, in some sort of way, they came all those miles to worship. Strange. But think how the tower must look to them, standing seventy feet above the water, the God-light flashing out from it, and the tower declaring itself with a monster voice. They never came back, those fish, but don't you think for a while they thought they were in the Presence?"

I shivered. I looked out at the long gray lawn of the sea stretching away into nothing and nowhere.

"Oh, the sea's full." McDunn puffed his pipe nervously, blinking. He had been nervous all day and hadn't said why. "For all our engines and so-called submarines, it'll be ten thousand centuries before we set foot on the real bottom of the sunken lands, in the fairy kingdoms there, and know *real* terror. Think of it, it's still the year 300,000 Before Christ down under there. While we've paraded around with trumpets, lopping off each other's countries and heads, they have been living beneath the sea twelve miles deep and cold in a time as old as the beard of a comet."

"Yes, it's an old world."

"Come on. I got something special I been saving up to tell you."

We ascended the eighty steps, talking and taking our time. At the top, McDunn switched off the room lights so there'd be no reflection in the plate glass. The great eye of the light was humming, turning easily in its oiled socket. The Fog Horn was blowing steadily, once every fifteen seconds.

"Sounds like an animal, don't it?" McDunn nodded to himself. "A big lonely animal crying in the night. Sitting here on the edge of ten billion years calling out to the Deeps. I'm here, I'm here, I'm here. And the Deeps *do* answer, yes, they do. You been here now for three months, Johnny, so I better prepare you. About this time of year," he said, studying the murk and fog, "something comes to visit the lighthouse."

"The swarms of fish like you said?"

"No, this is something else. I've put off telling you because you might think I'm daft. But tonight's the latest I can put it off, for if my calendar's marked right from last year, tonight's the night it comes. I won't go into detail, you'll have to see it yourself. Just sit down there. If you want, tomorrow you can pack your duffel and take the motorboat in to land and get your car parked there at the dinghy pier on the cape and drive on back to some little inland town and keep your lights burning nights, I won't question or blame you. It's happened three years now, and this is the only time anyone's been here with me to verify it. You wait and watch."

Half an hour passed with only a few whispers between us. When we grew tired waiting, McDunn began describing some of his ideas to me. He had some theories about the Fog Horn itself.

"One day many years ago a man walked along and stood

in the sound of the ocean on a cold sunless shore and said, 'We need a voice to call across the water, to warn ships; I'll make one. I'll make a voice like all of time and all of the fog that ever was; I'll make a voice that is like an empty bed beside you all night long, and like an empty house when you open the door, and like trees in autumn with no leaves. A sound like the birds flying south, crying, and a sound like November wind and the sea on the hard, cold shore. I'll make a sound that's so alone that no one can miss it, that whoever hears it will weep in their souls, and hearths will seem warmer, and being inside will seem better to all who hear it in the distant towns. I'll make me a sound and an apparatus and they'll call it a Fog Horn and whoever hears it will know the sadness of eternity and the briefness of life.' "

The Fog Horn blew.

"I made up that story," said McDunn quietly, "to try to explain why this thing keeps coming back to the lighthouse every year. The Fog Horn calls it, I think, and it comes. . . ."

"But—" I said.

"Sssst!" said McDunn. "There!" He nodded out to the Deeps.

Something was swimming toward the lighthouse tower.

It was a cold night, as I have said; the high tower was cold, the light coming and going, and the Fog Horn calling and calling through the raveling mist. You couldn't see far and you couldn't see plain, but there was the deep sea moving on its way about the night earth, flat and quiet, the color of gray mud, and here were the two of us alone in the high tower, and there, far out at first, was a ripple, followed by a wave, a rising, a bubble, a bit of froth. And then, from the surface of the cold sea came a head, a large head, dark-colored, with immense eyes, and then a neck. And then—not a body—but more neck and more! The head rose a full forty feet above the water on a slender and beautiful dark neck. Only then did the body, like a little island of black coral and shells and crayfish, drip up from the subterranean. There was a flicker of tail. In all, from head to tip of tail, I estimated the monster at ninety or a hundred feet.

I don't know what I said. I said something.

"Steady, boy, steady," whispered McDunn.

"It's impossible!" I said.

"No, Johnny, *we're* impossible. *It's* like it always was ten million years ago. *It* hasn't changed. It's *us* and the land that have changed, become impossible. *Us!*"

It swam slowly and with a great dark majesty out in the icy waters, far away. The fog came and went about it, momentarily erasing its shape. One of the monster eyes caught and held and flashed back our immense light, red, white, red, white, like a disk held high and sending a message in primeval code. It was as silent as the fog through which it swam.

"It's a dinosaur of some sort!" I crouched down, holding to the stair rail.

"Yes, one of the tribe."

"But they died out!"

"No, only hid away in the Deeps. Deep, deep down in the deepest Deeps. Isn't *that* a word now, Johnny, a real word, it says so much: the Deeps. There's all the coldness and darkness and deepness in the world in a word like that."

"What'll we do?"

"Do? We got our job, we can't leave. Besides, we're safer here than in any boat trying to get to land. That thing's as big as a destroyer and almost as swift."

"But here, why does it come *here*?"

The next moment I had my answer.

The Fog Horn blew.

And the monster answered.

A cry came across a million years of water and mist. A cry so anguished and alone that it shuddered in my head and my body. The monster cried out at the tower. The Fog Horn blew. The monster roared again. The Fog Horn blew. The monster opened its great toothed mouth and the sound that came from it was the sound of the Fog Horn itself. Lonely and vast and far away. The sound of isolation, a viewless sea, a cold night, apartness. That was the sound.

"Now," whispered McDunn, "do you know why it comes here?"

I nodded.

"All year long, Johnny, that poor monster there lying far out, a thousand miles at sea, and twenty miles deep maybe, biding its time, perhaps it's a million years old, this one creature. Think of it, waiting a million years; could *you* wait that long? Maybe it's the last of its kind. I sort of think that's true. Anyway, here come men on land and build this lighthouse, five years ago. And set up their Fog Horn and sound it and sound it, out toward the place where you bury yourself in sleep and sea memories of a world where there were thousands like yourself, but now you're alone, all alone in a world not made for you, a world where you have to hide.

"But the sound of the Fog Horn comes and goes, comes and goes, and you stir from the muddy bottom of the Deeps, and your eyes open like the lenses of two-foot cameras and you move, slow, slow, for you have the ocean sea on your shoulders, heavy. But that Fog Horn comes through a thousand miles of water, faint and familiar, and the furnace in your belly stokes up, and you begin to rise, slow, slow. You feed yourself on great slakes of cod and minnow, on rivers of jellyfish, and you rise slow through the autumn months, through September when the fogs started, through October with more fog and the horn still calling you on, and then, late in November, after pressurizing yourself day by day, a few feet higher every hour, you are near the surface and still alive. You've got to go slow; if you surfaced all at once you'd explode. So it takes you all of three months to surface, and then a number of days to swim through the cold waters to the lighthouse. And there you are, out there, in the night, Johnny, the biggest damn monster in creation. And here's the lighthouse calling to you, with a long neck like your neck sticking way up out of the water, and a body like your body, and, most important of all, a voice like your voice. Do you understand now, Johnny, do you understand?"

The Fog Horn blew.

The monster answered.

I saw it all, I knew it all—the million years of waiting alone, for someone to come back who never came back. The million years of isolation at the bottom of the sea, the insanity of time there, while the skies cleared of reptile-birds, the swamps dried on the continental lands, the sloths and saber-tooths had their day and sank in tar pits, and men ran like white ants upon the hills.

The Fog Horn blew.

"Last year," said McDunn, "that creature swam round and round, round and round, all night. Not coming too near, puzzled, I'd say. Afraid, maybe. And a bit angry after coming all this way. But the next day, unexpectedly, the fog lifted, the sun came out fresh, the sky was as blue as a painting. And the monster swam off away from the heat and the silence and didn't come back. I suppose it's been brooding on it for a year now, thinking it over from every which way."

The monster was only a hundred yards off now, it and the Fog Horn crying at each other. As the lights hit them, the monster's eyes were fire and ice, fire and ice.

"That's life for you," said McDunn. "Someone always waiting for someone who never comes home. Always someone loving some thing more than that thing loves them. And after a while you want to destroy whatever that thing is, so it can't hurt you no more."

The monster was rushing at the lighthouse.

The Fog Horn blew.

"Let's see what happens," said McDunn.

He switched the Fog Horn off.

The ensuing minute of silence was so intense that we could hear our hearts pounding in the glassed area of the tower, could hear the slow greased turn of the light.

The monster stopped and froze. Its great lantern eyes blinked. Its mouth gaped. It gave a sort of rumble, like a volcano. It twitched its head this way and that, as if to seek the sounds now dwindled off into the fog. It peered at the lighthouse. It rumbled again. Then its eyes caught fire. It reared up, threshed the water, and rushed at the tower, its eyes filled with angry torment.

"McDunn!" I cried. "Switch on the horn!"

McDunn fumbled with the switch. But even as he flicked

it on, the monster was rearing up. I had a glimpse of its gigantic paws, fishskin glittering in webs between the finger-like projections, clawing at the tower. The huge eye on the right side of its anguished head glittered before me like a caldron into which I might drop, screaming. The tower shook. The Fog Horn cried; the monster cried. It seized the tower and gnashed at the glass, which shattered in upon us.

McDunn seized my arm. "Downstairs!"

The tower rocked, trembled, and started to give. The Fog Horn and the monster roared. We stumbled and half fell down the stairs. "Quick!"

We reached the bottom as the tower buckled down to-ward us. We ducked under the stairs into the small stone cellar. There were a thousand concussions as the rocks rained down; the Fog Horn stopped abruptly. The monster crashed upon the tower. The tower fell. We knelt together, McDunn and I, holding tight, while our world exploded.

Then it was over, and there was nothing but darkness and the wash of the sea on the raw stones.

That and the other sound.

"Listen," said McDunn quietly. "Listen."

We waited a moment. And then I began to hear it. First a great vacuumed sucking of air, and then the lament, the bewilderment, the loneliness of the great monster, folded over and upon us, above us, so that the sickening reek of its body filled the air, a stone's thickness away from our cellar. The monster gasped and cried. The tower was gone. The light was gone. The thing that had called to it across a million years was gone. And the monster was opening its mouth and sending out great sounds. The sounds of a Fog Horn, again and again. And ships far at sea, not finding the light, not seeing anything, but passing and hearing late that night, must've thought: There it is, the lonely sound, the Lonesome Bay horn. All's well. We've rounded the cape.

And so it went for the rest of that night.

The sun was hot and yellow the next afternoon when the rescuers came out to dig us from our stoned-under cellar.

"It fell apart, is all," said Mr. McDunn gravely. "We had a few bad knocks from the waves and it just crumbled." He pinched my arm.

There was nothing to see. The ocean was calm, the sky blue. The only thing was a great algaic stink from the green matter that covered the fallen tower stones and the shore rocks. Flies buzzed about. The ocean washed empty on the shore.

The next year they built a new lighthouse, but by that time I had a job in the little town and a wife and a good small warm house that glowed yellow on autumn nights, the doors locked, the chimney puffing smoke. As for McDunn, he was master of the new lighthouse, built to his own specifications, out of steel-reinforced concrete. "Just in case," he said.

The new lighthouse was ready in November. I drove down alone one evening late and parked my car and looked across the gray waters and listened to the new horn sounding, once, twice, three, four times a minute far out there, by itself.

The monster?

It never came back.

"It's gone away," said McDunn. "It's gone back to the Deeps. It's learned you can't love anything too much in this world. It's gone into the deepest Deeps to wait another million years. Ah, the poor thing! Waiting out there, and waiting out there, while man comes and goes on this pitiful little planet. Waiting and waiting."

I sat in my car, listening. I couldn't see the lighthouse or the light standing out in Lonesome Bay. I could only hear the Horn, the Horn, the Horn. It sounded like the monster calling.

I sat there wishing there was something I could say.

ROBERT BLOCH
& EDGAR ALLAN POE

The Light-House

The author of more shivery tales of the supernatural than any other living writer, Robert Bloch was born in Chicago on April 5, 1917. An early fan of H.P. Lovecraft, Bloch became a regular contributor to Weird Tales, *selling his first story to that magazine two months after graduating from high school. He also writes much mystery and suspense. Indeed,* Psycho, *his best-known novel, was filmed by Alfred Hitchcock in 1959, and the resulting sensation propelled Bloch into a screen and television writing career that still continues.*

In this version of "The Light-House," which first appeared in Fantastic *in February 1953, Bloch completes Edgar Allan Poe's unfinished story.*

Edgar Allan Poe, the seminal genre writer of the nineteenth century, was born in Boston on January 19, 1809, and was raised by a foster family after his father ran away and his mother died. After two abortive tries at an army career, Poe began writing full-time. He was offered an editorial position after winning the 1833 Baltimore Sunday Visitor *short story contest with "Ms. Found in a Bottle." But his career did not prosper; he was invariably fired from his jobs because of his arrogance, strong views, and antisocial behavior.*

Poe moved to New York, where he lived and wrote in abject poverty as his cousin-bride wasted away. Masterpieces such as "The Raven" and

"The Purloined Letter" brought scant funds or were given away. Yet Poe was prolific, producing a short science fiction novel and several volumes' worth of poems and short stories in a brief period. In 1849, just as he seemed on the verge of straightening out his life, Poe apparently went on a spree and was found seriously ill in a Baltimore bar room. He died a few days later on October 7.

◻

The Light-House

NOTE: This story is the result of a suggestion from Professor T.O. Mabbott, the distinguished Poe scholar, who wrote me following publication of my *The Man Who Collected Poe*. He had been instrumental in publishing the unfinished version of Poe's last story, "The Light-House," in its definitive form, and was kind enough to suggest I try my hand at completing the tale. Poe's manuscript covers four leaves and ends with the notation from January 3, and it is here that my collaboration begins. Here, then, is the last story from the pen of Poe, with the humble apologies of yours truly—ROBERT BLOCH

Jan. 1, 1796. This day—my first on the lighthouse—I make this entry in my Diary, as agreed on with DeGrät. As regularly as I *can* keep the journal, I will—but there is no telling what may happen to a man all alone as I am—I may get sick or worse . . .

So far well! The cutter had a narrow escape—but why dwell on that, since I am *here,* all safe? My spirits are beginning to revive already, at the mere thought of being—for once in my life at least—thoroughly *alone*; for, of course, Neptune, large as he is, is not to be taken into consideration as "society." Would in Heaven I had ever found in "society" one half as much *faith* as in this poor dog;—in such case I and "society" might never have parted—even for a year . . .

What most surprises me, is the difficulty DeGrät had in getting me the appointment—and I a noble of the realm! It could not be that the Consistory had any doubt of my ability to manage he light. One man has attended it before now—and got on quite as well as the three that are usually put in. The duty is a mere nothing; and the printed instructions are as plain as possible. It would never have done to let Orndoff accompany me. I should never have made any way with my book as long as he was within reach of me, with his intolerable gossip—not to mention that everlasting meërschaum. Besides, I wish to be *alone* . . .

It is strange that I never observed, until this moment, how dreary a sound that word has—"alone"! I could half fancy there was some peculiarity in the echo of these cylindrical walls—but oh, no!—that is all nonsense. I do believe I am going to get nervous about my insulation. That will never do. I have not forgotten DeGrät's prophecy. Now for a scramble to the lantern and a good look around to "see what I can see." . . . To see what I can see indeed!—not very much. The swell is subsiding a little, I think—but the cutter will have a rough passage home, nevertheless. She will hardly get within sight of the Norland before noon tomorrow—and yet it can hardly be more than 190 or 200 miles.

Jan. 2. I have passed this day in a species of ecstasy that I find it impossible to describe. My passion for solitude could scarcely have been more thoroughly gratified. I do not say *satisfied*; for I believe I should never be satisfied with such delight as I have experienced today . . .

The wind lulled after day-break, and by the afternoon the sea had gone down materially . . . Nothing to be seen with the telescope even, but ocean and sky, with an occasional gull.

Jan. 3. A dead calm all day. Towards evening, the sea looked very much like glass. A few sea-weeds came in sight; but besides them absolutely *nothing* all day—not even the slightest speck of cloud . . . Occupied myself in exploring the light-house . . . It is a very lofty one—as I find to my cost when I have to ascend its interminable stairs—not quite 160 feet, I should say, from the low-water mark to the top of the lantern. From the bottom *inside* the shaft, however, the distance to the summit is 180 feet at least:—thus the floor is 20 feet below the surface of the sea, even at low-tide . . .

It seems to me that the hollow interior at the bottom

should have been filled in with solid masonry. Undoubtedly the whole would have been thus rendered more *safe*:—but what am I thinking about. A structure such as this is safe enough under any circumstances. I should feel myself secure in it during the fiercest hurricane that ever raged—and yet I have heard seamen say that, occasionally, with a wind at South-West, the sea has been known to run higher here than any where with the single exception of the Western opening of the Straits of Magellan.

No mere sea, though, could accomplish anything with this solid iron-riveted wall—which, at 50 feet from high-water mark, is four feet thick, if one inch . . . The basis on which the structure rests seems to me to be chalk . . .

Jan. 4. I am now prepared to resume work on my book, having spent this day in familiarizing myself with a regular routine.

My actual duties will be, I perceive, absurdly simple—the light requires little tending beyond a periodic replenishment of the oil for the six-wick burner. As to my own needs, they are easily satisfied, and the exertion of an occasional trip down the stairs is all I must anticipate.

At the base of the stairs is the entrance room; beneath that is twenty feet of empty shaft. Above the entrance room, at the next turn of the circular iron staircase, is my store-room which contains the casks of fresh water and the food supplies, plus linens and other daily needs. Above that—again another spiral of those interminable stairs!—is the oil room, completely filled with the tanks from which I must feed the wicks. Fortunately, I perceive that I can limit my descent to the storeroom to once a week if I choose, for it is possible for me to carry sufficient provisions in one load to supply both myself and Neptune for such a period. As to the oil supply, I need only to bring up two drums every three days and thus insure a constant illumination. If I choose, I can place a dozen or more spare drums on the platform near the light and thus provide for several weeks to come.

So it is that in my daily existence I can limit my movements to the upper half of the light-house; that is to say, the three spirals opening on the topmost three levels. The lowest is my "living room"—and it is here, of course, that Neptune is confined the greater part of the day; here, too, that I plan to write at a desk near the wall-slit that affords a view of the sea without. The second highest level is my bedroom and kitchen combined. Here the weekly rations of food and water are contained in cupboards for that purpose; at hand is the ingenious stove fed by the selfsame oil that lights the beacon above. The topmost level is the service room giving access to the light itself and to the platform surrounding it. Since the light is fixed, and its reflectors set, there is no need for me ever to ascend to the platform save when replenishing the oil supply or making a repair or adjustment as per the written instructions—a circumstance which may well never arise during my stay here.

Already I have carried enough oil, water and provender to the upper levels to last me for an entire month—I need stir from my two rooms only to replenish the wicks.

For the rest, I am free! utterly free—my time is my own, and in this lofty realm I rule as King. Although Neptune is my only living subject I can well imagine that I am sovereign o'er all I see—ocean below and stars above. I am master of the sun that rises in rubicund radiance from the sea at dawn, emperor of wind and monarch of the gale, sultan of the waves that sport or roar in roiling torrents about the base of my palace pinnacle. I command the moon in the heavens, and the very ebb and flow of the tide does homage to my reign.

But enough of fancies—DeGrät warned me to refrain from morbid or from grandiose speculation—now I shall take up in all earnestness the task that lies before me. Yet this night, as I sit before the window in the starlight, the tides sweeping against these lofty walls can only echo my exultation; I am free—and, at last, alone!

Jan. 11. A week has passed since my last entry in this diary, and as I read it over, I can scarce comprehend that it was I who penned those words.

Something has happened—the nature of which lies unfathomed. I have worked, eaten, slept, replenished the wicks twice. My outward existence has been placid. I can ascribe the alteration in my feelings to naught but some inner alchemy; enough to say that a disturbing change had taken place.

"Alone!" I, who breathed the word as if it were some mystic incantation bestowing peace, have come—I realize it now—to loathe the very sound of the syllables. And the ghastliness of meaning I know full well.

It is a dismaying, it is a dreadful thing, to be alone. Truly alone, as I am, with only Neptune to exist beside me and by his breathing presence remind me that I am not the sole inhabitant of a blind and insensate universe. The sun and stars that wheel overhead in their endless cycle seem to rush across the horizon unheeding—and, of late, unheeded, for I cannot fix my mind upon them with normal constancy. The sea that swirls or ripples below me is naught but a purposeless chaos of utter emptiness.

I thought myself to be a man of singular self-sufficiency, beyond the petty needs of a boring and banal society. How wrong I was!—for I find myself longing for the sight of another face, the sound of another voice, the touch of other hands whether they offer caresses or blows. Anything, anything for reassurement that my dreams are indeed false and that I am *not*, actually, alone.

And yet I *am*. I am, and I will be. The world is two hundred miles away; I will not know it again for an entire year. And it in turn—but no more! I cannot put down my thoughts while in the grip of this morbid mood.

Jan. 13. Two more days—two more centuries!—have passed. Can it be less than two weeks since I was immured in this prison tower? I mount the turret on my dungeon and gaze at the horizon; I am not hemmed in by bars of steel but by columns and pillars and webs of wild and raging water. The sea has changed; grey skies have wrought a wizardry so that I stand surrounded by a tumult that threatens to become a tempest.

I turn away, for I can bear no more, and descend to my room. I seek to write—the book is bravely begun, but of late I can bring myself to do nothing constructive or creative—and in a moment I fling aside my pen and rise to pace. To endlessly pace the narrow, circular confines of my tower of torment.

Wild words, these? And yet I am not alone in my affliction—Neptune, Neptune the loyal, the calm, the placid—he feels it too.

Perhaps it is but the approach of the storm that agitates him so—for Nature bears closer kinship with the beast. He stays constantly at my side, whining now, and the muffled roaring of the waves without our prison causes him to tremble. There is a chill in the air that our stove cannot dissipate, but it is not cold that oppresses him . . .

I have just mounted to the platform and gazed out at the spectacle of gathering storm. The waves are fantastically high; they sweep against the light-house in titanic tumult. These solid walls of stone shudder rhythmically with each onslaught. The churning sea is gray no longer—the water is black, black as basalt and as heavy. The sky's hue has deepened so that at the moment no horizon is visible. I am surrounded by a billowing blackness thundering against me from all sides . . .

Back below now, as lightning flickers. The storm will break soon, and Neptune howls piteously. I stroke his quivering flanks, but the poor animal shrinks away. It seems that he fears even my presence; can it be that my own features betray an equal agitation? I do not know—I only feel that I am helpless, trapped here and awaiting the mercy of the storm. I cannot write much longer.

And yet I will set down a further statement. I must, if only to prove to myself that reason again prevails. In writing of my venture up to the platform—my viewing of the sea and sky— I omitted to mention the meaning of a single moment. There came upon me, as I gazed down at the black and boiling madness of the waters below, a wild and wilful craving to become one with it. But why should I disguise the naked truth?—I felt an insane impulse to hurl myself into the sea!

It has passed now; passed, I pray, forever. I did not yield to this perverse prompting and I am back here in my quarters, writing calmly once again. Yet the fact remains—the hideous urge to destroy myself came suddenly, and with the force of one of those monstrous waves.

And what—I force myself to realize—was the meaning of my demented desire? It was that I sought escape, escape from loneliness. It was as if by mingling with the sea and the storm I would no longer be *alone*.

But I defy the elements. I defy the powers of the earth and of the heavens. Alone I am, alone I *must* be—and come what may, I shall survive! My laughter rises above all your thunder!

So—ye spirits of the storm—blow, howl, rage, hurl your watery weight against my fortress—I am greater than you in all your powers. But wait! Neptune . . . something has happened to the creature . . . I must attend him . . .

Jan. 16. The storm is abated. I am back at my desk now, alone—truly alone. I have locked poor Neptune in the store-room below; the unfortunate beast seems driven out of his wits by the forces of the storm. When last I wrote he was worked into a frenzy, whining and pawing and wheeling in circles. He was incapable of responding to my commands and I had no choice but to literally drag him down the stairs by the scruff of his neck and incarcerate him in the store-room where he could not come to harm. I own that concern for *my* safety was involved—the possibility of being imprisoned in this light-house with a mad dog must be avoided.

His howls, throughout the storm, were pitiable indeed, but now he is silent. When last I ventured to gaze into the room I perceived him sleeping, and I trust that rest and calm will restore him to my full companionship as before.

Companionship!

How shall I describe the horrors of the storm faced *alone*?

In this diary entry I have prefaced a date—January 16th—but that is merely a guess. The storm has swept away all track of Time. Did it last a day, two days, three—as I now surmise?—a week, or a century? I do not know.

I know only an endless raging of waters that threatened, time and again, to engulf the very pinnacle of the light-house. I know only an eternity of ebony, an aeon of billowing black composed of sea and sky commingled. I only know that there were times when my own voice outroared the storm—but how can I convey the cause of *that*? There was a time, perhaps a full day, perhaps much longer, when I could not bear to rise from my couch but lay with my face buried in the pillows, weeping like a child. But mine were not the pure tears of childhood innocence—call them, rather the tears of Lucifer upon the realization of his eternal fall from grace. It seemed to me that I was truly the victim of an endless damnation; condemned forever to remain a prisoner in a world of thunderous chaos.

There is no need to write of the fancies and fantasies which assailed me through those unhallowed hours. At times I felt that the light-house was giving way and that I would be swept into the sea. At times I knew myself to be a victim of a colossal plot—I cursed DeGrät for sending me, knowingly, to my doom. At times (and these were the worst moments of all) I felt the full force of loneliness, crashing down upon me in waves higher than those wrought by water.

But all has passed, and the sea—and myself—are calm again. A peculiar calmness, this; as I gaze out upon the water there are certain phenomena I was not aware of until this very moment.

Before setting down my observations, let me reassure myself that I am, indeed, *quite* calm; no trace of my former tremors or agitation yet remains. The transient madness induced by the storm has departed and my brain is free of phantasms—indeed, my perceptive faculties seem to be sharpened to an unusual acuity.

It is almost as though I find myself in possession of an additional sense, an ability to analyze and penetrate beyond former limitations superimposed by Nature.

The water on which I gaze is placid once more. The sky is only lightly leaden in hue. But wait—low on the horizon creeps a sudden flame! It is the sun, the Arctic sun in sullen splendour, emerging momentarily from the pall to incarnadine the ocean. Sun and sky, sea and air about me, turn to blood.

Can it be I who but a moment ago wrote of returned, regained sanity? I, who have just shrieked aloud, "Alone!"— and half-rising from my chair, heard the muffled booming echo reverberate through the lonely light-house, its sepulchral accent intoning *"Alone!"* in answer? It may be that I am, despite all resolution, going mad; if so, I pray the end comes soon.

Jan. 18. There will be no end! I have conceived a notion, a theory which my heightened faculties soon will test. I shall embark upon an experiment . . .

Jan. 26. A week has passed here in my solitary prison. Solitary?—perhaps, but not for long. The experiment is proceeding. I must set down what has occurred.

The sound of the echo set me to thinking. One sends out one's voice and it comes back. One sends out one's thoughts and—can it be that there is a response? Sound, as we know, travels in waves and patterns. The emanations of the brain, perhaps, travel similarly. And they are not confined by physical laws of time, space, or duration.

Can one's thoughts produce a reply that *materializes*, just as one's voice produces an echo? An echo is a product of a certain vacuum. A thought . . .

Concentration is the key. I have been concentrating. My supplies are replenished, and Neptune—visited during my venture below—seems rational enough, although he shrinks away when I approach him. I have left him below and spent the past week here. Concentration, I repeat, is the key to my experiment.

Concentration, by its very nature, is a difficult task: I addressed myself to it with no little trepidation. Strive but to remain seated quietly with a mind "empty" of all thought, and one finds in the space of a very few minutes that the errant body is engaged in all manner of distracting movement—foot tapping, finger twisting, facial grimacing.

This I managed to overcome after a matter of many hours—

my first three days were virtually exhausted in an effort to rid myself of nervous agitation and assume the inner and outer tranquility of the Indian *fakir*. Then came the task of "filling" the empty consciousness—filling it completely with *one* intense and concentrated effort of will. What echo would I bring forth from nothingness? What companionship would I seek here in my loneliness? What was the sign or symbol I desired? What symbolized to me the whole absent world of life and light?

DeGrät would laugh me to scorn if he but knew the concept that I chose. Yet I, the cynical, the jaded, the decadent, searched my soul, plumbed my longing, and found that which I most desired—a simple sign, a token of all the earth removed: a fresh and growing flower, a *rose*!

Yes, a simple rose is what I have sought—a rose, torn from its living stem, perfumed with the sweet incarnation of life itself. Seated here before the window I have dreamed, I have mused. I have then concentrated with every fibre of my being upon a rose.

My mind was filled with redness—not the redness of the sun upon the sea, or the redness of blood, but the rich and radiant redness of the rose. My soul was suffused with the scent of a rose: as I brought my faculties to bear exclusively upon the image these walls fell away, the walls of my very flesh fell away, and I seemed to merge in the texture, the odour, the color, the actual *essence* of a rose.

Shall I write of this, the seventh day, when heated at the window as the sun emerged from the sea, I felt the commanding of my consciousness? Shall I write of rising, descending the stairs, opening the iron door at the base of the light-house and peering out at the billows that swirled at my very feet? Shall I write of stooping, of grasping, of holding?

Shall I write that I have indeed descended those iron stairs and returned here with my wave-borne trophy—*that this very day, from waters two hundred miles distant from any shore, I have reached down and plucked a fresh rose?*

Jan. 28. It has not withered! I keep it before me constantly in a vase on this table, and it is a priceless ruby plucked from dreams. It is real—as real as the howls of poor Neptune, who senses that something odd is afoot. His frantic barking does not disturb me; nothing disturbs me, for I am master of a power greater than earth or space or time. And I shall use this power, now, to bring me the final boon. Here in my tower I have become quite the philosopher: I have learned my lesson well and realize that I do not desire wealth, or fame, or the trinkets of society. My need is simply this—Companionship. And now, with the power that is mine to control, I shall have it!

Soon, quite soon, I shall no longer be alone!

Jan. 30. The storm has returned, but I pay it no heed; nor do I mark the howlings of Neptune, although the beast is now literally dashing himself against the door of the store-room. One might fancy that his efforts are responsible for the shuddering of the very light-house itself; but no, it is the fury of the northern gale. I pay it no heed, as I say, but I fully realize that this storm surpasses in extent and intensity anything I could imagine as witness to its predecessor.

Yet it is unimportant; even though the light above me flickers and threatens to be extinguished by the sheer velocity of wind that seeps through these stout walls; even though the ocean sweeps against the foundations with a force that makes solid stone seem flimsy as straw; even though the sky is a single black roaring mouth that yawns low upon the horizon to engulf me.

These things I sense but dimly, as I address myself to the appointed task. I pause now only for food and a brief respite—and scribble down these words to mark the progress of resolution towards an inevitable goal.

For the past several days I have bent my faculties to my will, concentrating utterly and to the uttermost upon the summoning of a Companion.

This Companion will be—I confess it!—a woman; a woman far surpassing the limitations of common mortality. For she is, and must be fashioned, of dreams and longing, of desire and delight beyond the bounds of flesh.

She is the woman of whom I have always dreamed, the One I have sought in vain through what I once presumed, in my ignorance, was the world of reality. It seems to me now that I have always known her, that my soul has contained her presence forever. I can visualize her perfectly—I know her hair, each strand more precious than a miser's gold; the riches of her ivory and alabaster brow, the perfection of her face and form are etched forever in my consciousness. DeGrät would scoff that she is but the figment of a dream—but DeGrät did not see the rose.

The rose—I hesitate to speak of it—has gone. It was the rose which I set before me when first I composed myself to this new effort of will. I gazed at it intently until vision faded, senses stilled, and I lost myself in the attempt of conjuring up my vision of a Companion.

Hours later, the sound of rising waters from without aroused me. I gazed about, my eyes sought the reassurance of the rose and rested only upon a *foulness*. Where the rose had risen proudly in its vase, red crest rampant upon a living stem, I now perceived only a noxious, utterly detestable strand of ichorous decay. No rose this, but only seaweed; rotted, noisome and putrescent. I flung it away, but for long moments I could not banish a wild presentiment—was it true that I have deceived myself? Was it a weed, and only a weed I plucked from the ocean's breast? Did the force of my thought momentarily invest it with the attributes of a rose? Would anything I called up from the depths—the depths of sea or the depths of consciousness—be *truly* real?

The blessed image of the Companion came to soothe these fevered speculations, and I knew myself saved. There *was* a rose; perhaps my thought had created it and nourished it— only when my entire concentration turned to other things did it depart, or resume another shape. And with my Companion, there will be no need for focussing my faculties elsewhere. She, and she alone, will be the recipient of everything my mind, my heart, my soul possesses. If will, if sentiment, if love are needed to preserve her, these things she shall have in entirety. So there is nothing to fear. Nothing to fear . . .

Once again now I shall lay my pen aside and return to the great task—the task of "creation", if you will—and I shall not fail. The fear (I admit it!) of loneliness is enough to drive me forward to unimaginable brinks. She, and she alone, can save me, shall save me, *must* save me! I can see her now—the golden glitter of her—and my consciousness calls to her to rise, to appear before me in radiant reality. Somewhere upon these storm-tossed seas she exists, I know it—and wherever she may be, my call will come to her and she will respond.

Jan. 31. The command came at midnight. Roused from the depths of the most profound innermost communion by a thunderclap, I rose as though in the grip of somnambulistic compulsion and moved down the spiral stairs.

The lantern I bore trembled in my hand; its light wavered in the wind, and the very iron treads beneath my feet shook with the furious force of the storm. The booming of the waves as they struck the light-house walls seemed to place me within the center of a maelstrom of ear-shattering sound, yet over the demoniacal din I could detect the frenzied howls of poor Neptune as I passed the door behind which he was confined. The door shook with the combined force of the wind and of his still desperate efforts to free himself—but I hastened on my way, descending to the iron door at the base of the light-house.

To open it required the use of both hands, and I set the lantern down at one side. To open it, moreover, required the summoning of a resolution I scarcely possessed—for beyond that door was the force and fury of the wildest storm that ever shrieked across these seething seas. A sudden wave might dash me from the doorway, or, conversely, enter and inundate the light-house itself.

But consciousness prevailed; consciousness drove me forward.

I *knew.* I thrilled to the certainty that *she* was without the iron portal—I unbolted the door with the urgency of one who rushes into the arms of his beloved.

The door swung open—blew open—roared open—and the storm burst upon me; a ravening monster of black-mouthed waves capped with white fangs. The sea and sky surged forward as if to attack, and I stood enveloped in Chaos. A flash of lightning revealed the immensity of utter Nightmare.

I saw it not, for the same flash illuminated the form, the lineaments of *she* whom I sought.

Lightning and lantern were unneeded—her golden glory outshone all as she stood there, pale and trembling, a goddess arisen from the depths of the sea!

Hallucination, vision, apparition? My trembling fingers sought, and found, their answer. Her flesh was real—cold as the icy waters from whence she came, but palpable and permanent. I thought of the storm, of doomed ships and drowning men, of a girl cast upon the waters and struggling towards the succor of the light-house beacon. I thought of a thousand explanations, a thousand miracles, a thousand riddles or reasons beyond rationality. Yet only one thing mattered— my Companion was here, and I had but to step forward and take her in my arms.

No word was spoken, nor could one be heard in all that Inferno. No word was needed, for she smiled. Pale lips parted as I held out my arms, and she moved closer. Pale lips parted—and I saw the pointed teeth, set in rows like those of a shark. Her eyes, fishlike and staring, swam closer. As I recoiled, her arms came up to cling, and they were as cold as the waters beneath, cold as the storm, cold as death.

In one monstrous moment I *knew*, knew with uttermost certainty, that the power of my will had indeed summoned, the call of my consciousness had been answered. But the answer came not from the living, for nothing lived in this storm. I had sent my will out over the waters, but the will penetrates all dimensions, and my answer had come from *below* the waters. *She* was from below, where the drowned dead lie dreaming, and I had awakened her and clothed her with a horrid life. A life that thirsted, and must drink . . .

I think I shrieked, then, but I heard no sound. Certainly, I did not hear the howls from Neptune as the beast, burst from his prison, bounded down the stairs and flung himself upon the creature from the sea.

His furry form bore her back and obscured my vision; in

an instant she was falling backwards, away, into the sea that spawned her. Then, and only then, did I catch a glimpse of the final moment of animation in that which my consciousness had summoned. Lightning seared the sight inexorably upon my soul—the sight of the ultimate blasphemy I had created in my pride. The rose had wilted . . .

The rose had wilted and become seaweed. And now, the golden one was gone and in its place was the bloated, swollen obscenity of a thing long-drowned and dead, risen from the slime and to that slime returning.

Only a moment, and then the waves overwhelmed it, bore it back into the blackness. Only a moment, and the door was slammed shut. Only a moment, and I raced up the iron stairs, Neptune yammering at my heels. Only a moment, and I reached the safety of this sanctuary.

Safety? There is no safety in the universe for me, no safety in a consciousness that could create such horror. And there is no safety here—the wrath of the waves increases with every moment, the anger of the sea and its creatures rises to an inevitable crescendo.

Mad or sane, it does not matter, for the end is the same in either case. I know now that the light-house will shatter and fall. I am already shattered, and must fall with it.

There is time only to gather these notes, strap them securely in a cylinder and attach it to Neptune's collar. It may be that he can swim, or cling to a fragment of debris. It may be that a ship, passing by this toppling beacon, may stay and search the waters for a sign—and thus find and rescue the gallant beast.

That ship shall not find me. I go with the light-house and go willingly, down to the dark depths. Perhaps—is it perverted poetry?—I shall join my Companion there forever. Perhaps . . .

The light-house is trembling. The beacon flickers above my head and I hear the rush of waters in their final onslaught. There is—yes—a wave, bearing down upon me. It is higher than the tower, it blots out the sky itself, everything . . .

JACK VANCE

When the
Five Moons Rise

A writer noted for exceptional inspiration and style, John Holbrook Vance was born in San Francisco on August 28, 1916. After receiving his B.A. from the Univeristy of California at Berkeley in 1942, he served in the Merchant Marine during World War Two. He later worked on construction crews, played in jazz bands, and cranked out scripts for television's "Captain Video." A prolific author who has produced more than sixty books, Vance has won science fiction, fantasy, and mystery awards for his novels and short stories.

His selection in this anthology, "Where the Five Moons Rise," is our only interstellar lighthouse story. It was first published in Cosmos *in April 1954.*

◻

Seguilo could not have gone far; there was no place for him to go. Once Perrin had searched the lighthouse and the lonesome acre of rock, there were no other possibilities—only the sky and the ocean.

Seguilo was neither inside the lighthouse nor was he outside.

Perrin went out into the night, squinted up against the five moons. Seguilo was not to be seen on top of the lighthouse.

169

Seguilo had disappeared.

Perrin looked indecisively over the flowing brine of Maurnilam Var. Had Seguilo slipped on the damp rock and fallen into the sea, he certainly would have called out. . . . The five moons blinked, dazzled, glinted along the surface; Seguilo might even now be floating unseen a hundred yards distant.

Perrin shouted across the dark water: "Seguilo!"

He turned, once more looked up the face of the lighthouse. Around the horizon whirled the twin shafts of red and white light, guiding the barges crossing from South Continent to Spacetown, warning them off Isel Rock.

Perrin walked quickly toward the lighthouse; Seguilo was no doubt asleep in his bunk, or in the bathroom.

Perrin went to the top chamber, circled the lumenifer, climbed down the stairs. "Seguilo!"

No answer. The lighthouse returned a metallic vibrating echo.

Seguilo was not in his room, in the bathroom, in the commissary, or in the storeroom. Where else could a man go?

Perrin looked out the door. The five moons cast confusing shadows. He saw a gray blot—"Seguilo!" He ran outside. "Where have you been?"

Seguilo straightened to his full height, a thin man with a wise, doleful face. He turned his head; the wind blew his words past Perrin's ears.

Sudden enlightenment came to Perrin. "You must have been under the generator!" The only place he could have been.

Seguilo had come closer. "Yes . . . I was under the generator." He paused uncertainly by the door, stood looking up at the moons, which this evening had risen all bunched together. Puzzlement creased Perrin's forehead. Why should Seguilo crawl under the generator? "Are you . . . well?"

"Yes. Perfectly well."

Perrin stepped closer and in the light of the five moons, Ista, Bista, Liad, Miad, and Poidel, scrutinized Seguilo sharply. His eyes were dull and noncommittal; he seemed to carry himself stiffly. "Have you hurt yourself? Come over to the steps and sit down."

"Very well." Seguilo ambled across the rock, sat down on the steps.

"You're certain you're all right?"

"Certain."

After a moment, Perrin said, "Just before you . . . went under the generator, you were about to tell me something you said was important."

Seguilo nodded slowly. "That's true."

"What was it?"

Seguilo stared dumbly up into the sky. There was nothing to be heard but the wash of the sea, hissing and rushing where the rock shelved under.

"Well?" asked Perrin finally. Seguilo hesitated. "You said that when five moons rose together in the sky, it was not wise to believe anything."

"Ah," nodded Seguilo, "so I did."

"What did you mean?"

"I'm not sure."

"Why is not believing anything important?"

"I don't know."

Perrin rose abruptly to his feet. Seguilo normally was crisp, dryly emphatic. "Are you sure you're all right?"

"Right as rain."

That was more like Seguilo. "Maybe a drink of whisky would fix you up."

"Sounds like a good idea."

Perrin knew where Seguilo kept his private store. "You sit here, I'll get you a shot."

"Yes, I'll sit here."

Perrin hurried inside the lighthouse, clambered the two flights of stairs to the commissary. Seguilo might remain seated or he might not; something in his posture, in the rapt gaze out to sea, suggested that he might not. Perrin found the bottle and a glass, ran back down the steps. Somehow he knew that Seguilo would be gone.

Seguilo was gone. He was not on the steps, nowhere on the windy acre of Isel Rock. It was impossible that he had passed Perrin on the stairs. He might have slipped into the engine room and crawled under the generator once more.

Perrin flung open the door, switched on the lights, stooped, peered under the housing. Nothing.

A greasy film of dust, uniform, unmarred, indicated that no one had ever been there.

Where was Seguilo?

Perrin went up to the top-most part of the lighthouse, carefully searched every nook and cranny down to the outside entrance. No Seguilo.

Perrin walked out on the rock. Bare and empty; no Seguilo.

Seguilo was gone. The dark water of Maurnilam Var sighed and flowed across the shelf.

Perrin opened his mouth to shout across the moon-dazzled swells, but somehow it did not seem right to shout. He went back to the lighthouse, seated himself before the radio transceiver.

Uncertainly he touched the dials; the instrument had been Seguilo's responsibility. Seguilo had built it himself from parts salvaged from a pair of old instruments.

Perrin tentatively flipped a switch. The screen sputtered into light, the speaker hummed and buzzed. Perrin made hasty adjustments. The screen streaked with darts of blue light, a spatter of quick, red blots. Fuzzy, dim, a face looked forth from the screen. Perrin recognized a junior clerk in the Commission office at Spacetown. He spoke urgently, "This is Harold Perrin, at Isel Rock Lighthouse; send out a relief ship."

The face in the screen looked at him as through thick pebbleglass. A faint voice, overlaid by sputtering and crackling, said, "Adjust your tuning . . . I can't hear you. . . ."

Perring raised his voice. "Can you hear me now?"

The face in the screen wavered and faded.

Perrin yelled, "This is Isel Rock Lighthouse! Send out a relief ship! Do you hear? There's been an accident!"

". . . signals not coming in. Make out a report, send . . ." the voice sputtered away.

Cursing furiously under his breath, Perrin twisted knobs, flipped switches. He pounded the set with his fist. The screen flashed bright orange, went dead.

Perrin ran behind, worked an anguished five minutes, to no avail. No light, no sound.

Perrin slowly rose to his feet. Through the window he glimpsed the five moons racing for the west. "When the five moons rise together," Seguilo had said, "it's not wise to believe anything." Seguilo was gone. He had been gone once before and come back; maybe he would come back again. Perrin grimaced, shuddered. It would be best now if Seguilo stayed away. He ran down to the outer door, barred and bolted it. Hard on Seguilo, if he came wandering back. . . . Perrin leaned a moment with his back to the door, listening. Then he went to the generator room, looked under the generator. Nothing. He shut the door, climbed the steps.

Nothing in the commissary, the storeroom, the bathroom, the bedrooms. No one in the lighthouse. No one on the roof.

No one in the lighthouse but Perrin.

He returned to the commissary, brewed a pot of coffee, sat half an hour listening to the sigh of water across the shelf, then went to his bunk.

Passing Seguilo's room he looked in. The bunk was empty.

When at last he rose in the morning, his mouth was dry, his muscles like bundles of withes, his eyes hot from long staring up at the ceiling. He rinsed his face with cold water and, going to the window, searched the horizon. A curtain of dingy overcast hung halfway up the east; blue-green Magda shone through like an ancient coin covered with verdigris. Over the water oily skeins of blue-green light formed and joined and broke and melted. . . . Out along the south horizon Perrin spied a pair of black hyphens—barges riding the Trade Current to Spacetown. After a few moments they disappeared into the overcast.

Perrin threw the master switch; above him came the fluttering hum of the lumenifer slowing and dimming.

He descended the stairs, with stiff fingers unbolted the door, flung it wide. The wind blew past his ears, smelling of

Maurnilam Var. The tide was low; Isel Rock rose out of the water like a saddle. He walked gingerly to the water's edge. Blue-green Magda broke clear of the overcast; the light struck under the water. Leaning precariously over the shelf, Perrin looked down, past shadows and ledges and grottos, down into the gloom. . . . Movement of some kind; Perrin strained to see. His foot slipped, he almost fell.

Perrin returned to the lighthouse, worked a disconsolate three hours at the transceiver, finally deciding that some vital component had been destroyed.

He opened a lunch unit, pulled a chair to the window, sat gazing across the ocean. Eleven weeks to the relief ship. Isel Rock had been lonely enough with Seguilo.

Blue-green Magda sank in the west. A sulfur overcast drifted up to meet it. Sunset brought a few minutes of sad glory to the sky; jade-colored stain with violet streakings. Perrin started the twin shafts of red and white on their nocturnal sweep, went to stand by the window.

The tide was rising, the water surged over the shelf with a heavy sound. Up from the west floated a moon; Ista, Bista, Liad, Miad, or Poidel? A native would know at a glance. Up they came, one after the other, five balls blue as old ice.

"It's not wise to believe. . . ." What had Seguilo meant? Perrin tried to think back. Seguilo had said, "It's not often, very rare, in fact, that the five moons bunch up—but when they do, then there're high tides." He had hesitated, glancing out at the shelf. "When the five moons rise together," said Seguilo, "it's not wise to believe anything."

Perrin had gazed at him with forehead creased in puzzlement. Seguilo was an old hand, who knew the fables and lore, which he brought forth from time to time. Perrin had never known quite what to expect from Seguilo; he had the trait indispensable to a lighthouse-tender—taciturnity. The transceiver had been his hobby; in Perrin's ignorant hands, the instrument destroyed itself. What the lighthouse needs, thought Perrin, was one of the new transceivers with self-contained power unit, master control, the new organic screen, soft and elastic, like a great eye. . . . A sudden rain squall blanketed half the sky; the five moons hurtled toward the cloud bank. The tide surged high over the shelf, almost over a gray mass. Perrin eyed it with interest; what could it be?. . . About the size of a transceiver, about the same shape. Of course, it could not possibly be a transceiver; yet, what a wonderful thing if it were. . . . He squinted, strained his eyes. There, surely, that was the milk-colored screen; those black spots were dials. He sprang to his feet, ran down the stairs, out the door, across the rock. . . . It was irrational; why should a transceiver appear just when he wanted it, as if in answer to his prayer? Of course it might be part of a cargo lost overboard. . . .

Sure enough, the mechanism was bolted to a raft of Manasco logs, and evidently had floated up on the shelf on the high tide.

Perrin, unable to credit his good fortune, crouched beside the gray case. Brand new, with red seals across the master switch.

It was too heavy to carry. Perrin tore off the seals, threw on the power: here was a set he understood. The screen glowed bright.

Perrin dialed to the Commission band. The interior of an office appeared and facing out was, not the officious subordinate, but Superintendent Raymond Flint himself. Nothing could be better.

"Superintendent," cried out Perrin, "this is Isel Rock Lighthouse, Harold Perrin speaking."

"Oh, yes," said Superintendent Flint. "How are you, Perrin? What's the trouble?"

"My partner, Andy Seguilo, disappeared—vanished into nowhere; I'm alone out here."

Superintendent Flint looked shocked. "Disappeared? What happened? Did he fall into the ocean?"

"I don't know. He just disappeared. It happened last night—"

"You should have called in before," said Flint reprovingly. "I would have sent out a rescue copter to search for him."

"I tried to call," Perrin explained, "but I couldn't get the regular transceiver to work. It burnt up on me. . . . I thought I was marooned here."

Superintendent Flint raised his eyebrows in mild curiosity. "Just what are you using now?"

Perrin stammered, "It's a brand-new instrument . . . floated up out of the sea. Probably was lost from a barge."

Flint nodded. "Those bargemen are a careless lot—don't seem to understand what good equipment costs. . . . Well, you sit tight. I'll order a plane out in the morning with a relief crew. You'll be assigned to duty along the Floral Coast. How does that suit you?"

"Very well, sir," said Perrin. "Very well indeed. I can't think of anything I'd like better . . . Isel Rock is beginning to get on my nerves."

"When the five moons rise, it's not wise to believe anything," said Superintendent Flint in a sepulchral voice.

The screen went dead.

Perrin lifted his hand, slowly turned off the power. A drop of rain fell on his face. He glanced skyward. The squall was almost on him. He tugged at the transceiver, although well aware that it was too heavy to move. In the storeroom was a tarpaulin that would protect the transceiver until morning. The relief crew could help him move it inside.

He ran back to the lighthouse, found the tarpaulin, hurried back outside. Where was the transceiver?. . . Ah—there. He ran through the pelting drops, wrapped the tarpaulin around the box, lashed it into place, ran back to the lighthouse. He barred the box, and whistling, opened a canned dinner unit.

The rain spun and slashed at the lighthouse. The twin shafts of white and red swept wildly around the sky. Perrin climbed into his bunk, lay warm and drowsy. . . . Seguilo's disappearance was a terrible thing; it would leave a scar on his mind. But it was over and done with. Put it behind him; look to the future. The Floral Coast. . . .

In the morning the sky was bare and clean. Maurnilam Var spread mirror-quiet as far as the eye could reach. Isel Rock lay naked to the sunlight. Looking out the window,

Perrin saw a rumpled heap—the tarpaulin, the lashings. The transceiver, the Manasco raft had disappeared utterly.

Perrin sat in the doorway. The sun climbed the sky. A dozen times he jumped to his feet, listening for the sound of engines. But no relief plane appeared.

The sun reached the zenith, verged westward. A barge drifted by, a mile from the rock. Perrin ran out on the shelf, shouting, waving his arms.

The lank, red bargemen sprawled on the cargo stared curiously, made no move. The barge dwindled into the east.

Perrin returned to the doorstep, sat with his head in his hands. Chills and fever ran along his skin. There would be no relief plane. On Isel Rock he would remain, day in, day out, for eleven weeks.

Listlessly, he climbed the steps to the commissary. There was no lack of food, he would never starve. But could he bear the solitude, the uncertainty? Seguilo going, coming, going. . . . The unsubstantial transceiver. . . . Who was responsible for these cruel jokes? The five moons rising together—was there some connection?

He found an almanac, carried it to the table. At the top of each page five white circles on a black strip represented the moons. A week ago they strung out at random. Four days ago Liad, the slowest, and Poidel, the fastest, were thirty degrees apart, with Ista, Bista, and Miad between. Two nights ago the peripheries almost touched; last night they were even closer. Tonight Poidel would bulge slightly out in front of Ista, tomorrow night Liad would lag behind Bista. . . . But between the five moons and Seguilo's disappearance—where was the connection?

Gloomily, Perrin ate his dinner. Magda settled into Maurnilam Var without display, a dull dusk settled over Isel Rock, water rose and sighed across the shelf.

Perrin turned on the light, barred the door. There would be no more hoping, no more wishing—no more believing. In eleven weeks the relief ship would convey him back to Spacetown; in the meantime he must make the best of the situation.

Through the window he saw the blue glow in the east,

watched Poidel, Ista, Bista, Liad, and Miad climb the sky. The tide came with the moons. Maurnilam Var was still calm, and each moon laid a separate path of reflection along the water.

Perrin looked up into the sky, around the horizon. A beautiful, lonesome sight. With Seguilo he sometimes had felt lonely, but never isolation such as this. Eleven weeks of solitude. . . . If he could select a companion . . . Perrin let his mind wander.

Into the moonlight a slim figure came walking, wearing tan breeches and a short-sleeved white sports shirt.

Perrin stared, unable to move. The figure walked up to the door, rapped. The muffled sound came up the staircase. "Hello, anybody home?" It was a girl's clear voice.

Perrin swung open the window, called hoarsely, "Go away!"

She moved back, turned up her face, and the moonlight fell upon her features. Perrin's voice died in his throat. He felt his heart beating wildly.

"Go away?" she said in a soft puzzled voice. "I've no place to go."

"Who are you?" he asked. His voice sounded strange to his own ears—desperate, hopeful. After all, she was possible—even though almost impossibly beautiful. . . . She might have flown out from Spacetown. "How did you get here?"

She gestured at Maurnilam Var. "My plane went down about three miles out. I came over on the life raft."

Perrin looked along the water's edge. The outline of a life raft was barely visible.

The girl called up, "Are you going to let me in?"

Perrin stumbled downstairs. He halted at the door, one hand on the bolts, and the blood rushing in his ears.

An impatient tapping jarred his hand. "I'm freezing to death out here."

Perrin let the door swing back. She stood facing him, half-smiling. "You're a very cautious lighthouse-tender—or perhaps a woman-hater?"

Perrin searched her face, her eyes, the expression of her mouth. "Are you . . . real?"

She laughed, not at all offended. "Of course I'm real." She held out her hand. "Touch me." Perrin stared at her—the essence of night-flowers, soft silk, hot blood, sweetness, delightful fire. "Touch me," she replied softly.

Perrin moved back uncertainly, and she came forward, into the lighthouse. "Can you call the shore?"

She turned him a quick firefly look. "When is your next relief boat?"

"Eleven weeks."

"Eleven weeks!" she sighed a soft shallow sigh.

Perrin moved back another half-step. "How did you know I was alone?"

She seemed confused. "I didn't know. . . . Aren't lighthouse keepers always alone?"

"No."

She came a step closer. "You don't seem pleased to see me. Are you . . . a hermit?"

"No," said Perrin in a husky voice. "Quite the reverse. . . . But I can't quite get used to you. You're a miracle. Too good to be true. Just now I was wishing for someone . . . exactly like you. Exactly."

"And here I am."

Perrin moved uneasily. "What's your name?"

He knew what she would say before she spoke. "Sue."

"Sue what?" He tried to hold his mind vacant.

"Oh . . . just Sue. Isn't that enough?"

Perrin felt the skin of his face tighten. "Where is your home?"

She looked vaguely over her shoulder. Perrin held his mind blank, but the word came through.

"Hell."

Perrin's breath came hard and sharp.

"And what is Hell like?"

"It is . . . cold and dark."

Perrin stepped back. "Go away. Go away." His vision blurred; her face melted as if tears had come across his eyes.

"Where will I go?"

"Back where you came from."

"But"—forlornly—"there is nowhere but Maurnilam Var.

And up here—" She stopped short, took a swift step forward, stood looking up into his face. He could feel the warmth of her body. "Are you afraid of me?"

Perrin wrenched his eyes from her face. "You're not real. You're something which takes the shape of my thoughts. Perhaps you killed Seguilo . . . I don't know what you are. But you're not real."

"Not real? Of course I'm real. Touch me. Feel my arm." Perrin backed away. She said passionately, "Here, a knife. If you are of a mind, cut me; you will see blood. Cut deeper . . . you will find bone."

"What would happen," said Perrin, "if I drove the knife into your heart?"

She said nothing, staring at him with big eyes.

"Why do you come here?" cried Perrin. She looked away, back toward the water.

"It's magic . . . darkness. . . ." The words were a mumbled confusion; Perrin suddenly realized that the same words were in his own mind. Had she merely parroted his thoughts during the entire conversation? "Then comes a slow pull," she said. "I drift, I crave the air, the moons bring me up . . . I do anything to hold my place in the air. . . ."

"Speak your own words," said Perrin harshly. "I know you're not real—but where is Seguilo?"

"Seguilo?" She reached a hand behind her head, touched her hair, smiled sleepily at Perrin. Real or not, Perrin's pulse thudded in his ears. Real or not. . . .

"I'm no dream," she said. "I'm real. . . ." She came slowly toward Perrin, feeling his thoughts, face arch, ready.

Perrin said in a strangled gasp, "No, no. Go away. Go away!"

She stopped short, looked at him through eyes suddenly opaque. "Very well. I will go now—"

"Now! Forever!"

"—but perhaps you will call me back. . . ."

She walked slowly through the door. Perrin ran to the window, watched the slim shape blur into the moonlight. She went to the edge of the shelf; here she paused. Perrin felt a sudden intolerable pang; what was he casting away? Real or not, she was what he wanted her to be; she was identical to reality. . . . He leaned forward to call, "Come back . . . whatever you are. . . ." He restrained himself. When he looked again she was gone. . . . Why was she gone? Perrin pondered, looking across the moonlit sea. He had wanted her, but he no longer believed in her. He had believed in the shape called Seguilo; he had believed in the transceiver—and both had slavishly obeyed his expectations. So had the girl, and he had sent her away. . . . Rightly, too, he told himself regretfully. Who knows what she might become when his back was turned. . . .

When dawn finally came, it brought a new curtain of overcast. Blue-green Magda glimmered dull and sultry as a moldy orange. The water shone like oil. . . . Movement in the west—a Panapa chieftain's private barge, walking across the horizon like a water-spider. Perrin vaulted the stairs to the lightroom, swung the lumenifer full at the barge, dispatched an erratic series of flashes.

The barge moved on, jointed oars swinging rhythmically in and out of the water. A torn banner of fog drifted across the water. The barge became a dark, jerking shape, disappeared.

Perrin went to Seguilo's old transceiver, sat looking at it. He jumped to his feet, pulled the chassis out of the case, disassembled the entire circuit.

He saw scorched metal, wires fused into droplets, cracked ceramic. He pushed the tangle into a corner, went to stand by the window.

The sun was at the zenith, the sky was the color of green grapes. The sea heaved sluggishly, great amorphous sweeps rising and falling without apparent direction. Now was low tide: the shelf shouldered high up, the black rock showing naked and strange. The sea palpitated, up, down, up, down, sucking noisily at bits of sea-wrack.

Perrin descended the stairs. On his way down he looked in at the bathroom mirror, and his face stared back at him, pale, wide-eyed, cheeks hollow and lusterless. Perrin continued down the stairs, stepped out into the sunlight.

Carefully he walked out on the shelf, looked in a kind of fascination down over the edge. The heave of the swells distorted his vision; he could see little more than shadows and shifting fingers of light.

Step by step he wandered along the shelf. The sun leaned to the west. Perrin retreated up the rock.

At the lighthouse he seated himself in the doorway. To-night the door remained barred. No inducement could per-suade him to open up; the most entrancing visions would beseech him in vain. His thoughts went to Seguilo. What had Seguilo believed; what being had he fabricated out of his morbid fancy with the power and malice to drag him away? . . . It seemed that every man was victim to his own imaginings, Isel Rock was not the place for a fanciful man when the five moons rose together.

Tonight he would bar the door, he would bed himself down and sleep, secure both in the barrier of welded metal and his own unconsciousness.

The sun sank in a bank of heavy vapor. North, east, south flushed with violet; the west glowed lime and dark green, dulling quickly through tones of brown. Perrin entered the lighthouse, bolted the door, set the twin shafts of red and white circling the horizon.

He opened a dinner unit, ate listlessly. Outside was dark night, emptiness to all the horizons. As the tide rose, the water hissed and moaned across the shelf.

Perrin lay in his bed, but sleep was far away. Through the window came an electric glow, then up rose the five moons, shining through a high overcast as if wrapped in blue gauze.

Perrin heaved fitfully. There was nothing to fear, he was safe in the lighthouse. No human hands could force the door; it would take the strength of a mastodon, the talons of a rock choundril, the ferocity of a Maldene land-shark. . . .

He elbowed himself up on his bunk. . . . A sound from outside? He peered through the window, heart in his mouth. A tall shape, indistinct. As he watched it, it slouched toward the lighthouse—as he knew it would.

"No, no," cried Perrin softly. He flung himself into his

bunk, covered his head in the blankets. "It's only what I think up myself, it's not real. . . . Go away," he whispered fiercely. "Go away." He listened. It must be near the door now. It would be lifting a heavy arm, the talons would glint in the moonlight.

"No, no," cried Perrin. "There's nothing there. . . ." He held up his head and listened.

A rattle, a rasp at the door. A thud as a great mass tested the lock.

"Go away!" screamed Perrin. "You're not real!"

The door groaned, the bolts sagged.

Perrin stood at the head of the stairs, breathing heavily through his mouth. The door would slam back in another instant. He knew what he would see: a black shape tall and round as a pole, with eyes like coach-lamps. Perrin even knew the last sound his ears would hear—a terrible grinding discord. . . .

The top bolt snapped, the door reeled. A huge black arm shoved inside. Perrin saw the talons gleam as the fingers reached for the bolt.

His eyes flickered around the lighthouse for a weapon. . . only a wrench, a table knife.

The bottom bolt shattered, the door twisted. Perrin stood staring, his mind congealed. A thought rose up from some hidden survival-node. Here, Perrin thought, was the single chance.

He ran back into his room. Behind him the door clattered, he heard heavy steps. He looked around the room. His shoe.

Thud! Up the stairs, and the lighthouse vibrated. Perrin's fancy explored the horrible, he knew what he would hear. And so came a voice—harsh, empty, but like another voice which had been sweet. "I told you I'd be back."

Thud—thud—up the stairs. Perrin took the shoe by the toe, swung, struck the side of his head.

Perrin recovered consciousness. He stumbled to the wall, supported himself. Presently he groped to his bunk, sat down.

Outside there was still dark night. Grunting, he looked

out the window into the sky. The five moons hung far down in the west. Already Poidel ranged ahead, while Liad trailed behind.

Tomorrow night the five moons would rise apart.

Tomorrow night there would be no high tides, sucking and tremulous along the shelf.

Tomorrow night the moons would call up no yearning shapes from the streaming dark.

Eleven weeks to relief. Perrin gingerly felt the side of his head. . . . Quite a respectable lump.

DAN J. MARLOWE

All the Way Home

The author of more than twenty-five crime and espionage novels, Dan James Marlowe was born in Lowell, Massachusetts, on July 10, 1914. He was educated at the Bentley School of Accounting and Finance, and worked in accounting, insurance, and public relations. But after his wife died in 1957, he decided to become a full-time freelance writer. In 1970, one of his novels, Flashpoint *(or* Operation Flashpoint*), won the first Mystery Writers of America award for best paperback mystery. Marlowe died in Los Angeles in 1986.*

"All the Way Home" reflects the author's long sojourn in Harbor Beach, a tiny Michigan town on the shore of Lake Huron. This powerful story of marital passions was first published under the pseudonym of Jaime Sandoval in Ellery Queen's Mystery Magazine *in September 1965.*

◻

The hired man drove me back to the farm from the cemetery. Becky's funeral had taken a lot out of me, although at my age I should be used to them. I came back from my father's funeral in a horse and buggy, from my mother's in an old tin lizzie, and from Becky's in a many-horsed thunderbolt. I've lived too long.

My father's farm—my farm—is on a spit of land jutting

out into Lake Superior. It's a good farm. With a little help from the cows, it took care of all of us through the long years. I can't even leave it to kinfolk now. I'm the last of the Malcolms.

What still hurts me the most is knowing how Becky must have wondered why I never asked her to marry me. Especially since my mother died. Becky never let on, of course, and there was nothing I could do, or say. Not since that terrible night on Wild Swan Point so many years ago.

There used to be an old abandoned wooden lighthouse at the end of the causeway leading out to the point. It hasn't been there for a long time now, but at sunset when the west wind blows and the clouds are dark on the lake, I can sit by the kitchen window and look down the road, and once again a light seems to shine from the tiny window high up in the old lighthouse.

When I was twelve years old, the light shone there because my father had fixed up a room in the lighthouse for Miss Abby Hunter, up near the top where she wanted to be. My mother didn't like it at all when Miss Abby came back to live in our neighborhood again. Before she left, Miss Abby taught school and lived on the Brainard farm about a mile from us. I heard my mother say once after Miss Abby came to dinner at our house that some people were no better than they should be. My father heard her say it, too, and it made him angry. He told my mother later that she was a fool to believe all the gossip she heard.

We were at the supper table in our big farm kitchen when he said it. There were rusks and wild strawberry jam on the table. I wanted another rusk, but when I looked up and saw my father's face, I was afraid to ask for it. He was a big strong solid-looking man, with red cheeks and blue eyes and a temper that scared me sometimes. But his temper never scared my mother. She spoke right up to him all the time, but especially so after Miss Abby came back to live in the lighthouse.

I liked Miss Abby. She lent me books, but after my mother found out, I had to hide them. Miss Abby always looked dressed up. She was small and quick-moving and very pretty. She always wore a blue ribbon on her blond hair. When she was still teaching, she never seemed much older than the bigger kids in school.

The old lighthouse was a strange place to want to live in. It hadn't been used as a lighthouse for a long time. There wasn't much in the cobwebbed space at the bottom except a few bad-smelling battered oil drums. I never saw the room my father fixed up for Miss Abby at the top of the spiraling wooden staircase. She never invited me to see it, and I didn't know how to ask.

I came back to the farmhouse one morning after collecting the eggs in the coop and taking the cows down to the pasture by the lake, where we had a dock. My father's sailboat was always tied up at the dock during the summer. The dock was near the barn and the road, too, so I hadn't far to go. During the less busy seasons, in the spring and fall, my father used to go out on the lake with his nets and bring back whitefish, lake trout, pike, and perch.

He met me at our front gate, saying he wanted to talk to me. It made me feel important as soon as I saw he wasn't angry as he was so often those days. "Tommy," he said, "twice a week I want you to carry a pail of milk down to Miss Abby at the lighthouse. You can milk Daisy after supper, and get down and back before dark. Do it on Sunday and Wednesday nights. And let's keep it a secret, just between you and me." He put a finger to his lips, and winked at me.

It sounded fine to me. I had no brothers or sisters, and sometimes I got so lonely I welcomed the chance to talk to almost anyone. My mother was always busy in the kitchen after supper, and I was sure she wouldn't miss me. She was a tall, stout woman with black hair and snapping black eyes. She was almost pretty when she smiled, but she hardly ever smiled after Miss Abby came back to live at the lighthouse.

They argued a lot. More than once I overheard my father tell my mother that she'd better learn to control her tongue. My mother would get red in the face. Her eyes glared, and she usually left the room.

I could hardly wait to milk Daisy the first Sunday night and be on my way down to Wild Swan Point. My father had gotten me a special pail with a tight lid for the milk carrying. It didn't spill even when I ran. The sun was going down behind the lighthouse when I reached the point, and Miss Abby was sitting on a bench outside. She looked like a doll in her frilly white dress against the dirty wooden wall of the old lighthouse.

She greeted me warmly and asked me to sit down while she put the milk away. I could see that she was making a woodpile inside the big door. There was always driftwood on the shore, and I carried some inside and stacked it. Miss Abby thanked me when she came downstairs. It was almost dark when I reached home. I turned and looked back down the road and saw the high-up lighted window in the lighthouse, like a small and lonely star against the night.

The Brainards stopped by our place one Sunday afternoon in August. They had a boy a year older than me. His name was Nick, and I didn't like him. He was bigger than me, and he was always picking a fight. We sat in the front parlor, and Mrs. Brainard began talking about how queer it was for Miss Abby to come back and live in the old lighthouse when she was no longer teaching. Nick sat grinning at me from his chair across the parlor. He motioned with his head, finally, and we excused ourselves and went outside.

Nick headed for our outhouse. We had the nicest one in the area. It was painted green, and it had a kind of small porch with mosquito netting all around it. A wild cucumber vine grew across the top. Nick stayed inside a long time, and when he came out he had a piece of chalk in his hand.

"What have you been doing with the chalk?" I asked suspiciously.

"Go in and see," he sneered.

I went inside, and one look was enough. All down one wall he'd scribbled Miss Abby's name, and my father's name, and a lot of other things. He was all doubled up laughing when I charged out the door. I got him down, and we rolled on the ground, hitting and scratching and biting.

All of a sudden I felt myself swung up into the air. "Can't you damn kids get along without fighting?" my father hollered in my ear. Nick sat up, looking scared. He glanced at the open outhouse door, then looked away. My father stared at him, set me down, and went inside. Nick jumped up and streaked it for the front gate. My father ran out in time to see him vault the fence onto the road.

"I'll make his tail smoke when I get my hands on him!" my father declared. His lips were a thin hard line. He turned to me, and I stopped rubbing the eye that Nick's elbow had banged. "Sorry, Tommy. Run to the house and get something to wash—" He broke off when my mother came around the corner of the house and walked up to us.

Nobody said anything. My mother looked at each of us in turn. Two bright red spots blazed on her pale cheeks. My father was standing between her and the open door. She started to push past him. He half raised an arm to stop her, then shrugged and lowered it. My mother went inside.

I got out of there. I knew they'd say awful things to each other. I went in the back door to the kitchen, and in the mirror above the sink I tried to see if my eye looked as bad as it felt. It was getting dark outside, and I was late with the chores. I went out to the barn and started milking the cows. After a while my father came in and sat down on a stool beside mine and went to work without saying anything. His face was grim-looking in the lantern light.

I filled the special pail for Miss Abby and left the barn. My father still hadn't said a word. I walked down the path to the road gate, and I had just reached for the latch when my mother spoke to me from the darkness. "Where are you going?" she asked me. I nearly dropped the pail. She didn't wait for me to answer her. She took the pail away from me and carried it back to the barn.

I didn't know what to do. They didn't come out of the barn, and I knew they must be having a terrible row. I went back to the kitchen and waited for what seemed like a long time. I was hungry again, but I didn't want to be the only one eating. My mother came into the kitchen at last. She didn't speak to me. She walked as though her eyes weren't seeing anything. She passed through the kitchen and went upstairs. Outside, I could hear my father washing up at the pump, and then he walked down the path to the road.

I remembered the chalk-writing on the outhouse wall, and I wet a rag at the pump and went down to the barn for the lantern. The first step I took inside I saw the gaping stall in the lineup of placidly chewing cows. Daisy's stall was empty. Daisy was gone, and my father was gone. My stomach felt cold.

I finished up at the outhouse and then went back to the silent kitchen. I lighted the kerosene lamp and put it on the table by the window. I must have fallen asleep with my head on my arms on the table, because the sound of the parlor clock striking ten woke me up. There wasn't a sound in the house.

I went upstairs to bed, but I couldn't fall asleep again. I thought about my father and my mother, and the way it used to be before Miss Abby came. I wondered what would happen now. I wondered what my mother would do when she found out that Daisy was gone.

I didn't want to come downstairs in the morning, but I had to, finally. The big bedroom door was open when I passed it, and I thought that somehow everything might be all right. My mother was at the stove, and my father was at the table, eating, but they weren't speaking, even to me, and it wasn't all right.

I stayed away from the house all morning. In the afternoon I went out to the corncrib and got out the copy of *Wind in the Willows* that Miss Abby had lent me. I kept it hidden there so my mother wouldn't know. I went down the path to read under the big elm beside the road. The sun was shining, but clouds were forming in the west, and it was getting cooler.

I'd almost forgotten where I was when someone said, "Hey, kid!" I looked up and saw Joe Macy, the RFD mailman from Indian Bay. He was standing by our mailbox at the gate, and he had a letter in his hand. "Give this to your pa," he said to me. "It'll save me the hike to the point. He'll be glad of the chance to deliver it, no doubt."

I knew what it was even before I got up from the grass

and took it from him. The letter was addressed to Miss Abby.
Joe Macy grinned at me, a nasty grin. "Me, I aim to get on
back home before it storms," he said.

I stood there wishing I was bigger. I'd have taken the ugly
grin right off his ugly face. Over in the west the cloudbanks
were much larger, and it was beginning to blow. Dust eddied
in the roadside ditches. The big elm rustled loudly.

I wanted to hide the letter, but I was afraid. I put the book
back in the corncrib, then carried the letter to the house. My
mother was in the kitchen working the butter churn, one of
my usual jobs, and my father was oiling a trap. They had their
backs to each other. My father put the trap down as if he was
glad he had something else to do when I handed him the
letter. He looked at it, turning it over and over in his big
hands.

"Where'd this come from?" he asked in a strange voice.

"Joe brought it to the gate just now," I said. "He said you
could take it to Miss Abby while he got home before the
storm."

"No!" my mother screamed. It was such a piercing sound
that I ducked. "No, no, no! You're not going down there, Tom!
Are you trying to drive me out of my mind?"

"Don't tell me what I'm not going to do, woman!" he
shouted at her harshly. "Not in my own house!" He shoved
the letter into his pocket. "It will keep," he said to me in a
quieter tone. "I've got to get out on the lake and take my nets
in before the storm tears them up."

He stamped out of the house.

My mother sank down into a chair. She began to moan
and rock herself from side to side. I don't think she knew I
was still there. I couldn't stand it. I went outside, too. It was
almost dark, and blowing hard. Much too hard for my father
to be heading out in his boat to take in his nets.

I started to run to the dock, but I stopped after I turned the
corner of the barn. I could see the dock from there, and
silhouetted against the lake and the low-flying clouds I could
see the boat's stubby mast. My father hadn't gone out on the
lake. I knew where he'd gone.

Five minutes later it was so dark I couldn't see the dock,

let alone the boat. I went into the barn to get out of the wind. Daisy's empty stall reminded me of the way things were all over again. I could look down the road through a crack in the barn door left by a splintered hinge and see the light high up in the lighthouse on Wild Swan Point.

I couldn't stay in the barn, but I couldn't bear going back to the house either. The wind ripped at me out on the path. I reached the road and started to run. All along the causeway I could hear the big waves breaking against the rocks. I reached the lighthouse and sat down on the bench outside the door to catch my breath. I began to get chilled again in the fiercely gusting wind, and finally I went inside.

I couldn't find the door latch at first in the dark. The door opened easily, not creaking and groaning as it had when I was still delivering the milk. The hinges had been oiled. It was quiet inside, away from the soughing of the wind and the crashing of the waves. It was pitch-black inside, except for a single sliver of light at the top of the spiral staircase.

I felt around, trying to find something to sit on. I didn't feel like facing that wind again. I almost yelled out loud when I bumped into something big and warm. It took me a second to realize it was Daisy, tethered inside out of the storm. She butted me with her head the way she always did when she wanted to be milked. I moved away from her, afraid that she would moo.

I brushed against the railing at the foot of the stairs, and I looked up again to the crack of light at the top. I climbed the stairs silently, without really making up my mind that I intended to do it. I kept one hand on the railing, the other on the wall. I could hear Miss Abby's voice when I reached the top and stood outside the door. I could hear the wind again, that high up, but I could hear her, too.

". . . got to stop arguing with me, Tom," I could hear her saying. "You saw the letter. They can't keep the child any longer. I've got to go and get her and bring her back here with me. It's what I should do, anyway."

"No!" my father's voice exclaimed. "It's . . . it's no place for a child, Abby. Give me a few days. I'll . . . I'll think of something."

"The letter said right now, Tom." Miss Abby's voice was firm. "I'll leave tomorrow. You can think of something when I get back here."

"Good God, Abby, do you realize what you're doing to me?" My father's voice sounded like it did the time he hit his thumb with the maul. "It's impossible, I tell you! I can't—"

"You can, and you will. I've been patient long enough. Look at me, Tom. Are you saying you can't find a way? Are you telling me I should go and not come back at all?"

"No!"

Miss Abby's silvery laugh sounded after my father's hoarse exclamation. She murmured something I couldn't make out, and neither of them spoke again. The light under the edge of the door went out. I stared at the place where it had been. I felt like I did in church when the preacher talked about the end of the world: just plain scared. I crept back down the winding staircase in the pitch-black darkness and let myself out the big door at the bottom. All I could think of was what was going to become of us.

Outside it was a bit lighter. The moon showed fitfully through the racing clouds. The wind was higher than before, even, and the waves smashed solidly against the causeway. I started back to the house. I was too cold and too tired to do anything else.

I was two-thirds of the way along the causeway when I heard pebbles dislodged from the path ahead of me. I plunged down off the path on the land side without even thinking about it. I hid amidst big rocks dislodged by numerous lake storms. Above me a cloaked shadow passed by, on the way to the lighthouse. I knew it was my mother even before the moon came out again and showed me plainly. She was bent forward against the wind, and she was talking to herself. When she passed, I scrambled up onto the causeway path again and ran all the way to our house.

But when I got to the house I found I couldn't go inside. I couldn't stop thinking of my mother and father and Miss Abby at the lighthouse, and the dreadful things they'd say to each other. Nothing would ever be the same for us again.

I struggled against the wind down to the barn. I knew the

animal heat of the cows always kept it warm. I took down a pitchfork and piled fresh hay in a corner of Daisy's empty stall. I stretched out in the sweet-smelling hay, and I must have fallen asleep, because it seemed like a long time later that I heard a bell ringing. At first I thought it was a dream, but then it got louder and louder.

I jumped up and ran to the barn door. The floor shook from the thunder of horses' hoofs as the four-horse team from Indian Bay skittered down the road with the old fire pumper. Its iron bell was clanging steadily.

I whirled to look at our house, but it was safely dark. I turned then toward the point, but I think I knew before I looked. Great roaring sheets of flame were blowing out of the top of the lighthouse, hundreds of feet out over the lake.

I stood there shivering. My mother had intended to kill Miss Abby, but without knowing it she had killed my father, too. She thought he was out on the lake in his boat. What would she do to herself when she found out that he wasn't?

I ran down to the dock. I threw myself flat on my stomach on the rough pine planking and clawed at the hard knots in my father's snubbing ropes at the other end of which his boat pitched violently in the black choppy water. My fingernails were broken and bleeding when I finally got the ropes untied. I had a knife in my pocket, but I couldn't leave a cut rope-end showing. The boat lurched away into the whitecaps, and I got up and hurried to the house. I was in bed when the neighbors arrived.

No one but me ever knew everything that happened on Wild Swan Point that terrible night. The lighthouse burned flat. The fire was so fierce no one could get near it. The oil drums at the bottom burned for two days. It was another day before they could sift the ashes. They found human bones mixed with Daisy's, but not many of either from a fire that fierce. The human bones were buried as Miss Abby's. It never occurred to anyone that someone else could have been inside the lighthouse.

A trawler found my father's boat on the third day. It had capsized two miles out on the lake. They towed it into our dock.

My mother hadn't left the dock the whole time except for brief intervals. The lakemen told her gently that my father must have been washed overboard during the height of the storm.

My mother hired a man to help with the farm, after everything was done that had to be done. I did what I could, too. For two months my mother's eyes were sunk deeply into her head. The only person she talked to was me. Nights I could hear her praying behind her closed bedroom door.

She didn't show any sign of improvement, and I didn't know what to do. I knew she wasn't eating or sleeping much at all. I was sitting on our front steps one sunny afternoon, thinking about it all, when a man walked up our path with a battered satchel in one hand. He was leading a little girl with the other. "Mrs. Malcolm live here?" he asked me.

I nodded. I couldn't have got a word out. The girl was about three years old, with the bluest of eyes. She had a blue ribbon in her blond hair.

The man mopped his forehead before he knocked at the door. I could feel my heart beating while I waited for my mother to answer. When she did, she looked at the man inquiringly, but then she saw the little girl. My mother's features froze.

"Is Mrs. Malcolm home?" the man asked.

"I'm Mrs. Malcolm," my mother said.

"Oh, ahh—" The man was obviously taken aback. "Well, then, is the other Mrs. Malcolm here?"

"I'm the only—" my mother began then wrenched her eyes almost forcibly from the little girl's blue eyes and blond hair. "Come inside," she said curtly to the man. They went in and my mother closed the door.

I patted the step beside me. "Come sit here," I invited the girl. "What's your name?"

"Becky." That was all she said. She sat down beside me with a tired sigh. Her little white shoes were covered with road dust, and her thin face was pinched with weariness.

"I'm Tom," I told her. Even my mother had stopped calling me Tommy.

We sat in silence then. I wasn't staring directly at Becky,

but I heard her start to cry. She put her head down on her knees so I couldn't see her face. I didn't know what else to do, so I put my arm around her.

When my mother and the man came out of the house, the man was putting something into his pocket. He went down the path and up the road without saying anything, but he stopped twice to turn and look back at us. "Come along inside, dear," my mother said to Becky. She held out her hand to her. "It's time to milk the cows, Tom," she said to me in the same breath.

I knew then everything was going to be all right.

And for fifteen years it was, until my mother died of cancer. She didn't have an easy time. It almost seemed she didn't want an easy time. She never set foot inside church after that night on Wild Swan Point. She wouldn't let the preacher inside the house, either, but she sent Becky and me to Sunday school every week.

There were good years afterward, except I had to sit and watch Becky patiently waiting for me to ask her to marry me. I sent her away to college over her protests. She came back to the farm. My housekeeper complained for years about the waste of my money involved in the unnecessary young hired men I insisted on having on the place. Becky never seemed to see any of them in any way that mattered.

There was never an answer I could find, then or ever.

Now Becky's gone, too, and there's just me.

At least it won't be for much longer.

HUGH B. CAVE

The Door Below

One of the deans of living horror writers, Hugh Barnett Cave was born in Chester, England, on July 11, 1910, but his family emigrated to the United States when he was five. He started publishing while still in high school, and has been writing for more than sixty years. Although noted for short stories of supernatural horror, Cave has also written on a wide variety of other subjects, such as the West Indies, the American West, and the sea. His work has appeared in magazines as diverse as Dime Detective, Good Housekeeping, Scholastic, Redbook, *the* Saturday Evening Post, *and* Weird Tales. *His story in this collection, "The Door Below," first appeared in* Whispers III, *in 1981.*

¤

Lifting his gaze from the island lighthouse ahead to the gathering gray clouds above, the man stopped rowing and said, "It looks like rain, Wendy. Can't we do this some other time?"

The girl who shared the skiff with him said gaily, "Alan Coppard, I do believe you're scared! Why, we're nearly there!"

"You know I don't scare. But—"

"Oh, come on, Al. What if we do get a little wet? When we get back, I'll dry you and you dry me. Okay?"

In spite of his dark mood, Alan smiled. You had to smile

at this girl. She not only said things he had never heard a girl say before; she did things he hadn't known were done. Things that made him feel ten years younger than he was. Her age, instead of thirty-four.

He was a lucky man, he realized. Two weeks ago he had been mired in a miserable marriage with no hope of escape, never dreaming he would be here with the liveliest, best-looking girl on the *Star-News* payroll.

Of course, he had known he would be at the beach. He had rented the cottage a month ago, convinced that million-aire Roy Bolke's disappearance was a fake—and if he could prove it was, his future as a journalist would be assured. But he had never anticipated that by the time his vacation actually rolled around, dear Elaine would have walked out on him—calling him "crass" and "soulless," no less—to start proceedings for a divorce.

"Okay?" the barefoot girl in jeans and halter said again.

"Well, if you think—"

"You know what I really think, Al Coppard? You're not altogether convinced Danny Marshall was lying."

"The hell I'm not. Why else would I be giving up my vacation? I just don't think I'm going to get at the truth by snooping around an abandoned lighthouse."

"Well," she said, "you ought to see where it's supposed to have happened, even if it didn't."

Alan turned again to look at the island as he rowed toward it. It was visible from the cottage but didn't look the same close up. The distant view was like a hackneyed paint-ing, he thought, having no impact, being in fact rather homey and comfortable. Close up, there was something threatening in the way those huge rocks rose out of the sea. "Tread here at your risk," they seemed to challenge.

The lighthouse too was different at close range. It was not white, as he had supposed, but gray as a weathered granite graveyard marker, and now that it had been shut down, the glass at its top was, of course, dark. The shaft looked like a fairy-tale giant blinded in combat but still erect and grimly defiant, sullenly awaiting the return of its foe. Hey, he thought, that's pretty good. I must remember that and use it.

"Al," Wendy Corwin said.

"Yes?"

"I'm sorry. It *is* a creepy place. What did you say it's called?"

"Dolphinback. But when I get through tearing that kid's story apart, they'll be calling it Liars Light."

There were few places on the island where it was possible to tie up a boat and step ashore, he discovered. The best appeared to be a sheltered fissure, resembling a miniature ferry slip, that must have been used by the lighthouse keepers before the "incident." Some iron mooring rings had been set in the rock there.

"This must be where Joe Marshall and the boy tied up the *Ariel* when they brought her in," he said while looping the skiff's painter through a ring.

Nine-year-old Danny Marshall—if you accepted his story—had been fishing off the rocks when his grandfather came out of the lighthouse and told him there was a boat in trouble. Joe Marshall had been talking on the radio with the boat's owner, Roy Bolke, when suddenly the man broke off the conversation. Wondering what could have happened, Joe went to the tower to see if he could pick up the boat with binoculars. He could, but saw only one person on board—a woman who was running back and forth as though demented while the boat drifted.

So, according to Danny, the two had rowed out to see what was wrong. Not only because it was their duty to do so, but because Joe knew Roy Bolke well. Joe had been the millionaire's chauffeur for years, and had become keeper here only after smashing himself up in one of Bolke's fancy sports cars.

The rope fast, Alan helped his companion ashore, admiring the competent way she used her pretty feet. "Watch your step now," he cautioned. "We don't want any accidents in this godforsaken place."

With the agility of a ballerina she danced up the natural stone staircase and turned with hand outthrust to wait for him. When he had toiled up to her, she said, "There's a thing I'm not clear about, Al. Danny and his grandfather rowed out

to the yacht from here, and when they got there, the woman
Joe had been watching through the glasses had vanished?"

"That's what the kid said. There were just the two bodies—Bolke at the wheel and his wife in the cabin. Their
clothes were in shreds, and both bodies had small deep marks
all over them—punctures of some sort, Danny insisted—but
there was no blood anywhere. The missing woman's clothes
were on the deck and not torn, he said. We're supposed to
believe she stripped them off and tried to swim ashore or to
the island here."

"So Danny and Joe brought the yacht here?"

"If you believe the boy. But night had fallen by then so
they decided to wait till morning before doing anything more.
Then when Danny awoke in the morning he found Joe dead
in bed. Right in the same room with him—if you're a believer
in fairy tales—Joe had been killed by the same thing or things
that killed the two on the boat. Pajamas shredded, same
puncture marks on the body, same unexplained absence of
blood. Anyway, the kid says he jumped into their dinghy and
rowed ashore to tell the police."

Solemnly nodding—which meant she didn't believe a
word of it either—Wendy took him by the hand and tugged
him toward the lighthouse. But Alan resisted.

"Hold on a minute. Now we're here, let's have a look at
the island first."

"You said it was going to rain."

"*You* said if we got wet, we'd dry each other. So let it rain."

The place hardly deserved to be called an island, Alan
noted. It was a mass of stone half an acre in extent, its top a
field of smooth planes tipped at assorted angles and its edges
nearly everywhere plunging precipitously into the sea. It
must have been a depressing place for a partially crippled
man like Joe Marshall. If Bolke had indeed offered him a
profitable escape from here in return for a tale that would
cover up a murder—as he, Alan Coppard, firmly believed—
Danny's grandfather could almost be excused for snatching it.

The background for what he believed was simple. Roy
Bolke, millionaire founder of a cosmetic empire, was sixty-

seven. His wife Amanda had been sixty-five. A few weeks before the happenings at the light here, Bolke had brought back with him, from a visit to Madrid, a stunning, twenty-four-year-old Spanish model named Maria Oviedo. When her English improved he would make her a sex symbol for his cosmetics, he said.

But, of course, the role of public sex symbol was not what Bolke had in mind. Sex, certainly—and no mere symbol. Public, no way.

What Alan Coppard believed, and intended to prove, was that Bolke and his Spanish kitten had conspired to do away with Amanda. Why the elaborate hoax with the help of former chauffeur Joe Marshall? Two reasons. First, Amanda Bolke for years had been deeply involved in spirit-world doings, claiming to have talked time and again with the dead. Second, Dolphinback had a sinister story, dating back forty-odd years, of mysterious drownings and disappearances. Amanda herself had written a book about it.

As they made their way over the canted planes of stone, Wendy was a child at play and Alan a reluctant explorer held back by his feeling that the trip was a waste of time. But as they neared the lighthouse the girl said with a sudden frown, "When the police came out here to investigate Danny's story, what did they find, exactly?"

"The yacht."

"You mean *only* the yacht?"

"That's right. No bodies on board. No trace of Joe Marshall's body, which the boy said was in the lighthouse."

"What about the Spanish girl's clothes?"

"Well, they did find those where Danny said they would, on the *Ariel*. But I figure Bolke and Maria were smart enough to leave them there to back up the tale the boy had been coached to tell."

"So with the help of Joe Marshall, Bolke and Maria are far away by now, and Amanda is dead at the bottom of the sea, huh? That's what you think?"

"That's it. And when I prove it—"

"Where's Danny now?"

"Living with his mother, Joe's daughter, in the village. And he's one tough kid, I can tell you. But he'll crack." Alan suddenly realized he had allowed himself to be led to the lighthouse doorway and was about to be walked inside. Annoyed, he took a step backward.

"Come on now," Wendy said with a pretty pout. "You promised."

There was no way he could back down without risking an unwanted change in their relationship, he realized. There was not even a door to deter them. Someone, probably curious visitors, had forced it open despite a No Trespassing notice that must have been nailed up by the police.

Unwillingly he surrendered. It was stupid, though, he felt. He would get his story from the boy, not from prowling around a stupid lighthouse.

Curiosity seekers had been here, he saw as he and Wendy entered a living room of sorts. The stone floor, only partly covered with a worn carpet, was littered with cigarette stubs. There appeared to be little damage, however. Perhaps the callers had not stayed long.

For one thing, the room was dark. Though the afternoon still had an hour to run, the windows were small and the panes so coated with salt they let in little light. And heavy, dark ceiling beams added to the uncomfortable feeling one got that the place was a dungeon.

Wondering if the power had been shut off when the lighthouse was closed down—Dolphinback was fed by an undersea cable—Alan hopefully tried a light switch. Nothing happened.

He turned to study the room. It contained a worn sofa and two shabby overstuffed chairs, a smattering of small tables. On the wall were instruments of some sort, perhaps designed to warn the keeper of any malfunction in the light chamber above. An old bookcase, built to fit the curved wall, contained volumes whose titles intrigued him. *Lorna Doone*? Sophocles? *Tarzan and the Jewels of Opar? Amanda Bolke's The Mysteries of Dolphinback?* Strange assortment. But then, the local people must have donated their surplus books from time to time.

"What's upstairs, Al?" Wendy asked, startling him a little as she broke the long silence.

"Other rooms, I've been told. Kitchen, bedroom, store-room—right on up to the light itself."

"Come on, then." She grabbed his hand and pulled him toward a narrow wooden staircase.

"Wendy, don't you think—"

"Oh, don't be *old*, Al Coppard!"

That did it. He followed her up the stairs into a kitchen and stood patiently, hands in pockets, while she satisfied her curiosity. It took her some time to complete her snooping—there were more cupboards and drawers than one would have thought to find in such cramped quarters—and all the while she kept up a running conversation with herself which he found amusing. Then like an eager child on a treasure hunt she climbed the next flight of stairs, and, following, he found himself in a bedroom.

It was here Joe and Danny Marshall had slept, and here the boy had awakened to find his grandfather dead that morning—if you accepted his pack of lies. The small, circular room contained two cots, two straight-backed chairs, a table, and a closet. The closet door was locked, Wendy discovered when like a moth to a flame she went straight to it and tried to open it.

"Sorry," Alan said dryly. "Joe Marshall's daughter has the key."

"Huh?"

"Investigators came out here, did what they were supposed to do, then told her she could remove Joe's belongings. Her answer was that as long as she lived she would never set foot on this island again. So they locked Joe's personal things in the bedroom closet here and gave her the key, telling her to come when she felt like it."

Obviously disappointed, Wendy turned toward the next flight of stairs. But Alan, with a frown, held up a hand and said, "Hold on. Isn't that rain I'm hearing?"

It certainly was something. Muffled by the thick walls of

the lighthouse, it was loud enough to be disconcerting.

Wendy's enthusiasm for adventure at last seemed to wane. "Gee, Al, it *is* rain!"

"Let's get out of here."

The rain had brought premature darkness, and they had to be careful descending the steep flights of stairs to the base of the tower. It took a surprisingly long time, with both of them stumbling as the darkness thickened. With the increase of gloom came an amplification of the noise, so that when Alan at last groped through the lower room to the door by which they had entered, he was all but deafened by the roar.

There in the doorway he halted, stared out at a wall of falling water, and shook his head in disbelief. "We're not going anywhere," he announced. "Not in this."

Wendy clung to his hand. "Oh, Al, it's my fault."

"Forget it. Come sit down till it eases off a bit."

They returned to the living room and sat, but the room was even more oppressive now than it had been. As the darkness deepened, Alan found he could no longer read the titles in the bookcase, or even see very clearly the face of his companion, though he could see enough to know she was now both contrite and frightened.

Rising from the overstuffed chair he had plopped himself down in, he searched the room for something to relieve the gloom. "There *must* be some lamps around here, in case the power went off," he said. "At least a flashlight." But he could find nothing.

Now for a long time both he and Wendy just sat in silence.

When the roar of the downpour seemed to diminish somewhat, Alan looked at his watch. "Oh Lord, it's after six-thirty. Be dark soon even without this blasted rain. Look, I'm going to bail out the skiff. It'll be half full by now. Give me five or ten minutes, then you come too."

"I'm not staying here," she said quickly. "I'm going with you!"

He glanced around the room and realized he wouldn't enjoy being left alone in it either. Not in darkness. "Okay, come on."

Through the still-pounding rain they groped across the treacherous no-man's-land of stone to where the skiff was tied. There, in a state of shock, they stood hand in hand, silently gazing down into an empty cleft. The tide had risen. With each incoming wave a rush of snarling gray foam covered the iron ring with its frayed foot of yellow rope attached. The skiff was nowhere to be seen.

Lifting his head, Alan surveyed the stretch of angry, rain-whipped sea between island and shore. Wendy was a first-class swimmer and might make it, but hardly in the dark under conditions such as this. He was no swimmer at all. "Seems we're stuck for the night," he said, wanting to add a few choice expletives but aware he probably shouldn't, because the girl whose hand he held was frightened.

"Oh, Al," she sobbed.

"Take it easy now. It's not the end of the world. We have shelter, and we'll find a light if we look hard enough, I'm sure. Come on, girl. You wanted adventure. Now you've got it."

He spent only a few minutes more searching the living room for a light, then turned to the stairs. It was ironical, he thought. A hell of a note, really. Here they were in a light-house, of all places, and with a wet black night coming down on them they couldn't even find a candle. Ha!

He did have a book of paper matches. With those he searched the kitchen, finding nothing, and then with Wendy at his heels climbed the stairs to the bedroom.

"Our last hope," he muttered as he produced a pocket knife and tried to jimmy the locked door of the closet.

It would not open. Stepping back, he gave it an angry kick that persuaded it. "Ah," he breathed, reaching for a lantern on one of the crowded shelves.

When he shook the lantern, it gurgled. He applied a match and the room filled with yellow light and a smell of kerosene. He let his breath out in a sigh of relief. "Not much, but better than nothing," he said as he sank wearily onto one of the cots. "Whew! For a while there I wasn't too sure."

Wendy sat too. But after a moment of silence she went to

the closet and began to investigate its contents. "Here's a radio of some kind, Al. Look." She stepped aside so he could see it on the shelf.

Alan got up. "One of those citizens-band things, I guess."

"The kind people talk to each other with? Can we use it to call for help?"

"If I knew anything about them. Afraid I don't. Anyway, the power's off—remember?"

"Oh."

It probably worked on DC too, Alan thought. But even if old Marshall had some source of DC power around for emergencies—they had it on boats, didn't they?—and even if he recognized it when he saw it, he wouldn't know how to hook it up.

There was another gadget on the shelf, however. "Now this," he said, reaching for it, "I know about. It's a tape recorder. Uses cassettes. Got batteries in it, too," he added after flipping the back open. "Maybe we can have some music while we wait. You see any cassettes in the closet here?"

She found some and he carried them, with the recorder, back to the cot from which he had risen. In a moment the little bedroom with its flickering yellow light and smell of kerosene was filled with music.

"Beds and Beethoven," Alan said. "Even light of a sort. Not bad for a start. Marshall had good taste in music, anyway."

Wendy was actually smiling again. "And I saw some cans of food in the kitchen, if we get hungry. The stove's electric, though. We'll have to eat the stuff cold."

Alan rose again. "I'll bring some on my way back. Want to get that Amanda Bolke book and see what she said about this place." He reached for the lantern and realized he had a problem. If he took their only light, Wendy would be left in darkness. "Guess you'd better come with me," he said.

They descended to the living room, Alan holding the light high as he led the way. The book in hand, he said, "Hold on a minute," and stepped to the door to size up the weather. The rain was still unrelenting, the night black as pitch now. He could hear the sea assaulting the island: a circle of sound like a ring of wild animals with Wendy and himself helpless in the center.

He was glad to go back upstairs. Somehow the bedroom, high up in the tower, seemed a better refuge.

With the lantern on the table between them, they lay on the cots, Alan with his book, Wendy with her hands clasped behind her head and her gaze fixed on the ceiling as she listened to the music. But presently Wendy got up again, saying, "I just thought of something, Al."

"What?"

"This rowing out to the *Ariel*, finding bodies on board, and bringing the yacht back here. Wouldn't a lighthouse keeper write up a report of a thing like that if he actually did it?"

"Don't be a dope. Joe Marshall didn't write any report."

"Read your book. I'm going to have a good look in this closet."

She really hoped to find something, Alan realized with amusement as he watched her assault the closet's contents. She actually believed at least part of the boy's story. Losing interest, he returned to Amanda Bolke's *Mysteries of Dolphinback*.

A strange woman, Amanda Bolke. Like other very wealthy women he could think of, she seemed to have ridden her hobby with fantastic determination. "Wendy, listen to this," he said, and began reading from the book aloud. " 'It should be obvious to anyone who has delved deeply enough into the history of Dolphinback Island—even before the construction of the lighthouse—that here is one of several very special places where the known and unknown worlds are in juxtaposition. There have been too many unexplained happenings here for us to believe otherwise. If one acknowledges the existence of demons, as one must, of course, if not cursed with a rigidly shut mind, then here is one of the gateways by which such creatures are able to penetrate our world.' "

"Who published that nonsense?" Wendy demanded, pausing in her exploration of the closet.

Alan looked. "She did, herself."

"Ha!"

"Wait. 'One day when the time is propitious,' she goes on,

'a believer in these matters, with a proper background of study and self-training, will make an effort to deliberately summon these spirit-world creatures from their habitat in this area. It is my own firm belief that their dwelling place, or at least the gateway to it, lies under the sea in the vicinity of the island.' "

"She's nuts," Wendy said, "but she gives me the creeps."

Alan grinned. "Sure she's nuts. But all this will make my story bigger and better when I break it. And I'll break it, don't worry. This time next month you'll be seeing Al Coppard's name all over the place."

"The new journalism you were talking about, huh?"

"That's it, woman. All you need to do today is get the goods on some well-known character and drag him down. When he's down, you're up."

"Well, all right," Wendy said. "But if you want to read that book, kindly read it to yourself and let me listen to the music."

When the Beethoven ended, Alan tried another tape from the closet. This was a live Boston Pops concert, apparently recorded by Marshall himself from a radio program. It lasted long enough for Wendy to finish taking the closet apart—without finding a single item of interest, she was forced to admit—and when the Pops tape gave way to a professional recording of Mahler, Wendy returned to her cot.

Only for a moment, though. Rising again, she frowned down at the cot and said, "You know, I'll bet *I've* got the bed Danny found his grandfather dead in that morning."

"Danny didn't find anyone dead."

"Well, we don't *know*. Anyway—" Walking over to his cot, she stood there impishly gazing down at him. "Move over, huh? You can even read to me if you like."

Alan didn't read to her. When she was nicely snuggled up to him with her head on his shoulder, he dropped the book and put his arm around her. They lay that way in silence for a time, then undressed and made love.

It was when they were quietly side by side again that Wendy suddenly said, "Al, listen!"

He did so but was aware of nothing unusual—only a

diminution of earlier sounds to which he had become accustomed with the passing of time. "Rain seems to have stopped," he said. "Sea's subsiding. That what you mean?"

"No. Listen."

It was hardly a time to confess that his hearing was less than acute. He really tried to absorb what she apparently was hearing but received nothing.

"You don't hear a scratchy noise like—like footsteps?" She was frightened now, he realized. Her warm, moist body—they were both still undressed—had begun to tremble in his embrace.

"Probably water dripping somewhere. From the rain."

"Uh-uh. It isn't water." She slipped from his arms and hurriedly put her blue jeans and white halter back on. As she did so, he saw what looked like a bit of silver chain dangling from a pocket of the jeans and reached out for it.

To his surprise he found himself holding a small cross, apparently of sterling, with a crucified Christ on it. To the brief length of chain was attached a small safety pin of the same metal. Apparently the cross was meant to be pinned to the wearer's clothing.

"Where did this come from?" he demanded, certain it was not hers.

She seemed annoyed. "I found it in the closet."

"Oh-oh. You *are* shy of scruples, aren't you?" He turned the cross over and saw something stamped in the metal, and, his sight being sharper than his hearing, was just able to read it. " 'Cedillo, Guadalajara.' Must be the maker."

"Guadalajara's in Mexico," Wendy said, pouting. "I've been there." She took the cross out of his hand and with a look of defiance thrust it back into her pocket. Then suddenly she said, "Al, listen!"

Obediently he did so but heard nothing.

"Downstairs!" she insisted. "What's wrong with you, Al? Can't you hear *anything*?"

Rising, Alan went naked to the door and opened it. Annoyed by her censure of him, he stood there fully a minute, straining to hear what she said she had heard.

Nothing.

He realized suddenly that she was at his side, peering into the darkness down there at the foot of the steep stairs. "Well?" he demanded.

"It—it's gone, whatever it was. But I *heard* it. Something was moving around down there, Al. Making the same scratchy footsteps I heard before. Only—only I'm sure there was more than one this time."

Alan was tempted to take the lantern and go down the stairs with it to show her there was nothing down there in the kitchen. His nakedness dissuaded him, and so did his awareness that her hearing was better than his. He shut the door and said, "What we need is some lively music, don't you think?" Music she was familiar with, he thought. Something to take her mind off what was supposed to have happened here. Otherwise she might crack up.

She had discovered a dozen or more tapes in the closet and he had played parts of some already. He looked at the others now. Most were prerecorded symphonies, opera excerpts, chamber music. Even the ones bought blank were filled with the same kind of music, according to the scribbled notes on the boxes. One box, however, had no index. Hopefully he inserted that tape into the player.

A man's voice came scratchily from the speaker. ". . . so what we did, Joe, we decided to take the *Ariel* and get away from those pests for a while. You know what bastards they can be with their questions; you used to keep them at bay for me. Since Watergate, every two-bit newsman in the country thinks he's the Spanish Inquisition. So I said to Maria, 'Come on, let's take off and let them find someone else to harass.' And here we are. You know we're close enough I could almost talk to you without this radio, Joe . . .

"You're what? Taping my part of this? Well, I'll have to say something for posterity then, won't I? Maybe I should ask Amanda for some deathless words. You'd get a laugh if you were aboard this boat right now, Joe. You know what she always said about Dolphinback? That crazy book she published? Well, for the past hour she's been in the cabin going through some kind of crazy routine that's supposed to prove everything. Right this minute she's bellowing out some lunatic chant. Can you hear it? Listen while I keep quiet a minute."

There was a faint background sound of chanting on the tape. Then the voice of Roy Bolke intruded again. "You hear it, Joe? Yeah? Well, it's been going on like that for an hour. Can you imagine? Maria is scared half to death. These Spanish gals are high-strung, you know. For half an hour she's been begging Amanda to stop it, telling her something awful will happen if she keeps it up. A while ago she came and begged *me* to stop it, and I noticed blood on her blouse where she'd pinned a cross on herself. It was for protection, she said, in case Amanda succeeded in opening that gateway she's been going on about. What I mean, the poor gal is so scared and nervous, she stuck the brooch right into herself, Joe. Right into her breast. But hold on a minute, will you? What is it, Maria?"

Here another voice, a woman's, was audible for a few seconds but was too far from the microphone to be intelligible. Too shrill, too. "What?" Bolke said in reply. "Hell, I can't come now. Somebody has to run this scow. Go tell her I—"

The next sound on the tape was not his, nor could it have come from the girl to whom he was talking. It was a prolonged scream that obviously came from a distance. Then Bolke's voice, returning, was a hoarse yell. "Oh, Christ! Oh, my God . . ."

And silence.

When the silence had endured long enough to indicate the taping was at an end, Alan stopped staring at the recorder and muttered what he knew was a stupid remark. It was the only one he could think of that would not make matters worse.

"The cross didn't come from Mexico," he said. "There's a Guadalajara in Spain."

Wendy, too, seemed to realize they must control their emotions. "How do you suppose it got here, Al? To the lighthouse, I mean."

"That's more than I can figure out."

It wasn't more than Wendy could figure out, though. After a few moments of silence she said, "Al, I think I know what happened. I mean I really do."

"What?"

"Well, in the first place Amanda Bolke, with her crazy chanting and whatever else she was doing on board the yacht, opened that door or gateway she believed in and conjured something up out of the depths. She and her husband were killed by it, but the Spanish girl was protected by the crucifix she wore. Demons and vampires and such are supposed to fear a crucifix, aren't they?"

"You're nuts," Alan said.

She ignored the comment. "But Maria made a mistake. When she found herself alone with two dead bodies, she stripped off her clothes—with the crucifix pinned to her dress—and tried to swim ashore. Not to make it, because she was unprotected then. You see?"

"You're wasting your time working for the *Star-News*, pal. You ought to be writing shudder movies."

"So we come to Joe Marshall and his grandson," Wendy stubbornly continued. "They rowed out to the yacht and found the two bodies and Maria's clothes. They took the yacht to the island here. Then while examining the Spanish girl's garments Danny saw the cross and fancied it, just as I did when I discovered it in the closet. He took it. And that night, when whatever boarded the Ariel came here to the lighthouse, Danny survived because he had the cross in his possession. When he rowed ashore in the morning he must have left it behind for fear he'd be questioned about it."

"You're a genius," Alan said. "So what about the tape? How did it get into the closet here?"

"Well . . . when Joe and Danny went out to the yacht to see what was wrong, Joe must have left the radio and recorder running in case Bolke came back on the air. That makes sense. Then when they got back here Joe was pretty shook up, and my hunch is he just didn't bother listening to the tape until later, when Danny was in bed. Realizing the police would want to hear it, he rewound it intending to take it ashore in the morning. But in the morning he was dead, and Danny didn't take the tape because he had no idea it was important."

"Ha."

"Well, can you think of a better explanation? When the police came out here after hearing Danny's story, they wouldn't have thought anything of finding the tape. More than likely there were others around, all of music, so why should that one be special? When the time came to gather up Joe's things and lock them in the closet, the tape went in with everything else, and that was the end of it."

"You know," Alan said, shaking his head in not-so-mock amazement, "I never dreamed you had a mind like that. I almost hate to shut you up. The fact is, however, the tape is a fake, a hoax, part of the whole elaborate plot to enable Roy Bolke to escape from a dull marriage and run off with his Spanish doll. Newsmen think they're the Spanish Inquisition, do they? Ha. He'll find out. Now if you'll just stop your fantasizing for a moment and—"

A new sound had filled the room. The recorder, left running, had come alive again after a long silence. A girl's voice was screaming hysterically in Spanish.

Screaming for *help*, Alan realized with an ego-shattering shock as his knowledge of the tongue came back to him. His Spanish was the South American version, acquired during a year in Venezuela, but it was adequate.

"They're coming back!" she was screaming. "Oh Jesus, Mary, and Joseph, they're coming back for me! Oh, they're horrible, horrible—I can see four of them coming up over the side. Oh God, I can't stay here! I have to go!"

The rest was a scream that diminished in volume as the girl ran from the yacht's radio. Ran out on deck to strip off her clothes and leap into the sea. *If* this wasn't just a continuation of the fairy tale . . .

Again the recorder was silent. While Alan struggled with his convictions and Wendy sat like a figure carved from wood, it ran on for another minute or two, gently humming, then clicked as the tape came to an end. Total silence filled the room.

I better put my clothes on, Alan thought. This whole thing is phony, but I can't be like this if anything happens. He had always enjoyed the sensation of being naked, but now it filled him with dread. He felt defenseless.

But Wendy's hand was on his thigh, her sharp nails tearing at him as she whispered frantically, "Al! There's something downstairs again! Oh, my God!"

As before, he strained to hear—and this time *did* hear a rhythmic, rasping sound as though someone were shuffling toward them over a stone floor strewn with sand. But it was not in the kitchen below. It was on the stairs just outside the door.

Wendy screamed. Snatching the Spanish girl's cross from her pocket and thrusting it blindly out in front of her, she leaped to her feet and raced to the door. She jerked it open. Something massive and dark out there—something man-shaped but taller than any man—recoiled from her with a hissing sound as she jabbed the cross at it. Alan had only a glimpse of huge webbed feet and a scaly torso, of upflung arms terminating in long, curled fingers that resembled the talons of a bird of prey.

"Wait!" he wailed. "For God's sake, Wendy, wait for me!"

But she was past the thing and gone. He could hear her shrieking at others, on the stairs, to get out of her way. Could hear the slap of her bare feet as she fled through the dark kitchen below. Had she forgotten there was no skiff? Probably she had, but it made no difference. She had the cross, and she could swim . . .

He stopped thinking about Wendy then. Poised for flight, he stared at the doorway and felt his naked body shrivel. The thing at the top of the stairs filled the doorway now, and the lantern's light revealed even more of it. The scales and talons were not its most frightful features. He found himself staring at a huge, scaly head with great bulbous fish-eyes and cavernous nostrils. And he had not believed!

With a hoarse cry, Alan snatched the lantern and raced for the stairs at the rear of the bedroom—stairs leading up to chambers he and Wendy had not explored. As he clawed his way to the next room above, he looked back and saw one of the cots go crashing into the wall as the plodding creature kicked it aside instead of walking around it. It was the cot on which he and Wendy had made love.

Behind that horror came a second, and a third.

The stairs ended and Alan found himself in a storeroom, stumbling past a standby generator and drums of fuel . . . past a workbench and mounds of boxes. No refuge here. He groped across it to the next flight of stairs and again looked back as he climbed.

There were four of the things now, shuffling on in single file, awful in their unhurried but relentless pursuit. Four monsters from the same ghastly mold. And now as their hissing swelled to a snakepit chorus he noticed the mouths from which the sound spewed forth. Each was an obscene slit equipped with two long, needle-pointed fangs.

Staggering into the room at the top of the tower, he saw he could go no farther. It was the smallest chamber of all. Its walls were of glass. The space left for running was only a circular catwalk around the lamp.

He, Alan Coppard, new-style mediaman, was trapped in the blind eye of the fairy-tale giant that was, after all, only a prison.

As the first of the creatures plodded inexorably forward, he turned wildly to face it and screamed. But the scream came out a whimper as he sank naked to his knees and covered his eyes with his hands.

JOE R. LANSDALE

By the
Hair of the Head

Popular young horror writer Joe Richard Lansdale was born in Glade-
water, Texas, on October 28, 1951, and, under the encouragement of his
mother, began writing at the age of nine. He attended the University of
Texas at Austin and Stephen F. Austin State University, then worked
briefly as a custodial foreman before becoming a full-time freelance
writer in 1981. Although horror and fantasy are his main love—he
won a Bram Stoker Award for his novel The Drive-In *(1988)—he*
also writes mysteries, westerns, and mainstream stories.

"By the Hair of the Head," an uncomfortable story about remorse,
twisted love, and witchcraft, was first published in the original anthol-
ogy Shadows 6 *(1983).*

◻

The lighthouse was gray and brutally weathered, kissed each
morning by a cold, salt spray. Perched there among the rocks
and sand, it seemed a last, weak sentinel against an encroach-
ing sea; a relentless, pounding surf that had slowly swallowed up the shoreline and deposited it in the all-consuming
belly of the ocean.

Once the lighthouse had been bright-colored, candy-
striped like a barber's pole, with a high beacon light and a
horn that honked out to the ships on the sea. No more. The

217

lighthouse director, the last of a long line of sea watchers, had cashed in the job ten years back when the need died, but the lighthouse was now his and he lived there alone, bunked down nightly to the tune of the wind and the raging sea.

Below he had renovated the bottom of the tower and built rooms, and one of these he had locked away from all persons, from all eyes but his own.

I came there fresh from college to write my novel, dreams of being the new Norman Mailer dancing in my head. I rented in with him, as he needed a boarder to help him pay for the place, for he no longer worked, and his pension was as meager as stale bread.

High up in the top was where we lived, a bamboo partition drawn between our cots each night, giving us some semblance of privacy, and dark curtains were pulled round the thick, foggy windows that traveled the tower completely around.

By day, the curtains were drawn and the partition was pulled. I sat at my typewriter, and he, Howard Machen, sat with his book, and his pipe swelled the room full of gray smoke the thickness of his beard. Sometimes he rose and went below, but he was always quiet and never disturbed my work.

It was a pleasant life, agreeable to both of us. Mornings we had coffee outside on the little railed walkway and had a word or two as well, then I went to my work and he to his book, and at dinner we had food and talk and brandies; sometimes one, sometimes two, depending on mood and the content of our chatter.

We sometimes spoke of the lighthouse, and he told me of the old days, of how he had shone that light out many times on the sea. Out like a great, bright fishing line to snag the ships and guide them in; let them follow the light in the manner that Theseus followed Ariadne's thread.

"Was fine," he'd say. "That pretty old light flashing out there. Best job I had in all my born days. Just couldn't leave her when she shut down, so I bought her."

"It is beautiful here, but lonely at times."

"I have my company."

I took that as a compliment, and we tossed off another brandy. Any idea of my writing later I cast aside. I had done four good pages and was content to spit the rest of the day away in talk and dreams.

"You say this was your best job," I said as a way of conversation. "What did you do before this?"

He lifted his head and looked at me over the briar and its smoke. His eyes squinted against the tinge of the tobacco. "A good many things. I was born in Wales. Moved to Ireland with my family, was brought up there, and went to work there. Learned the carpentry trade from my father. Later I was a tailor. I've also been a mason—note the rooms I built below with my own two hands—and I've been a boat builder and a ventriloquist in a magician's show."

"A ventriloquist?"

"Correct," he said, and his voice danced around me and seemed not to come from where he sat.

"Hey, that's good."

"Not so good really. I was never good, just sort of fell into it. I'm worse now. No practice, but I've no urge to take it up again."

"I've an interest in such things."

"Have you now?"

"Yes."

"Ever tried a bit of voice throwing?"

"No. But it interests me. The magic stuff interests me more. You said you worked in a magician's show?"

"That I did. I was the lead-up act."

"Learn any of the magic tricks, being an insider and all?"

"That I did, but that's not something I'm interested in," he said flatly.

"Was the magician you worked for good?"

"Damn good, m'boy. But his wife was better."

"His wife?"

"Marilyn was her name. A beautiful woman." He winked at me. "Claimed to be a witch."

"You don't say?"

"I do, I do. Said her father was a witch and she learned it and inherited it from him."

"Her father?"

"That's right. Not just women can be witches. Men too."

We poured ourselves another and exchanged sloppy grins, hooked elbows, and tossed it down.

"And another to meet the first," the old man said and poured. Then: "Here's to company." We tossed it off.

"She taught me the ventriloquism, you know," the old man said, relighting his pipe.

"Marilyn?"

"Right, Marilyn."

"She seems to have been a rather all-around lady."

"She was at that. And pretty as an Irish morning."

"I thought witches were all old crones, or young crones. Hook noses, warts . . ."

"Not Marilyn. She was a fine-looking woman. Fine bones, agate eyes that clouded in mystery, and hair the color of a fresh-robbed hive."

"Odd she didn't do the magic herself. I mean, if she was the better magician, why was her husband the star attraction?"

"Oh, but she did do magic. Or rather she helped McDonald to look better than he was, and he was some good. But Marilyn was better.

"Those days were different, m'boy. Women weren't the ones to take the initiative, least not openly. Kept to them-selves. Was a sad thing. Back then it wasn't thought fittin' for a woman to be about such business. Wasn't ladylike. Oh, she could get sawed in half, or disappear in a wooden crate, priss and look pretty, but take the lead? Not on your life?"

I fumbled myself another brandy. "A pretty witch, huh?"

"Ummmm."

"Had the old pointed hat and broom passed down, so to speak?" My voice was becoming slightly slurred.

"It's not a laughin' matter, m'boy." Machen clenched the pipe in his teeth.

"I've touched a nerve, have I not? I apologize. Too much sauce."

Machen smiled. "Not at all. It's a silly thing, you're right. To hell with it."

"No, no, I'm the one who spoiled the fun. You were telling me she claimed to be the descendant of a long line of witches."

Machen smiled. It did not remind me of other smiles he had worn. This one seemed to come from a borrowed collection.

"Just some silly tattle is all. Don't really know much about it, just worked for her, m'boy." That was the end of that. Standing, he knocked out his pipe on the concrete floor and went to his cot.

For a moment I sat there, the last breath of Machen's pipe still in the air, the brandy still warm in my throat and stomach. I looked at the windows that surrounded the lighthouse, and everywhere I looked was my own ghostly reflection. It was like looking out through the compound eyes of an insect, seeing a multiple image.

I turned out the lights, pulled the curtains and drew the partition between our beds, wrapped myself in my blanket, and soon washed up on the distant shore of a recurring dream. A dream not quite in grasp, but heard like the far, fuzzy cry of a gull out from land.

It had been with me almost since moving into the tower.

Sounds, voices . . .

A clunking noise like peg legs on stone . . .

. . . a voice, fading in, fading out . . . Machen's voice, the words not quite clear, but soft and coaxing . . . then solid and firm: "Then be a beast. Have your own way. Look away from me with your mother's eyes."

". . . your fault," came a child's voice, followed by other words that were chopped out by the howl of the sea, wind, the roar of the waves.

". . . getting too loud. He'll hear . . ." came Machen's voice.

"Don't care . . . I . . ." lost voices now.

I tried to stir, but then the tube of sleep, nourished by the brandy, came unclogged, and I descended down into richer blackness.

•

Was a bright morning full of sun, and no fog for a change. Cool clear out there on the landing, and the sea even seemed to roll in soft and bounce against the rocks and lighthouse like puffy cotton balls blown on the wind.

I was out there with my morning coffee, holding the cup in one hand and grasping the railing with the other. It was a narrow area but safe enough, provided you didn't lean too far out or run along the walk when it was slick with rain. Machen told me of a man who had done just that and found himself plummeting over to be shattered like a dropped melon on the rocks below.

Machen came out with a cup of coffee in one hand, his unlit pipe in the other. He looked haggard this morning, as if a bit of old age had crept upon him in the night, fastened a straw to his face, and sucked out part of his substance.

"Morning," I said.

"Morning." He emptied his cup in one long draft. He balanced the cup on the metal railing and began to pack his pipe.

"Sleep bad?" I asked.

He looked at me, then at his pipe, finished his packing, and put the pouch away in his coat pocket. He took a long match from the same pocket, gave it fire with his thumbnail, lit the pipe. He puffed quite awhile before he answered me. "Not too well. Not too well."

"We drank too much."

"We did that."

I sipped my coffee and looked at the sky, watched a snowy gull dive down and peck at the foam, rise up with a wriggling fish in its beak. It climbed high in the sky, became a speck of froth on the crystal blue.

"I had funny dreams," I said. "I think I've had them all along, since I came here. But last night they were stronger than ever."

"Oh?"

"Thought I heard your voice speaking to someone. Thought I heard steps on the stairs, or more like the plunking of peg legs, like those old sea captains have."

"You don't say?"

"And another voice, a child's."

"That right? Well . . . maybe you did hear me speakin'. I wasn't entirely straight with you last night. I do have quite an interest in the voice throwing, and I practice it from time to time on my dummy. Last night must have been louder than usual, being drunk and all."

"Dummy?"

"My old dummy from the act. Keep it in the room below."

"Could I see it?"

He grimaced. "Maybe another time. It's kind of a private thing with me. Only bring her out when we're alone."

"Her?"

"Right. Name's Caroline, a right smart-looking girl dummy, rosy cheeked with blonde pigtails."

"Well, maybe someday I can look at her."

"Maybe someday." He stood up, popped the contents of the pipe out over the railing, and started inside. Then he turned: "I talk too much. Pay no mind to an old, crazy man."

Then he was gone, and I was there with a hot cup of coffee, a bright, warm day, and an odd, unexplained chill at the base of my bones.

Two days later we got on witches again, and I guess it was my fault. We hit the brandy hard that night. I had sold a short story for a goodly sum—my largest check to date—and we were celebrating and talking and saying how my fame would be as high as the stars. We got pretty sicky there, and to hear Machen tell it, and to hear me agree—no matter he hadn't read the story—I was another Hemingway, Wolfe, and Fitzgerald all balled into one.

"If Marilyn were here," I said thoughtlessly, drunk "why we could get her to consult her crystal and tell us my literary future."

"Why that's nonsense, she used no crystal."

"No crystal, broom, or pointed hat? No eerie evil deeds for her? A white magician no doubt?"

"Magic is magic, m'boy. And even good intentions can backfire."

"Whatever happened to her? Marilyn, I mean."

"Dead."

"Old age?"

"Died young and beautiful, m'boy. Grief killed her."

"I see," I said, as you'll do to show attentiveness.

Suddenly, it was as if the memories were a balloon over-loaded with air, about to burst if pressure were not taken off. So, he let loose the pressure and began to talk.

"She took her a lover, Marilyn did. Taught him many a thing, about love, magic, what have you. Lost her husband on account of it, the magician, I mean. Lost respect for herself in time.

"You see, there was this little girl she had, by her lover. A fine-looking sprite, lived until she was three. Had no proper father. He had taken to the sea and had never much enter-tained the idea of marryin' Marilyn. 'Keep them stringing' was his motto then, damn his eyes. So he left them to fend for themselves."

"What happened to the child?"

"She died. Some childhood disease."

"That's sad," I said, "a little girl gone and having only sipped at life."

"Gone? Oh, no. There's the soul, you know."

I wasn't much of a believer in the soul and I said so.

"Oh, but there is a soul. The body perishes but the soul lives on."

"I've seen no evidence of it."

"But I have," Machen said solemnly. "Marilyn was deter-mined that the girl would live on, if not in her own form, then in another."

"Hogwash!"

Machen looked at me sternly. "Maybe. You see, there is a part of witchcraft that deals with the soul, a part that believes the soul can be trapped and held, kept from escaping this earth and into the beyond. That's why a lot of natives are superstitious about having their picture taken. They believe once their image is captured, through magic, their soul can be contained.

"Voodoo works much the same. It's nothing but another

form of witchcraft. Practitioners of that art believe their souls can be held to this earth by means of someone collecting nail parin's or hair from them while they're still alive.

"That's what Marilyn had in mind. When she saw the girl was fadin', she snipped one of the girl's long pigtails and kept it to herself. Cast spells on it while the child lay dyin' and again after life had left the child."

"The soul was supposed to be contained within the hair?"

"That's right. It can be restored, in a sense, to some other object through the hair. It's like those voodoo dolls. A bit of hair or nail parin' is collected from the person you want to control, or if not control, maintain the presence of their soul, and it's sewn into those dolls. That way, when the pins are stuck into the doll, the living suffer, and when they die the soul is trapped in the doll for all eternity, or rather, as long as the doll with its hair or nail parin's exists."

"So she preserved the hair so she could make a doll and have the little girl live on, in a sense?"

"Something like that."

"Sounds crazy."

"I suppose."

"And what of the little girl's father?"

"Ah, that sonofabitch! He came home to find the little girl dead and buried and the mother mad. But there was the little gold lock of hair, and knowing Marilyn, he figured her intentions."

"Machen," I said slowly. "It was you, was it not? You were the father?"

"I was."

"I'm sorry."

"Don't be. We were both foolish. I was the more foolish. She left her husband for me and I cast her aside. Ignored my own child. I was the fool, a great fool."

"Do you really believe in that stuff about the soul? About the hair and what Marilyn was doing?"

"Better I didn't. A soul once lost from the body would best prefer to be departed I think . . . but love is sometimes a brutal thing."

We just sat there after that. We drank more. Machen smoked his pipe, and about an hour later we went to bed.

There were sounds again, gnawing at the edge of my sleep. The sounds that had always been there, but now, since we had talked of Marilyn, I was less able to drift off into blissful slumber. I kept thinking of those crazy things Machen had said. I remembered, too, those voices I had heard, and the fact that Machen was a ventriloquist, and perhaps, not altogether stable.

But those sounds.

I sat up and opened my eyes. They were coming from below. Voices. Machen's first. ". . . not be the death of you, girl, not at all . . . my only reminder of Marilyn . . ."

And then to my horror. "Let me be, Papa. Let it end." The last had been a little girl's voice, but the words had been bitter and wise beyond the youngness of the tone.

I stepped out of bed and into my trousers, crept to the curtain, and looked on Machen's side.

Nothing, just a lonely cot. I wasn't dreaming. I had heard him all right, and the other voice . . . it had to be that Machen, grieved over what he had done in the past, over Marilyn's death, had taken to speaking to himself in the little girl's voice. All that stuff Marilyn had told him about the soul, it had gotten to him, cracked his stability.

I climbed down the cold metal stairs, listening. Below I heard the old, weathered door that led outside slam. Heard the thud of boots going down the outside steps.

I went back up, went to the windows, and pulling back the curtains section by section, finally saw the old man. He was carrying something wrapped in a black cloth and he had a shovel in his hand. I watched as, out there by the shore, he dug a shallow grave and placed the cloth-wrapped object within, placed a rock over it, and left it to the night and the incoming tide.

I pretended to be asleep when he returned, and later, when I felt certain he was well visited by Morpheus, I went downstairs and retrieved the shovel from the tool room. I went out to where I had seen him dig and went to work, first turning over the large stone and shoveling down into the pebbly dirt. Due to the freshness of the hole, it was easy digging.

I found the cloth and what was inside. It made me flinch at first, it looked so real. I thought it was a little rosy-cheeked girl buried alive, for it looked alive . . . but it was a dummy. A ventriloquist dummy. It had aged badly, as if water had gotten to it. In some ways it looked as if it were rotting from the inside out. My finger went easily and deeply into the wood of one of the legs.

Out of some odd curiosity, I reached up and pushed back the wooden eyelids. There were no wooden painted eyes, just darkness, empty sockets that uncomfortably reminded me of looking down into the black hollows of a human skull. And the hair. On one side of the head was a yellow pigtail, but where the other should have been was a bare spot, as if the hair had been ripped away from the wooden skull.

With a trembling hand I closed the lids down over those empty eyes, put the dirt back in place, the rock, and returned to bed. But I did not sleep well. I dreamed of a grown man talking to a wooden doll and using another voice to answer back, pretending that the doll lived and loved him too.

But the water had gotten to it, and the sight of those rotting legs had snapped him back to reality, dashed his insane hopes of containing a soul by magic, shocked him brutally from foolish dreams. Dead is dead.

The next day, Machen was silent and had little to say. I suspected the events of last night weighed on his mind. Our conversation must have returned to him this morning in sober memory, and he, somewhat embarrassed, was reluctant to recall it. He kept to himself down below in the locked room, and I busied myself with my work.

It was night when he came up, and there was a smug look about him, as if he had accomplished some great deed. We spoke a bit, but not of witches, of past times and the sea. Then he pulled back the curtains and looked at the moon rise above the water like a cold fish eye.

"Machen," I said, "maybe I shouldn't say anything, but if

you should ever have something bothering you. If you should ever want to talk about it . . . Well, feel free to come to me."

He smiled at me. "Thank you. But any problem that might have been bothering me is . . . shall we say, all sewn up."

We said little more and soon went to bed.

I slept sounder that night, but again I was rousted from my dreams by voices. Machen's voice again, and the poor man speaking in that little child's voice.

"It's a fine home for you," Machen said in his own voice.

"I want no home," came the little girl's voice. "I want to be free."

"You want to stay with me, with the living. You're just not thinking. There's only darkness beyond the veil."

The voices were very clear and loud. I sat up in bed and strained my ears.

"It's where I belong," the little girl's voice again, but it spoke not in a little girl manner. There was only the tone.

"Things have been bad lately," Machen said. "And you're not yourself."

Laughter, horrible little girl laughter.

"I haven't been myself for years."

"Now, Catherine . . . play your piano. You used to play it so well. Why, you haven't touched it in years."

"Play. Play. With these!"

"You're too loud."

"I don't care. Let him hear, let him . . ."

A door closed sharply and the sound died off to a mumble; a word caught here and there was scattered and confused by the throb of the sea.

Next morning Machen had nothing for me, not even a smile from his borrowed collection. Nothing but coldness, his back, and a frown.

I saw little of him after coffee, and once, from below—for he stayed down there the whole day through—I thought I heard him cry in a loud voice, "Have it your way then," and then there was the sound of a slamming door and some other sort of commotion below.

After a while I looked out at the land and the sea, and

down there, striding back and forth, hands behind his back went Machen, like some great confused penguin contemplating the far shore.

I like to think there was something more than curiosity in what I did next. Like to think I was looking for the source of my friend's agony; looking for some way to help him find peace.

I went downstairs and pulled at the door he kept locked, hoping that, in his anguish, he had forgotten to lock it back. He had not forgotten.

I pressed my ear against the door and listened. Was that crying I heard?

No. I was being susceptible, caught up in Machen's fantasy. It was merely the wind whipping about the tower.

I went back upstairs, had coffee, and wrote not a line.

So day fell into night, and I could not sleep but finally got the strange business out of my mind by reading a novel. A rollicking good sea story of daring men and bloody battles, great ships clashing in a merciless sea.

And then, from his side of the curtain, I heard Machen creak off his cot and take to the stairs. One flight below was the door that led to the railing round about the tower, and I heard that open and close.

I rose, folded a small piece of paper into my book for a marker, and pulled back one of the window curtains. I walked around pulling curtains and looking until I could see him below.

He stood with his hands behind his back, looking out at the sea like a stern father keeping an eye on his children. Then, calmly, he mounted the railing and leaped out into the air.

I ran. Not that it mattered, but I ran, out to the railing . . . and looked down. His body looked like a rag doll splayed on the rocks.

There was no question in my mind that he was dead, but slowly I wound my way down the steps . . . and was distracted by the room. The door stood wide open.

I don't know what compelled me to look in, but I was

drawn to it. It was a small room with a desk and a lot of shelves filled with books, mostly occult and black magic. There were carpentry tools on the wall, and all manner of needles and devices that might be used by a tailor. The air was filled with an odd odor I could not place, and on Machen's desk, something that was definitely not tobacco smoldered away.

There was another room beyond the one in which I stood. The door to it was cracked open. I pushed it back and stepped inside. It was a little child's room filled thick with toys and such: jack-in-the-boxes, dolls, kid books, and a toy piano. All were covered in dust.

On the bed lay a teddy bear. It was ripped open and the stuffing was pulled out. There was one long strand of hair hanging out of that gutted belly, just one, as if it were the last morsel of a greater whole. It was the color of honey from a fresh-robbed hive. I knew what the smell in the ashtray was now.

I took the hair and put a match to it, just in case.

DELIA SHERMAN

Land's End

A relatively new writer, Delia Sherman was born on June 22, 1951, in Tokyo. She received her baccalaureate degree from Vassar College in 1972 and her Ph.D. in English from Brown University in 1981. She has been publishing fantastic short stories since 1985 and has two novels (Through a Brazen Mirror, *1989, and* The Porcelain Dove, *1993) to her credit. A resident of Massachusetts, she teaches Freshman Composition and Fantasy part-time to support her writing habit.*

"Land's End," which she wrote in Maine after being inspired by a painting, first appeared in The Magazine of Fantasy and Science Fiction *in October 1991.*

◻

The Land's End Light flashed out into the pale gray dawn. Forty-second beam. Twenty-second eclipse.

Aboard the clipper *White Goddess*, the lookout shouted, "Land ho!" The men of the watch raised a hoarse cheer, which did not penetrate to the second mate's cabin, where Joshua Saltree dozed and woke and dozed again.

The sleeping was better than the waking, for the pain wasn't so troublesome when he was asleep, nor the dead weight of his leg, wrapped and tied like a broken spar. He groaned in protest when the ship's surgeon woke him to give

231

him a dose of laudanum and the news that land was in sight.

"We'll make port by noon. Captain's going to look after you." Dr. Coffin's voice was dry as a ship's biscuit. "He's that grateful. See you're grateful back, Joshua Saltree; that's all I have to say."

Grateful? Saltree couldn't think why. The laudanum eased the pain some, but slowed his mind and his tongue more. He wanted to tell Dr. Coffin that Joshua Saltree wasn't dependent on any man, that he had a place to go and a few dollars laid by. But all he could get out was, "Rooming house."

Dr. Coffin laughed. "Mrs. Peabody's a sight too busy to nurse a man hurt bad as you are," he said. "Drink up."

"Don't hurt," Saltree protested, but he drank the bitter stuff down, and a moment later, or maybe half a day, he opened his eyes to find the captain and Dr. Coffin hanging over him like he was lying at the bottom of a well.

"Well, lad," said the captain heartily. "Time to go ashore."

Saltree tried to sit up, found himself prevented by the weight of his leg and Dr. Coffin's hand on his shoulder. "Damn young fool," the surgeon snapped. "Bones're near sticking out your shin, and you want to walk ashore. Try it and be damned to you, but don't be surprised if you wake up one morning with no leg at all."

"It's splintered; no, s-splinted, Devil take it."

Captain Mayne sighed louder than he needed to. "You'll be carried on a litter from here to my house. . . ."

A woman's voice finished the sentence: "And that's an order, mister."

"Mary!" Captain Mayne's teeth flashed through his beard, and he turned away from the berth as fast as his bulk and the narrow cabin would let him.

"Seth." A woman's white hands slid around the captain's neck and pulled down his head. Saltree closed his eyes in shame and almost drifted off again, but a cool touch on his forehead brought him around.

Mrs. Mayne was bending over him, smiling. "Well, Mr. Saltree," she said. "This is a fine state for a sailor to be in."

Saltree frowned at her and feebly twitched his hand away

from the tickling fringe of her shawl. He should be looking down at her, not up, should be saluting her from the rigging or standing by while the bo'sun piped her aboard, not lying here useless as a torn sail. She was a pretty woman—or had been, twenty years ago. Saltree smiled. A very pretty woman. And he and the captain were the only men aboard who'd seen her without her corsets.

That wasn't quite true. The whole crew had seen her bare bosom, but most of them hadn't the first notion that the *White Goddess*'s figurehead was the spitting image of the captain's lady. Oh, the carver had given the figurehead greeny brown hair and draped a fancy white sheet under her round, high breasts. But anyone looking close at her face would see Mrs. Mayne's straight nose and dark, long-lidded eyes. Stuck out under the bowsprit as she was, hardly anyone'd notice. But he'd noticed.

On calm days he used to scramble out the jib guys and stare out over the sea with one arm around the Goddess's sun-warm shoulders. He liked listening to the thutter of the bow over the swell, and watching the water glitter and foam under the keel. Ahead, always ahead, were ocean, weather, unknown shores, and he liked the way she breasted them with her carved lips parted and smiling. Why was she frowning now? Saltree moaned and closed his eyes.

After that, time passed in a blur of pain, heat, fear, and strange dreams. From time to time, Saltree was dimly aware of lying propped in a wide bed in a large room fitted with windows and curtains and gentle hands that brought him water and tended to his needs. But mostly he swam a pathless ocean, buffeted by storm. Lightning pulsed; sharks looked at him hungrily out of the eyes of dead sailors and rolled to snap at his feet. Salt water clogged the air, crushed his chest so that he gasped and flailed. A ship loomed—at her prow the White Goddess, decked out in seaweed. Her face was shadowed; her naked breasts rose and fell with the ship's breathing; her eyes streamed salt tears.

"Man overboard!" Saltree shouted; and she reached down

her wooden arms to him. Sometimes he caught her fingers—slick and cool as varnished wood—and sometimes he did not, but in either case he always woke wheezing and coughing and retching like a man hauled in from drowning.

It was deep night when finally he opened his eyes to see a fire burning in the grate, and a woman sewing by a shaded lamp. He felt light-headed, and all his limbs were limp as rope yarn. A glass and a pitcher stood on a table nearby, with a brown bottle, a spoon, and a tin basin.

"Thirsty," he said, and was startled to hear how rusty his voice sounded.

The woman got up and came to the bed, her skirts hushing. "I'm not surprised to hear it, Joshua Saltree, for you've been sweating like a pig all night." She touched her hand against his forehead before pouring a glass of water and holding it to his lips. "The fever's nearly gone. You'll sleep quieter now."

Saltree swallowed the water gratefully. The woman busied herself plumping the pillows and smoothing the sheets. As she moved around the bed, the firelight fell on her face: dark, long-lidded eyes above a straight nose. His heart began to race.

"Goddess?"

"Don't try to talk now. You've had pneumonia and ship fever and I don't know what all else, and very nearly died. You're in Captain Mayne's house, and I'm Mrs. Mayne, as you'll remember just fine when you're feeling better. Go to sleep now. That's right. Sleep."

The next time Saltree woke up, Captain Mayne sat by the bed, sucking on an empty pipe and regarding him gravely. "Glad to see you back with us, my lad," he said.

"The *Goddess*?"

"She's up in dry dock, getting overhauled as good as new, if not better. A new mainmast's the heaviest expense, but eight members of the Pioneer Mining Association of Auburn're taking passage to San Francisco at fifty dollars a head, so she'll pay for her repairs and more soon enough. Owner's glad we brought her home at all, and he's real grateful to you in particular, as well he should be."

Saltree frowned. That's not what he meant. A broad hand gripped his arm, lying helpless on the white counterpane. "Don't you remember the storm?" asked Captain Mayne kindly. "Well, well, that's no loss to you. Never you worry, lad; the *Goddess* is safe and sound. You sleep now."

Once the fever was gone, Saltree was not long mending. The *White Goddess* had made port on the second of May. By the end of the month, Saltree could hobble from the bed to the window to the fireplace and back again; in the second week of June, he asked respectfully whether he better not be moving on.

"You've been dreadful kind—kinder than there's any call for," he said awkwardly, fearing to seem ungrateful.

"Nonsense," said Captain Mayne. "We're glad to have you, Mrs. Mayne and I. You mayn't remember going aloft with Tom Harris when the mainmast started to crack, but I do. The pair of you saved my ship, lad, for which I'm grateful; and my hide, for which Mrs. Mayne is grateful. Now Tom's dead and gone: we can't show him we're grateful. So let's hear no more of you leaving, at least not until you've got someplace better'n Mrs. Peabody's Rooming House to leave to."

What could Saltree do but thank him and work out his restlessness in learning to walk again. His leg had healed twisted and gaunt. It bore him, with the help of two sticks, and Dr. Coffin promised he'd be able to dispense with at least one of them in time. But it would keep him off a ship, except perhaps as steward or ship's cook—a comedown in the world, and no mistake.

As the spring days passed, despair gathered over him like a thunderhead. To be a cripple, only twenty-five years old and condemned to live ashore like an old man. It hardly bore thinking on. Mornings, when he pulled his pants over his twisted leg and his shirt over arms wasted by fever, Saltree ground his teeth and envied Tom Harris from the bottom of his heart.

Mrs. Mayne did her best to amuse him, and Saltree knew she meant it kindly. But whenever he saw her approaching with her hands folded around a fat black Bible, such rage swelled his breast that he liked to have burst from the force of it. Her motherly smile, her knitting, the hint of a double chin overlapping her lace collar—all were wormwood and gall to him.

Saltree didn't know why he should have taken so strongly against Mrs. Mayne, who'd nursed him like a mother. All he knew was that he didn't like being beholden, and he didn't know how he could stop being beholden, and what with one thing and another, he began to look near as peaked as he had when he was knocking at death's door.

Mary Mayne told her husband she feared Mr. Saltree might be sickening again.

Captain Mayne shook his head. "I doubt it's his body, my dear. It's hard on the lad, being land-bound at his age with no prospect of shipping out again."

"You'd think he'd be glad to be safe ashore and quit of storms."

"Saltree, well, Saltree's a queer bird. A fine seaman, but a queer bird nonetheless. He likes climbing masts, and he fair loves storms. The higher the sea, the better he's pleased; and the nearer he comes to death, the more he laughs. Tom Harris and he were a fine pair of fools, racing up the mainmast when anybody with an eye in his head could see she was cracked. But if they hadn't managed to cut loose the topgallant and trim the storm sails, we'd've run slap bingo into Bermuda Island." Seth Mayne sighed. "A fine seaman. It won't be easy to find him a living won't be the death of him. I'll have to stir my stumps."

And stir his stumps the captain did. One fine June morning, he drove all the way to Portland to see a friend he thought might have some pull with the Lighthouse Board down Washington way. Two days later he returned like a cheerful gale, blowing down Main Street and into the garden where Saltree was hobbling back and forth between two fruit trees.

"Ahoy there, Mr. Saltree," shouted the captain. "Double grog for all hands and plum duff for dinner." He took the astonished Saltree by the hand and pumped vigorously. "I've news for you—the best. It seems Elisha Tully, who keeps the

Land's End Light, is wanting an assistant. I told my old shipmate Captain Drinkwater about you, leg and all, and the long and short of it is that you've the job if you want it. Nobody's saying it's a ship, but it's the sea and plenty to do in a storm." Captain Mayne clasped his hands behind him, very pleased with himself. "It's a good life by all accounts—time to think and time to work and a dry place to lay your head off-watch. When my sailing days are over, we might like to keep a light ourselves, Mrs. Mayne and me."

No more than a week later, Saltree sat on his sea chest on the public pier, waiting for Elisha Tully to row in from Land's End Rock to fetch him. Piled around him were boxes of provisions, a keg of rum, and a small wooden crate marked "Chimneys: Fragile." Round about midmorning, a fat, red-faced man in a torn navy blouse clambered up onto the pier. He stared at Saltree, his sea chest, his groceries, and his "Chimneys: Fragile," and tongued a wad of tobacco from one cheek to the other. "Name of Saltree?"

"Ayuh."

"Elisha Tully. Lighthouse Keeper." Tully bent and heaved Saltree's sea chest onto his shoulder. "Dory's below."

They loaded the dory, Tully handing down crates and Saltree disposing them neatly along the gunwales. When all were stowed, Saltree sat himself down on the rower's bench.

Tully, still on dock, spat thoughtfully into the gray water. "Thought you'd had 'neumony," he said.

"Ayuh," said Saltree, and unshipped the oars.

Tully coiled the bow line and climbed down into the stern. "Not much of a hand at nursemaiding," he remarked.

"No call for it."

"Sure?" Tully squinted doubtfully at him.

"Sure." Saltree pushed off from the pilings and turned the dory around with two economical strokes, then set off slow and steady. He was blown before he'd gone a hundred yards, and by the time they made Land's End Rock, he felt like he'd been flogged. But when they landed, he hoisted the "Chimneys: Fragile" onto his shoulder and carried it over the rocks, steadying himself with his stick. He'd give no man a reason to say that Joshua Saltree was a helpless cripple, twisted leg or no.

"Keepers used to live in the Light," said Tully as they came near it. "There was a room below the watch room, all right and tight. But the new revolving gear took up the watch room, so two, three years back, they built the house." Tully glared for a second at the comfortable shingle house and the horse weather vane trotting bravely on the roof. "Good nor'easter'll snap it into matchsticks one day. Matchsticks!"

Tully lugged Saltree's sea chest inside and led him up a wooden ladder to the assistant keeper's room. Its window looked out onto the light tower and headland beyond. Saltree could see sky in plenty, but no more water than from his room at Captain Mayne's house. He shrugged. He was a landsman now, not a sailor, and he'd best get used to the sight of land.

Downstairs, Tully led Saltree through a short, roofed passage to the iron-bound door of the light itself. There were windows cut in the walls, but they were sealed tight with wooden shutters, and the tower was black as a ship's hold. Groping in the gloom for the rail, Saltree laid his hand on the pitted wall and brought it away chilled and glistening with damp.

Tully's boots clanged upward, and his voice echoed flatly between iron and stone.

"This here's the oil tank, and this here above it's the watch room." Tully opened a manhole into a wilderness of tables and boxes and tools piled higgledy-piggledy on every flat surface. The watch room reeked as strongly as the forecastle of a bad ship, with an unfamiliar metallic tang mixed in with the general stink of sweat, wet wool, and neglect. Saltree frowned.

Tully spat in the direction of a spattered, stinking bucket. "It ain't so bad, really," he said defensively. "Needs a bit of tidying, is all. Man can't keep everything shipshape when he's all on his own like I been. I can put my hand on what I need when I need it." He poked through the flotsam, found a bull's-eye lantern, lit it, and hung it from a hook on the wall, where it smoked sullenly.

"Extry chimneys there and there. Wicks, scissors, tool case for the clockwork, clock oil, tripoli, spirits of wine, chamois cloths, brushes, oil carriers."

His grubby forefinger stabbed into the shadows, seemingly at random. Saltree stood and watched until at last Tully said, "What the hell. You'll find all that when you need it. Light's up here."

Slowly, for his leg was aching fiercely, Saltree followed Tully's ample rump up another staircase to a door that led them into a circular gallery. Tully slapped the inner wall. "Lantern base." They mounted a last, flimsy curl of steps.

Remembering how the sun dazzled on the water, Saltree squinted cautiously. Then he stepped into a warm, golden fog and blinked. The whole dome was swathed in cloth: yellow shades blinded the windows; a linen cover shrouded the lens. With a professional twitch, Tully unveiled a thing like a glass cage, tiers of long, louverlike prisms held in place with iron clips. Even in the dim light, it sparkled some.

"Seems sunlight's not good for her," said Tully, "So we keep her covered, days. She's all ready to go. Lighting her's nothing. Real work's in the morning. You'll see."

Saltree did see, the next morning and every morning after. Tully's idea of training was to have his assistant do all the cleaning, polishing, oiling, and adjusting while he, Tully, sat on a crate with his feet on another and nursed a cup of strong coffee laced with rum.

"Not a speck of dust, now," he'd say. "Dust is hell on clockwork. Dust'll throw off a fly governor faster'n rust, and that's saying some. Have you oiled the carriage rollers yet? Well, hop to it, boy. It's gone twelve noon, and you ain't even drained the oil cistern."

Unless there was a storm, Tully insisted on keeping the night watch alone. He'd light the lantern in the evening and eat a plate of hardtack and boiled beef in the kitchen. Come about nine o'clock, he'd get up, scratch in his thick beard, and take the bull's-eye down from the chimney piece. "There's a wreck, I'll wake you," he'd say, and disappear aloft.

Alone, Saltree would smoke a pipe, maybe put an extra polish on a brass oilcan, darn a sock, look at a newspaper if they had one, and then go up to his attic room and watch the light pulsing its forty-second beam, twenty-second eclipse. The light, gathered and refracted by those hundred carefully ground prisms, cut through the night like lightning—its illumination self-contained, unrevealing. Beam. Eclipse. Beam. Here are rocks, it seemed to say. Here is harbor. Beam. Eclipse. Beam. Here . . . Am . . . I.

Compared to being second mate on a clipper, it was an easy berth. No long watches, no standing perched on an icy yardarm hauling at wet canvas with numb and swollen hands. No captain to curse at him, no first mate to lord it over him, no seamen to get uppity. No yarns, no songs, no jigs amidships. An easy berth. but a solitary one.

In October a carrier pigeon brought the news that the *White Goddess* had been cleared for San Francisco, and that Captain Mayne sent his kind regards and was counting on seeing Mr. Saltree and his light again sometime before midsummer. Though as a rule he wasn't a drinking man, Saltree locked himself in his attic that night with a blanket thrown over the window and dined on Tully's rum. He drank until his head spun and his leg no longer pained him. He drank until he like to have drowned, but the liquor, whistling in his ears like wind in the rigging, could not drown the pain of the Goddess skimming the wave crests without him.

By November, Saltree had polished every oil carrier, honed every knife and scissors blade, arranged all the tools and glass chimneys in gleaming, ordered rows, and generally overhauled the watch room until everything about it was entirely shipshape and Bristol fashion. The days were dull, though they went by quickly enough. Lighthouses take a good deal of keeping, what with swabbing the lens with spirits of wine, greasing the clockwork of the turning mechanism, dusting and trimming and winding all the gears and wicks, rollers and fittings of brass and iron that together create that forty-second beam and twenty-second eclipse.

But the nights were long and filled with dreams.

No sooner did Saltree lay down his head, than he was aloft on the rigging of the *White Goddess* or striding down her deck. His legs were strong, and under his bare brown feet, the timbers shone clean and white as flax. His watch—the larboard watch—set up rigging, tarred down the spars. The sun was warm on his shoulders. Gulls and terns wheeled in the wide sky, blue, then gray, then black with clouds foaming and churning like the black water that licked at the crosstrees. Rope between his hands, salt water to his waist, clutching his feet, chilling his bones, his heart pounding fast and hard, Tom Harris beside him, grinning wider and wider until his whole face was teeth and bone and wisps of rotted hair.

Other dreams rang with cries of "Man overboard!" and Captain Mayne at the leeward rail, pointing down at the heaving waves. "For God's sake, man. He saved your life!" Making for the rail, laboring on one leg, lurching. Tom below, laughing, and in his arms the Goddess, carved lips parted and smiling. Wood and living flesh entwined, they rolled upon the swell like sleeping birds, then she drew Tom down, down below the black water.

Saltree always woke from these dreams half-strangled with unuttered shouts. He'd rub the sweat from his face, then sit at the edge of his bed and watch the light's signal pattern. Beam. Eclipse. Beam. Eclipse. Forty seconds' light. Twenty seconds' dark. Steady, sure as a heartbeat. The Land's End Light.

The first day of the New Year, Tully went ashore to buy provisions. The sky threatened snow, but they were down to their last mouthful of salt beef and moldy bread, so off he sculled. He left just after daybreak, in plenty of time to buy what was needful, raise a tankard or three at the Mermaid's Tale, and row back to the Rock again before dark.

Midafternoon, the wind rose and the sea with it. It grew bitter cold, and Saltree stopped puttering with the clockwork to climb out on the parapet and rub the windows with glycerin and spirits of wine to keep them from icing over. Before he was half-done, heavy flakes of snow began to slap at his cheeks. Tully'd be a fool to row back in this, when there was beer and company and a warm bed at the Tale.

Tully always kept a hammock rigged in the watchroom, and about midnight, Saltree climbed into it. The storm had settled into a steady blow, nothing that should give any trouble to a captain worth his brandy. He couldn't sleep, of course, but he had to rest his leg, which was aching like billy hell from the cold. In an hour or so, he'd get up and rewind the fog bell.

Within the granite tower, the sound of the storm was muted to a whistle and a far grumble of breaking waves. Saltree climbed the mainmast in a brisk wind with all canvas shown. Saint Elmo's fire danced ghostly on the crosstrees, and a flight of petrels canted and mewed above the skysail. Tom Harris clung one-handed to the topgallant yard.

"Land ho!" he cried, and pointed into the gathering clouds. A cheer below, and all the sails bellied full as the *Goddess* rose above the swell and flew over the wave-crests like a skipped stone. It was snowing now, land ahead, and nothing to say where. Perched among the shrouds, Saltree squinted into the blizzard. Where were the lights? Every coast had lights. Did the snow hide them? Then where were the fog bells? And why was Captain Mayne running blind before a gale into land?

A crash and a shudder spilled Saltree from his hammock, dazed and half-convinced he was still aboard the *Goddess,* and she was breaking up on the rocks of some unknown coast. The waves made a deafening roar, and a cold wind flooded down the turret stairs. That, or guilt at falling asleep, chilled him to the bone. He shivered like a beaten dog and blinked. Was that snow, coming down inside the tower? And what was that hullabaloo?

A good sailor leaps to what needs doing, and Saltree leaped now, swarming up the stairs like rigging. In the dome, wind and snow eddied, blinding white, then ghostly as the lens turned slowly on its carriage. It took Saltree a full two cycles of beam and eclipse to see the broken pane of glass and the bird that had broken it flapping through the shards.

"Bloody stupid bird," Saltree swore, and lunged. The bird was farther from him than he'd thought, but his hand closed on one powerfully flailing wing. It whipped its head around to peck at him with a bill like a marlinespike, and he ducked. Big gull, he thought. Looks like—the wing jerked from his grasp—an albatross.

"Devil take it." It was almost a prayer. There were tales of shipwreck and sudden death caused by killing the bird that brought fair winds and guided ships blown off-course to safe harbors. Saltree knew that the greater part of these tales were nothing but so much rope yarn spun on the off-watch by bored seamen, but there was no denying that albatross were uncanny birds. He had seen them asleep on the water off Cape Horn, riding the swells from crest to trough. He had seen them perched on the masthead, so white in the sun that they seemed lit from inside. The sight of this one, bedraggled and blood-splattered, frightened him more than a twenty-foot wave.

While Saltree hung fire, the albatross flapped and heaved its way inside the glass cage of the lens and up onto the lantern base. Briefly, it mantled with the light behind it, and the lens distorted it into a giant thing with wings like sails and an eye like the moon in eclipse.

Gears ground. The carriage, slowed, strained; and the albatross, screaming, battered its wings. A chimney broke. One wick went out; the others flickered wildly. Saltree found the trimming knife and crawled toward the bird. He was a lighthouse keeper now, he told himself, and his light was threatened. It didn't matter whether a gull or an albatross or a mermaid or King Neptune himself was sitting in that lantern. It didn't belong there, and it was up to him, Saltree, to get it out.

Saltree crooked one arm across his face to protect his eyes, and wormed his way into the lens.

Inside was a second storm of feathers and blood. The albatross's feet were entangled in the turning mechanism, and it attacked the clockwork with wings and darting beak.

Shadows and light glittered in Saltree's eyes until he could have sworn that a thousand albatross were trapped in the prisms. He thrust blindly with the knife. A final scream, a convulsive flutter. The light flared, and a thousand albatross scattered into the snowy darkness. The last wick went out.

Moving painfully, Saltree crawled out of the lantern and toward the door, cursing himself for not bringing up the extra lamp. It should have been instinctive, like carrying rope up the rigging. Crews were counting on him: it took no time at all for a ship to run aground.

Downstairs at last, Saltree snatched up an extra lantern, lit it with trembling hands, settled the chimney on it, and pulled himself up the stairs again, hop-and-heave as fast as he could go. It was only a small flame under a glass chimney, hardly bright enough to reach across the dome. But when he slid it into the empty holder, a clear, strong beam leaped into the darkness.

Saltree sighed in relief and turned his attention to the dead albatross. Its wings were singed and bloody, tattered as an old shawl. Carefully, so as not to endanger the lamp, he disentangled the yellow legs from the clockwork. They were thoroughly caught in the gears, and his sweater and hands were slimy with blood before he worked the bird free. He dragged it out of the lens, hoisted it up into his arms, and limped to the window with its feathers trailing against his knees. Under his cold fingers, the body was warm and yielding. Saltree shuddered and threw it from him, out the broken window and into the treacherous wind.

Clearing blood and feathers from the clockwork and the lens took him the rest of the night. Just before dawn the wind dropped to nothing, but the snow continued heavy and the seas rough. Tully'd not come back today.

Alone, Saltree tacked in a temporary window, cleaned as much of the apparatus as he could without dismounting the frame, and oiled the carriage so it could turn again. He drove himself to wrench the heavy gears apart, strained his back and his legs manhandling wooden boards up the narrow stair. If he hadn't fallen asleep, if he'd killed the albatross right of, then the light wouldn't have gone out. Sure, there was no harm done this time. But what if the *Goddess* had been out there? What if other keepers were as careless, as unfit, as he?

By nightfall, Saltree was wet through and more dog-tired than he'd ever been on ship. He knew he'd have to spend another night in the watch room, but he thought he'd get himself a dry shirt. Then, once he got to his attic room, he thought he'd change his socks. He took a pair from the sea chest, sat on the edge of the bed to put them on, leaned wearily against the wall. He frowned. What if the *Goddess* had been out there?

He woke after moonset, feeling oddly peaceful. From the sound of the waves on the rocks, it was ebb tide, with a light sea running. He was lying on the bed, fully clothed. "Son of a bitch," he said. But his guilt was as dead as the albatross. His stolen sleep had been deep and dreamless.

A scrape, like a heavy object being dragged over the roof, brought Saltree upright. Silence. The window was luminous with snow light and the lantern's intermittent dazzle. He shrugged. Maybe, as long as he was awake, he'd best get to the tower. Saltree swung his legs to the floor. Between one flash and the next, he caught an odd shadow drifting down the window.

Saltree blinked. Too slow for a gull—and even an albatross wasn't that big. Another—a strange shape. Long, heavy, with strange knots and bulges. Another.

As a fourth shadow swam across the window, Saltree limped painfully across the rough planks. His hands met and clutched the window frame; his face approached the glass. Eclipse: he saw his own reflection staring back at him out of shadowed eyes. Beam: his gaze focused on the dome.

Figureheads: dripping seaweed, some far gone in decay, others still bright with paint. They clustered around the lantern like wingless and awkward moths, yearning toward the light. Some were headless, and stretched only their long necks, questing eyelessly for comfort. Some were snapped off at the waist, mere torsos. Most pathetic of all were the ones that retained their faces, for they were openmouthed, drowned, and their wooden eyes stared at the light with a dreadful and accusing intelligence.

One of these figureheads was not so sea-changed as the rest. She hovered between Saltree and the lantern so that at first he saw only her back and the dirty front of her clothes. Then she drifted outside the crowding school of figureheads and showed Saltree her profile. Straight nose; high, round, naked breasts: the white Goddess.

There was a swath of seaweed drapped around her shoulders and tossed across her throat like a bedraggled feather boa, which gave her a rakish look, like a dockside whore. Saltree's hands tightened on the window frame. The Goddess drifted farther around, and he saw that half her wooden head had been sheared away, one breast and shoulder splintered.

Saltree threw open the sash and leaned far out the window. "Goddess!" he shouted, and held out his hand to her.

The White Goddess floated nearer, bobbing with a long swell. Dark water dripped from her like blood. Her eye glittered wetly. Her hand that had held back the carved folds of her drapery released them and reached for him.

Beautiful. She was so beautiful, and as she drew near Saltree, she brought with her the smells of salt and sun-warmed tar and varnish and newly scrubbed decks. His breath came fast; his fingers trembled.

The revolving lens flickered slowly. Forty-second beam: twenty-second eclipse. The figurehead hovered just out of his reach, stretching her fingers to him.

Saltree flung his good leg over the sill, braced the other against his sea chest, and hung from the sash by the length of his arm.

Beam. Eclipse. Beam.

An inch, no more, separated their hands. Eclipse. In the brief darkness, Saltree touched the slick coolness of varnished wood. Beam. His fingers closed on hers, and his muscles strained to pull her into his arms.

Eclipse. Beam. Eclipse.

She was his now, wild sea smell, smooth breasts and all,

clinging to his neck like kelp and smiling into his eyes. He felt her body yield to his hand like flesh, but cold, so cold. Entwined, buoyant as gulls, they rolled upon the waves, sliding from crest to trough out to the open sea. They sailed beyond the breakers to black water, and then she drew him down with her, gently down to her cold ocean bed.

EDWARD WELLEN

The Driven Snow

A consummate professional who has written many original stories for us, Edward Paul Wellen was born in New Rochelle, New York, on October 2, 1919. He attended Shrivenham American University, in England, and City college of New York. During World War Two he was awarded seven battle stars and served in the Chemical Warfare Service. Since then he has been a mail-order stamp dealer, an advertising consultant, a freelance writer, and a writing instructor.

In love with both mystery and science fiction, Wellen has spent twenty-five years fusing the two genres in strong, complex, and fast-paced novellas memorable for their rich, almost Joycean, language. His story "The Driven Snow" is published here for the first time.

◻

The snowman saw it all with his coals.

Though the coal pile diminished to scrapings, the kid would not dream of taking back the snowman's eyes for the fire burning low in the coal stove that heated the lighthouse. The snowman was packed solid to see the Maine winter through. For three days now, it had stood tall and firm, though the kid had waited in vain for his mother to take notice of it and commend him on it—or at least glance at it and laugh. That was the thing he loved best about her, her laugh.

He had even taken her black gloves for the snowman, so that when she asked the world where in hell her black gloves had gone to he could point to the snowman and she could see what he had built. He guessed her black gloves were too thin for this cold spell and so she had not missed them yet. Meanwhile, they stood the snowman in good stead, dramatizing the snowman's folded-arms stance. The snowman did not look afraid of anything or anyone. With his narrow build and taper, he stood guarding the coast like a miniature lighthouse alongside the real one that was their home.

For during the winter, when no one else wanted it, the kid and his mother lived in a decommissioned lighthouse on Penobscot Bay that his mother rented from an old man in Town. Only yesterday, the old man, Mr. Stornoway, had come out to collect back rent—fruitlessly, as it proved, because the kid's mother (maybe because she had wind of the old man's coming) had stayed in Town. Anyway, Mr. Stornoway had noticed the snowman and commented favorably.

Then he had come in to warm his hands and backside at the coal stove (and maybe to see for himself that the kid's mother was truly out) and that had put him in mind of the old days. They burned oil then, he said, in the time when the Treasury Department's lighthouse supply-ship *Armeria* made its annual call. As the *Armeria* rounded the headland, the keeper hurriedly donned full uniform and his wife her best calico, and the keeper sounded the deep-throated steam foghorn in moaning welcome.

The kid's eyes shone. Be something if he could bring the foghorn back to life! Maybe one day . . .

When old Mr. Stornoway was convinced that the kid was all alone, that put him in mind of another young boy left all alone in this very lighthouse.

It was before they had built the causeway. A long wooden bridge joined the lighthouse rock to the mainland. The young boy was the son of the keeper, and this day the keeper left him alone in the lighthouse while the father crossed the bridge to

Town for provisions. A sudden storm came up before the father could return, and wind and wave tore the bridge away. The gale raged for three weeks, but there were no wrecks, because the light shone steadily. When the seas died down, the father rowed out in a borrowed boat. The boy was weak for lack of sleep and food, but still tending the light.

With a smile that turned sad, Mr. Stornoway looked at the kid and shook his head. Then he left, with a nice parting word for the snowman.

Yet the kid's own mother had not noticed the snowman enough to say anything about it to the kid even though she had to pass it on her way out in the late afternoon when she left for work in Town. Maybe she had seen it, going out, and meant to say something about it to the kid but it kept slipping her mind. And each night by the time she got back home maybe it had been too dark out for her to see it again to remind her to say something about it. Though the headlights of whatever car she got a lift in would surely pick it out, she'd probably be too busy brushing off a man's paws and trying to get out with just a goodnight peck. Maybe she'd see it tonight.

He sat up by the stove, nibbling a chocolate bar, and when the stove went dead and cold he still sat up by it, though he wrapped himself in blankets and the memory of heat, waiting for his mother. She might not be the best of mothers, to go by what the other kids he met at school—he lived too far out to play with them after school—said their folks said of her, but she was his mother. She worked as a barmaid, and the bar she worked in might not be the best in Town, but at least it was a job, and she said it was the best she could do.

He did not let himself dream his dream of a better time and a better place for the two of them because dreaming would put him to sleep. He could not let himself fall asleep, however late the hour of her coming, till she had come safely home and thrown herself on her bed and moaned or cursed herself to sleep. Tonight least of all.

Tonight the clouds had melted away like snow from the glow of the moon and the snowman stood sharp and bright.

Snow had a way of blurring sharp outlines, but the outline of the kid's snowman was sharp and threw a sharp shadow on the smooth whiteness covering the yard. She would not miss seeing the snowman tonight.

Meanwhile, he was not all alone like that earlier kid—he had the snowman for company. The snowman was a lighthouse—only *his* eyes cast beams of darkness.

The snowman saw the car first. But then the kid heard the snow-softened rumble of the car over the causeway and left the stove, almost tripping on the blankets he had wrapped around himself, and looked out the front window and watched the car swing off the road and head up the little more than a track toward the lighthouse.

The kid twisted around for a glance at the clock. He had to wave his breath away to see the hour clear. The hands reached for midnight. It seemed early for his mother. But it could be his mother if she had knocked off work on time for once and had got a lift straight home.

She often got a lift home, though more often than not he had to listen to and live through an endless time of whisperings and rustlings on the doorstep; endless till his mother laughed, more or less irritationfully or promisefully, and said, "Not now, not here. The kid." Then finally she would come in alone and the car would drive away.

But this car carried only the driver. The kid's heart went hard and cold as a rock-centered snowball. The kid knew the car. And he knew the driver by his bulk and by the masterful one-handed way he swung the car back and forth to park it heading back the way it had come.

The car backed right into the front yard to pull around, and likely would have even if the picket fence still stood in the way. The last few pickets still standing had gone into the stove to heat the house one bitter night last winter, his mother having then, too, forgotten to leave the kid money to pay the cash on delivery for the coal and the coal having gone away still loaded on the truck. The warmest thing he remembered about that night last winter was his mother laughing and saying that it was too bad it wasn't like when *she* was a kid and trains used coal. If coal-stoked trains passed on nearby tracks, the two of them could have stood down by the tracks and thrown rocks and got back coal. If, she said, if. Bread upon the water, she said, bread upon the water.

The headlights shone full upon the snowman before the driver swung the car around, so the driver had to have seen the snowman.

The snowman saw the car back up into it but could do nothing to save itself. It fell over on one side and its packed body cracked and broke apart.

The driver had done it out of hundred-proof drunken meanness. The kid balled his fists but had nothing at hand to pound that would do any good. If there had been, if the man's ribs had been in reach, the kid would not have minded the hurt to his hands.

The kid had been unable to protect his snowman. How could he protect his mother? The man had beaten his mother and had threatened worse. That would be why the man had come tonight.

Coal being what it is, the remains of living plants, the snowman's eyes had stored up the memory of mild air and leafy millennia. But now looking sideways at the world, they saw only night sky on the one hand and a soiled whiteness on the other. In the soiled whiteness the snowman saw the car that had knocked it down, and saw the dull red glow of the exhaust pipe. The driver idled the car to keep the heater going. It would be much warmer in the car than in the house. The snowman could make out the man's head as the man tossed it back to drink from a bottle still in a paper bag. The snowman could see the man settle down to wait for the kid's mother to come home. The snowman could see the man drink and drink and work up a murderous hate.

The kid saw all this too, and fear rose to hate in the kid as in the man. But the kid's hate remained a futile dull glow like the tailpipe's. David and Goliath worked only in the Bible.

Then the coal eyes sent forth beams of darkness and a

thought from the snowman warmed the kid as he eyed the tailpipe.

If he stole out to the car to do what needed doing, his tracks would show, and they would continue to stand out because the sky held no promise of more snowfall to cover them. But the warmth grew into a brightness of seeing how he might do the thing he had to do and yet make no tracks.

The kid pulled the blankets tight around himself and went through the lighthouse to the back door. He stepped outside and scooped up handfuls of snow from the back stoop. The kid molded snowballs in his bare hands. His hands burned with cold and he had to stop often to blow on them. But he finally had a pyramid of snowballs that he carried back through the lighthouse in a rust-pinholed old dishpan. He stepped out onto the front step, put the pan down, and knelt on the step and freed his throwing arm from the blankets.

The man started at the thud of the first snowball to hit his car. He spotted the kid on the step winding up for another throw. He ducked away from the closed window, then cursed himself for flinching and the kid's aim was way off. The snowball smacked home far elsewhere on the car. The man smiled.

Last winter, or the one before that, the kid and the man, in one of the man's rare moods of palship, had waged snowball war. Winning had cost the kid a face-rub in the snow. The man couldn't take it that the kid threw straighter. The snowfight had lost the nature of play. But now the kid's aim was off a mile.

Still, it was his car the kid dared to throw snowballs at, and the kid was keeping it up even though he had given the kid the glare and the shaken fist. He put his hand on the door release, but then sat back. He felt too comfortable in the car to chase after the kid in all that cold out there. Besides, he wanted to save his anger for the two-timing woman. So he merely smiled and nodded at the kid. *Just you wait, kid. I'll get around to you later. After I take care of your ever-loving mother.*

The kid threw another snowball, again nowhere near the

driver's window. The driver nodded again at the kid. *Just keep it up, kid.*

The kid kept it up and each time the driver nodded at the kid.

Then he just nodded.

Then he just sat still with his chin on his chest.

Only now did the kid begin to feel cold to the bone. Still shivering, he had just put the empty dishpan out on the back stoop when another car rumbled over the causeway and headed for the lighthouse.

The kid hurried back through the lighthouse to the front window. He made it in time to see the two in the front seat break apart as though they had suddenly spotted the waiting car.

His mother got out, and the man who had brought her home hurriedly backed the car down to the road without allowing her time to close the door. The slam of it came from down the road, then the car rumbled over the causeway and vanished from hearing.

Then came the crunch of snow crust as the woman hesitantly approached the waiting car. With a frightened-sounding intake of breath she gathered herself to greet the man. Then she saw the man's chin rested on his chest and that his eyes were shut. She laughed softly with relief and pulled herself righteously together and opened the car door. She spoke the man's name, then spoke it again, louder. Then she shook him. She screamed as the man fell out at her feet.

The boy opened the front door at her scream. She turned and from far out of reach pushed at him to go back in. She joined him inside long enough to get him into his bed. She noted aloud absently that his hands were like ice.

She chafed them while she told him not to worry but something bad had happened and she would have to go right out again and hike over the causeway to the nearest house with a phone.

He fell asleep but he wakened when the Maine State Police came, so he knew it wasn't all a dream. They didn't want to waken him but he got up himself and answered sleepily the few questions they thought he could answer, though they knew already what had happened and how it had happened.

"Did you make the snowman?"

"Yes."

"Did you see the car back into the snowman?"

"Yes."

That seemed to satisfy them. One of them who said he had a kid the kid's age shook the kid's hand, but by now the kid's hand was no longer like ice. That one said he would see about getting them some coal.

They took flash pictures of the man and of the car and of the snow all around the car. The snowman appeared in some of the pictures. Then some other men bagged the body and took it away.

His mother explained it to the kid in thready mists of breath the way the police had explained it to her.

"The tire tracks show how it happened. He backed his car into that stupid snowman of yours and that plugged up the exhaust. He never knew. He just fell asleep for good."

She covered the kid with an extra blanket and the kid fell asleep. He did not hear his mother ask the world, "Where in the hell did my black gloves go to? I need them for the kid's father's funeral."

The air grew milder toward dawn. If the unseasonable warmth held for a spell, the snowman would begin to melt sooner than later. In any case, the snowman's destiny was to melt into silence. Two coals only would remain, with the memory newly frozen into them already dying out: the sight of the kid hurling snowball after snowball into the raw mouth of the tailpipe, sealing it with snow so that the carbon monoxide would seep into the body of the car and into the body of the man. The snowman had seen it all with his coals but he would say nothing.